DRUGS FOR LIFE

EXPERIMENTAL FUTURES
Technological Lives, Scientific Arts, Anthropological Voices

A SERIES EDITED BY
Michael M. J. Fischer
and Joseph Dumit

DRUGS FOR LIFE

How Pharmaceutical Companies Define Our Health

Joseph Dumit

Duke University Press | Durham and London | 2012

© 2012 Duke University Press

All rights reserved

Printed in the United States of America on acid-free paper ♾

Designed by Heather Hensley

Typeset in Scala by Tseng Information Systems, Inc.

Library of Congress Cataloging-in-Publication Data appear on
the last printed page of this book.

for Sylvia

CONTENTS

ILLUSTRATIONS

ACKNOWLEDGMENTS

I've been working on the research and writing of this book for over eight years and have accumulated so many debts and therefore so many relations.

I am deeply grateful to all of the fictional persons I interacted with (i.e., corporations, agencies, institutions and other collectives; financial support, spaces of presentation, and constant ethnographic engagement; warm receptions, all while being fiercely critical; the little and big provocations in Q&A sessions and over meals have inspired so many parts of my work). These interactions took place at the Massachusetts Institute of Technology; the Department of Social Medicine at Harvard Medical School; Wenner Gren Sweden; the Center for Technology and Ethics; Davis Humanities Institute; RxID; Oxidate; ModLab@UCDavis; the Psychiatry Department at Alta Bates Medical; Massachusetts General Hospital Psychiatry; Mental Health Services at MIT; the Berkeley Anthropology and Geography Departments; Cornell Science and Technology Studies (STS); Pembroke Center at Brown; the departments of Communication, Anthropology, and STS at the University of California at San Diego; the Department of Anthropology at Stanford; Harvard's History of Science Department; Duke's Anthropology Department; and the University of California, Davis.

To the nonfictional persons, or readers and interlocutors, it has been so exciting to think with you all and to continue to do so virtually and in meatspace whenever we can. Thank you to Vincanne Adams, Naira Ahmad, Étienne Balibar, Andrés Barragán, João Biehl, Charlotte Biltekoff, Tom Boellstorff, Regula Burri, Candis Callison, Angie Chabram,

Anita Chan, Tim Choy, Tim Claffey, Adele Clarke, Lawrence Cohen, Lucy Corin, Marisol de la Cadena, William DiFede, Lawrence Diller, Don Donham, Gary Downey, Mark Driscoll, Barbara and Thomas Dumit, Jeanette Edwards, Michael Fischer, Kim Fortun, Mike Fortun, Sarah Franklin, Paula Gardner, Cristiana Giordano, Byron Good, Mary-Jo Delvecchio Good, Jeremy Greene, Nathan Greenslit, Jim Griesemer, Hugh Gusterson, Orit Halpern, Clara Han, Donna Haraway, Susan Harding, Anita Hardon, Penny Harvey, Cori Hayden, David Healy, Deborah Heath, Stefan Helmreich, Linda Hogle, Dirk Hommrich, Jean Jackson, Erica James, Sheila Jasanoff, David Jones, David Kaiser, Nina Kessler, Nick King, Alan Klima, Chris Kortright, Jake Kosek, Cathy Kudlick, Andrew Lakoff, Kyra Lanzelius, Jieun Lee, Margaret Lock, Anne Lovell, Emily Martin, Joe Masco, Bill Maurer, Sarah McCullough, Jonathan Metzl, Colin Milburn, Lynn Morgan, Michelle Murphy, Natasha Myers, Diane Nelson, Jackie Orr, Esra Ozkan, Heather Paxson, Jesper Petersson, Adriana Petryna, Anne Pollock, Rima Praspaliauskiene, Rachel Prentice, Dan Price, Paul Rabinow, Rayna Rapp, Erika Rivas, Elizabeth Roberts, Nikolas Rose, Roger Rouse, Camilo Sanz, Suzana Sawyer, Bern Shen, Susan Silbey, Tania Simoncelli, Ilina Singh, Carol Smith, Natalie Speer, Susan Leigh Star, Karen Starback, Michelle Stewart, Kaushik Sunder Rajan, Miriam Ticktin, Sharon Traweek, Peter Wade, Nina Wakeford, Ethan Watters, Carl Whithaus, Allan Young, Li Zhang, the advertising and pharma marketers who remain anonymous, the many folks at direct-to-consumer (DTC) and medical meetings who helped me understand what I was reading, my seven classes and more than six hundred students for "Drugs, Science and Culture," and so many more people than I can remember.

Lastly, I am grateful to the personal drugs of my life: caffeine, my steadfast supporter anytime day or night; Xanax, for early mornings and redeye flights; the iPhone, for memory enhancement; meditation, for alphawaves during meetings; ibuprofen, for when meditation isn't enough; yoga and tai chi, for when ibuprofen isn't enough; Airborne, for real and imaginary bio-protection; alcohol, when needed; massage, when possible; Andrew, for games and inspiration; and Sylvia, for love and everything else.

INTRODUCTION

A doctor tells his patient, "Your blood pressure is off the chart, you're overweight, out of shape, and your cholesterol is god-awful. In short I find you perfectly normal."

A doctor tells his patient, "The good news is that your cholesterol level hasn't gone up. The bad news is the guidelines have changed."

These two jokes are both funny, and their intersection points to a new kind of health, one in which to be normal is to have symptoms and risk factors you should worry about, and at the same time to not know whether you should be worrying about yet more things. In fact, to not worry about your health, to not know as much as you can about it, and to not act on that knowledge is to be irresponsible. Some public relations campaigns feature people who are the "picture of health" but yet warn, "You might look and feel fine, but you need to get the inside story" (fig. 1). It appears to be that feeling healthy has become a sign that you need to be careful and go in for screening. To be normal, therefore, is to be insecure: this is the subject of my book.

Health in America today is defined by this double insecurity: never being sure enough about the future—always being at risk—and never knowing enough about what you could and should be doing. Paradoxically, the insecurity continues to grow despite there being an equal growth in research about risks, screening, and treatments and constant growth in the amount of medicine consumed each year—as

FIGURE 1 "'Are You the Picture of Health?'" poster for the Centers for Disease Control and Prevention's Screen for Life Campaign. *Source*: Centers for Disease Control and Prevention, Campaign for Colorectal Cancer Screening (retrieved May 5, 2005, from www.cdc.gov/screenforlife).

if the more we know, the more we fear; and the more we fear, the more preventive actions and medications we need to take. In the first joke, what is not revealed is how many prescriptions the patient will be given for being "perfectly normal." The growth in pharmaceutical consumption is actually quite astounding. Put simply, Americans are on drugs. The average American is prescribed and purchases somewhere between nine and thirteen prescription-only drugs per year, totalling over 4 billion prescriptions in 2011 and growing.[1] The range is wide, however, and many people are prescribed few or no drugs each year.

According to medical data companies and national surveys, 8 percent of Americans aged twenty to fifty-nine, and 44 percent of those over sixty were prescribed cholesterol-lowering statins in 2008. More than 20 percent of women over forty were taking monthly antidepressants in 2005–2008, and more than 6 percent of adolescents were prescribed attention-deficit disorder drugs (fig. 2).[2] These people are us, the generalized "you" of the jokes and the object of pharmaceutical marketing. These numbers are the flipside of the cost of healthcare. Overall healthcare costs were over $2 trillion in 2011, prescription drugs accounting for about 10 percent, or $203 billion, of that amount.

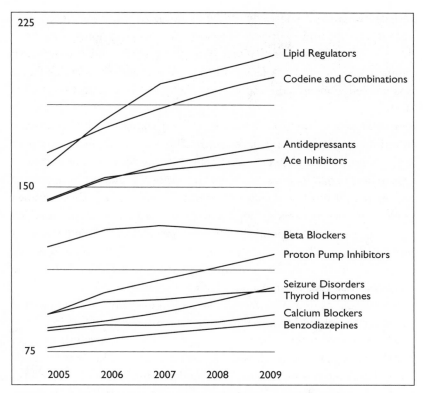

225

Lipid Regulators

Codeine and Combinations

Antidepressants
Ace Inhibitors

150

Beta Blockers

Proton Pump Inhibitors

Seizure Disorders
Thyroid Hormones

Calcium Blockers
Benzodiazepines

75

2005　　2006　　2007　　2008　　2009

FIGURE 2 The top therapeutic classes of drugs by U.S. dispensed prescriptions (in millions), 2010. *Source*: IMS National Prescription Audit PLUS, IMS Health.

If our health is so insecure, why are such jokes like the ones mentioned above funny? One reason they make us laugh is that they reveal the anxieties we feel about our health, and they carry the trace of how it has changed. The first joke reminds us that being overweight and having high cholesterol is normal now because the average American has these characteristics. The doctor diagnoses the patient as being typical, despite the symptoms. The other joke often earns even more nervous laughter because many of us have experienced finding out from our doctors or from the newspaper that new guidelines issued by national committees for health mean we are now at risk and in need of remediation. We joke among ourselves about the constant stream of new findings that tell us we are now at high risk, or that another drug has newly discovered side effects, or that a food we like is now carcinogenic. We joke also because we are essentially helpless in the face of a stream of information that reveals our current knowledge to be incomplete and maybe even dangerous. Normal and healthy are severed, and this is anxiously funny because it didn't used to be that way. Fifty years ago we didn't even know about cholesterol as a risk factor. In fact, the very concept of a risk factor was created alongside the innovation of large-scale prospective clinical studies.

In the 1950s, medicine began to rely on statistics. The large-scale Framingham Heart Study tracked the habits, health, and illnesses of over 5,000 members of a town in Massachusetts for decades. Public health researchers began to amass evidence that smoking "caused" lung cancer and increased mortality, although it was not universal.[3] These studies helped produce notions of populations "at risk." They represented an essential movement of public health from vaccinations, which definitely prevented some illnesses, to statistics, a shift in which biomarkers like cholesterol and high blood pressure correlated with health problems. The result was that risk became a target of medical intervention.

The 1950s also saw the rise of a new form of study: the randomized control trial, a clinical trial that in its ideal form was a double-blind study in which one treatment, usually a drug, was compared to another or to a placebo such that neither the doctors nor the patients knew what treatment the patients were getting. This rendered the trial a fair and objective test in which the only difference was the treatment. The advantages of these clinical trials were many, including the ability to detect incredibly minute differences between two treatments. For example, one could determine that one treatment worked 3 percent better than another one, which often meant that one treatment might help 103 out of 1,000 get better and the other treatment only 100 out of 1,000. This was both a stunning form of objective measurement and a bizarre one at the time: it meant that the treatments were so similar in effectiveness that no doctor or patient would be able to experience the difference but instead would have to rely on the results of the clinical trial to tell them which drug was better. Many doctors rebelled against such medicine by statistics, but the government, the drug companies, and other medical professionals as well as doctors and public health officials were thrilled to have a clear-cut way of knowing what worked.[4]

At the same time, the postwar pharmaceutical industry was getting started, growing out of prewar medicine companies but newly empowered by expansion during the war into national prominence and by the Food and Drug Administration's (FDA) granting of status to prescription-only drugs, which had not existed before. This new industry lost no time in imagining mass markets for drugs and in targeting doctors as the gate-keepers to this market.[5] The pharmaceutical industry and its armies of detail men, or drug representatives, invented many now-classic sales tactics and strategies.

The industrialization of clinical trials happened because drugs could be paired with risk factors: for example, Diuril with hypertension, Orinase with diabetes, Mevacor with high cholesterol. The drugs would be taken not to cure the condition but to reduce the risk factor and potential future events, such as heart disease or heart attacks. And the drugs would be taken chronically, every day. The pharmaceutical industry had found diagnoses whose markets could be grown to massive proportions.[6]

Clinical trials can increase the productivity of prescriptions, creating more drugs for more people for longer periods of time. According to pharmaceutical industry analysts, "Clinical trials are the heart of the pharmaceutical industry,"[7] and, conversely, pharmaceutical companies are the main force behind clinical trials. Pharmaceutical companies make money by selling medicines for which they hold a patent and FDA approval to market. The FDA approves drugs on the basis of evidence from the clinical trial, which allows the patent owner to sell it exclusively until the patent runs out. This can be up to fourteen years, but usually it is less. Pharma companies are therefore constitutionally insecure, continually losing their products and needing to come up with a constant stream, or pipeline, of new drugs to be thoroughly tested through clinical trials.

Because they see clinical trials as investments, pharma companies start with the question of how to research a treatment so it can be indicated for the largest possible market. They do this because they measure the value of clinical trial research via the total number of potential treatments that can be sold over the patent life of the drug. This has a number of consequences. Chronic treatments, especially long-term risk-reduction prescriptions, will generate a much larger market than acute treatments. One-time treatments like vaccines that actually prevent illness are "more likely to interfere with the spread of the disease than are drug treatments, thus reducing demand for the product,"[8] while mental illness treatments are highly valued precisely because these illnesses "share the distinction of not being cured by these pharmacological treatments. This makes the market even more attractive. The patients have to take the drugs chronically."[9]

With these clinical trials in hand, the pharma companies' and advertisers' objective is to "maximize the number of new prescriptions" and to make sure consumers stay on their medication as long as possible. In their accounting, potential patients who are not taking medication are counted as prescription loss. Making us aware and personalizing this risk so that we see our need for treatment are two of their strategies. Others involve getting us to ask our doctors about these conditions and drugs and developing relationships with us so that we keep taking our meds. These processes may seem harsh and uncaring, as they are manifestly prioritizing profits over health—but this is their job: maximizing sales of treatments. Marketers explicitly celebrate such growth.

These three trends—risk factors as targets of public health intervention, clinical trials as instruments to pinpoint smaller and smaller health risks for treatments, and growth in the power and size of the pharmaceutical industry—interacted with each other. And they came to generate the new notion of health that we laugh at in doctor–patient jokes. The sheer size of the pharmaceutical industry meant that it could afford to pose questions of smaller and smaller health risks and of risks in the more distant future. It also meant that government would be more or less compelled to let industry conduct the research because otherwise it was too expensive. Today, clinical trials can include more than one hundred thousand patients and can span hundreds of hospitals and doctors in many countries.

Medical observers have noticed that the vast majority of illnesses today are treated as chronic and that being at risk for illness is often treated as if one had a disease requiring lifelong treatments, drugs for life. Today, chronic diseases are said to affect 133 million Americans, one out of every two adults.[10] These are not the chronic illnesses studied by medical anthropologists that painfully disorder one's life and disrupt one's biography.[11] The recent reformulation of chronicity represents a shift in the basic paradigm of health and disease, a paradigm shift away from an inherently healthy body. The old paradigm assumes that most people are healthy at their core and that most illnesses are temporary interruptions in their lives, identified by persons as the experience of suffering. Chronic and genetic diseases like diabetes, cystic fibrosis, and Huntington's, although well-known counterexamples, were exceptions to the basic paradigm of inherent health. Beginning in the 1960s and 1970s and becoming common by the 1990s, a very different notion of illness took center stage, one in which bodies are inherently ill, whether genetically or through lifestyles or traumas. Health for the chronically ill is not an existential term in that they are never absolutely healthy; rather, it is a temporal, relative, experiential term, that is, they feel healthy today. In the words of Elizabeth Beck-Gernsheim, "All of us are affected, all of us all risk carriers."[12]

Diabetes is regularly invoked as a paradigmatic template for many conditions that were previously not thought of as illnesses. The older notion and examples of chronic illness are not gone; these notions coexist, and we are quite good at inhabiting and switching between the paradigms. But the new notion of illness is more prevalent because it is now promoted to us in advertisements and in awareness campaigns throughout our daily life. As an index of this paradigm shift, health itself is starting to disappear in pharmaceutical reports. The word often appears in quotation marks. A report in 2005 on pharmaceutical consumption trends by Express Scripts stated "2004 was in fact a 'healthier' year than 2003." It placed *healthier* in quotation marks because only five of the top twenty-five most widely consumed drug types decreased in use: these were the five classes given for acute conditions like infections, in which a patient calls a doctor. For all other classes of drugs, like cholesterol-lowering, antidepressant, and antihypertensive medicine, there was significant growth in both the percentage of people taking them and in the number of pills each person consumed. Increased consumption of a preventive or chronic drug confounds the analysis of health. If you find out you have high cholesterol and start taking a statin, are you sick because you have an elevated risk? Or are you healthier because you are reducing that risk? The distinction between healthy treatment and chronic illness seems to be dissolving. So *healthy* is in quotes as if it were literally a legacy term, one that no longer has meaning.

When the risk of a disease comes to be seen as a disease in itself, then clinical trials can be designed to test lifelong treatments for that risk factor, and this is a vastly bigger market. Treatments that reduce risk ostensibly could be indicated for all of us since we are all at risk for most diseases. Even a small risk can be targeted by a clinical trial, and its reduction can be measured if the trial is large enough. The result is a set

TABLE 1 **Health Models**

INDIVIDUAL HEALTH MODEL	MASS HEALTH MODEL
Symptoms interrupt the patient's life and drive him or her to the doctor.	Little or no experience of symptoms until attention is called to them.
Doctor takes history and examines patient to make diagnosis.	Patient or doctor takes checklist or screening test and discovers treatable risks.
Doctor prescribes treatment.	Clinical trials indicate treatments.
Treatment returns patient to health and is discontinued.	Treatment often has no discernible effect and is indefinite.

of facts about treatable risks, facts we then must act on or ignore at our peril. Even if we question the relevance of those facts to ourselves as individual patients, if there are no other facts to contradict them, we must act on the facts we have.

All the pieces for understanding the jokes and this book are now in place: the jokes are funny because they mark the transition from an old to a new notion of health (see table 1). The old idea is based on symptoms you feel that make you call on the doctor, symptoms the doctor reads to diagnose you as being ill and to prescribe treatment for you that ideally cures you and returns you to health. In place of this older paradigm we have a new mass health model in which you often have no experience of being ill and no symptoms your doctor can detect, but you or your doctor often discover that you are at risk via a screening test based on clinical trials that show some efficacy of a treatment in reducing that risk; you may therefore be prescribed a drug for life that will have no discernible effect on you, and by taking it you neither return to health nor are officially ill, only at risk. The first joke marks the irony of this transition: you are normal even while you have many illnesses that need treatment, and you stay the same while coming to be newly diagnosed and in need of treatments. The terms health and illness do not appear in the jokes because they are old-model terms; in their place are biomarkers of risk like cholesterol and chronic treatment guidelines.

Along with this transformation in health is the remarkable fact that the prescription rates are projected to keep growing. Healthcare spending has been growing and is expected to continue to grow around 4 to 8 percent per year through 2020; drug growth is expected to be more

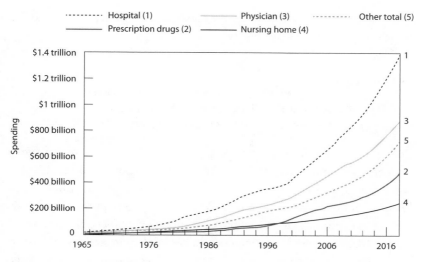

FIGURE 3 Personal healthcare expenditures, by type of expenditure, 1965–2018, based on data from the U.S. Department of Health and Human Services, 2009. *Source*: RAND Health (retrieved December 10, 2010, from www.randcompare.org).

than 7 percent per year; and personal healthcare spending is growing by about 6 percent per year (fig. 3).[13] The growth rates for almost all classes of drugs have been in the low double digits for a decade, with prescription rates for children growing the fastest. Similarly, both the prevalence (the number of people on each drug) and the intensity (the size of the yearly prescription) are projected to continue to grow in all drug categories for the foreseeable future.[14] The figures match our fears, and according to many surveys Americans are spending more time, more energy, more attention, and more money on health.[15] Health is not simply a cost to the nation to be reduced; contradictorily, it is also a market to be grown.

A notion of health driven by market forces seems like a dystopian science fiction story. On one side it seems crazy that so many kids could really be so sick and need lifelong medicines and that so many of the rest of us are on so many drugs, with all of these rates increasing. On the other side, there are facts to back up these claims, epidemiological surveys to show the growing prevalence of illnesses and clinical trials to demonstrate the need to treat. If anything, the facts imply that we are not doing enough screening and treating. Too much and too little at the same time. My research has been aiming to understand this double bind of ever-increasing diagnosis and pharmaceutical consumption in the United States and to discover the consequences of our redefinition of health and illness over the past two decades.

WHY YOU SHOULD READ THIS BOOK

"'Get well soon'? We prefer, 'Stay healthier longer.'" (see fig. 4)
—MAGAZINE AND SUBWAY ADVERTISEMENT FROM PFIZER (2007)

This is a book about the current American, middle-class, commonsense view of health and illness, risk and treatment, and how it works. It is also about how this view resulted in people consuming more and more drugs for life. The book is for everyone who takes a prescription despite not feeling sick, and for anyone who has wondered why there are almost no studies that help people or their doctors know when to stop taking a drug (see chapter 5). It is a book for expert patients, who comb the internet for information and think they know how to get to the bottom of facts and make the right decision (see chapters 1 and 6). It is for those who wonder why the cost of healthcare keeps going up and why most of the solutions seem to result in even more screening tests and more drugs (see chapters 3 and 4). And it is a book for those who think there is something fishy about all of those pharmaceutical commercials on television and in magazines suggesting that you really should do a mini-self-diagnosis and go talk to your doctor (see chapter 2).

Explaining this continual growth in drugs, diagnoses, costs, and insecurity can take many forms. One key approach involves following the money and tracing connections between the profits of pharmaceutical companies and disease expansion. Even though the FDA has probably the safest regulatory standards in the world, it also controls the largest market in the world. So the incentives to cheat are staggering. Recent books by Don Light, Marcia Angell, Jerry Avorn, Ray Moynihan, David Healy, and others and the detailed reporting by the *Seattle Times* in the series of articles entitled "Suddenly Sick" are all worth mining to discover how many ways the health system is manipulated: from controlling research results, to ghostwriting medical articles allegedly written by doctors, to influencing guideline committees, to hyping clinical trials, to funding disease awareness campaigns and activist groups in order to drive drug sales. The fact that most biomedical research is underwritten by private industry and therefore that most drugs are produced first for profit and

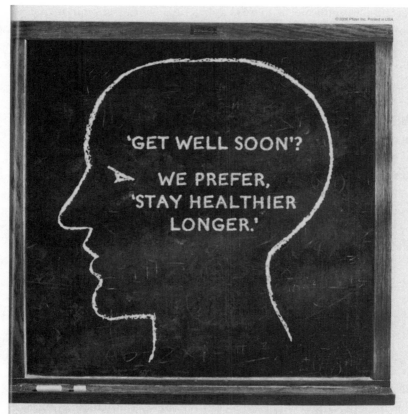

think of it. Americans are living longer and spending more on healthcare. In fact, spending has risen to more than two trillion dollars a year. At Pfizer we're working on ways to help - with innovative medicines that help prevent illnesses and reduce the cost of treating them. We also have programs that provide our medicines to people without prescription coverage.

But we know we have to go further. Across America, Pfizer is partnering with health care providers, state governments and local communities to bring personalized, quality, preventive health solutions to patients; measures like providing personal care managers, 24 hour-a-day nurse call centers, and health education

such as diabetes workshops and other group health classes. And the results are clear. These programs are helping keep people healthy and reducing the economic burden of disease, in some cases decreasing hospital stays by as much as 52%.

Today, Pfizer is working toward solutions that mean a happier, healthier tomorrow for us all.

Working for a healthier world™
www.pfizer.com

FIGURE 4 "'Get well soon'? We prefer, 'Stay healthier longer.'" Advertisement by Pfizer, *New Yorker*, February 12, 2007, 23.

second for health means there is a structural contradiction in medicine, one requiring vigilant watchdogs.[16]

I want to take a different approach here. For the past eight years I have been conducting fieldwork on pharmaceutical marketing—attending conferences; talking with marketers, researchers, doctors, and patients; and surveying the extensive literature produced by marketers about their strategies. I have concluded that underlying the continual growth in drugs, diseases, costs, and insecurity is a relatively new understanding of ourselves as being inherently ill. Health has come to be defined as re-duction in risk. Treatment is prevention, and we have an increasingly in-secure notion of our well-being because we have outsourced its evidence to clinical trials. Together these definitions are reinforced and amplified by the pharmaceutical industry, which sees clinical trials as investments, and measures the value of those investments by the size of the market in treatments it will define.

My interest was in how we enter into relationships with these mass health facts and how their logics come to seem natural. This led to a sys-temic study of how pharmaceutical facts are defined and how they circu-late. Pharmaceutical marketers in particular have a highly developed set of strategies not only for directly managing the manufacture of clinical trials so that they produce the largest number of potential patients, but also for ensuring that the discussions of clinical trials in the media, in doctors' offices, and online constantly reinforce a sense that any measur-able health risks must be treated immediately, as if the risks themselves were diseases.

The interaction between the redefinition of health and the growth of treatment was on my mind when I attended a neuroethics meeting in 2002 at which questions of informed consent, brain privacy from scan-ning, and lie detection were the main topics. The increasing mass pre-scription of psychopharmaceuticals as an ethical concern was not a topic, however. So after one talk I went up to a leading clinical researcher (a medical doctor with a PhD) and asked whether he was worried at all that the average American was on at least five prescriptions per year. His re-sponse was quick and sure:

> I think being on five or more drugs for life is a minimum! Based on the latest clinical trials, almost everyone over thirty should be on cholesterol-lowering drugs.

At the time I could not believe my ears. I was astonished at how easily he pronounced these phrases, how natural he found it that clinical trials could seriously suggest that every adult be put on lifelong statins.[17] Each part of his comment assumed a world in which biomedical facts in the form of trials set thresholds for asymptomatic biomarkers like cholesterol or even age that obligated preventive pharmaceutical treatment. This meant that almost all of these average Americans would not feel ill or experience any symptoms, and most of them would not even suffer a heart attack. They would know only that they were ill or at risk when they were tested and found out they had a score below the threshold for health as defined by the clinical trial. Or they would find out that being over thirty meant they were now at high risk. And why thirty? I'm over thirty, why wasn't I on a statin? Shouldn't I know my cholesterol score at least?

When I speak of this encounter with other doctors, I am told over and over that this is how things are. But even they are a bit disturbed when we start to work out the implications of this view of facts.

First, illness is not felt, and there are no symptoms that drive a person to the doctor. Instead, as we'll see in the next chapter, some sort of screening test determines whether or not that person has crossed a line and needs to be treated. The line measures not a state of illness or ill health, but a state of risk as well as a treatment that would ideally reduce that risk. It is ambiguous whether the person who should be on the cholesterol-lowering drug is ill, but it is clear that it would be healthier to be on the drug because it would reduce the risk of getting heart disease in the future. The historian Robert Aronowitz called this the preventive revolution: if a health risk can be reduced, it should be.[18] Health is thus not exactly a state one is in but a relative category: you would be healthier if you were on the drug, especially if you are over thirty.

Second, the principal agent in the statement is not you, the drug, or the age limit, but the clinical trials. The trials are where the experience of illness seems to have gone when it left the body. They provide the researcher with the answer as to whether someone needs treatment or not. Like the person himself, the doctor in this case cannot tell whether she is ill. The doctor does not even diagnose. Rather, she uses the same algorithm that everyone else does: if a person is over thirty, then he or she should probably be put on cholesterol-lowering drugs. Neither health nor illnesses are states of being: they are states of knowledge; they are epistemic. This means that the questions asked by the clinical trials determine what counts as illness and risk and treatment. And the control of these design questions, as we'll see in chapters 4 through 6, has shifted from doctors to clinical researchers to pharmaceutical company researchers to pharmaceutical company marketers.

Furthermore, the disempowerment of the doctor is compounded by many of the direct-to-consumer advertising campaigns such as TV commercials. These ads often portray active consumers-become-patients who paid attention to the TV or a website and recognized a risk that their doctors missed or even misdiagnosed. Consumers can self-diagnose online or even by listening to their symptoms as defined in the ad, and increasingly they are arriving at their doctors' offices with demands rather than questions. Doctors, in turn, because of the multiple pressures of limited patient time, keeping up with rapidly changing information, and the constraints of health maintenance organizations and insurance, are quite vulnerable to these demands.[19]

Third, the relation of the researcher to the state of knowledge is narrated as one of deep submission. Referring to "the latest" clinical trial may seem like an authoritative move, but it implies that what the researcher may have told the patient the day before is now false. Here the jokes are more sinister: health and illness and treatment are continually subject to revision. The consumer as being potentially at risk must maintain vigilance with regard to health information. Health must become a preoccupation. And indeed it has.[20]

Finally, it may not be surprising that the latest clinical trials almost always recommend more treatment for more people. But the researcher's happy sense of the trend quoted above, "Five or more drugs for life is a minimum!" is still disturbing. Declaring a minimum implies an open-endedness to the number of drugs we should be on for life. Given the logic and authority of his claim, it seems that only large-scale clinical trials can help determine whether someone would actually benefit from a treatment. As we will see in chapter 4, because large-scale trials are run by pharmaceutical companies as investments, the only trials they can afford to run are those that, if successful, will return that investment through indicating more treatments.

These characteristics of mass health—chronic treatments for risk reduction, health as known through limited clinical trials, ever-increasing numbers of drugs—are the subject of this book. They are not secret, except that they are taken for granted and therefore hidden in plain sight. But they were quite controversial when they were emerging. Just sixty years ago most doctors fiercely opposed all of these developments, insisting on symptomatic diagnosis, etiological treatment, the ability to personally diagnose, and the idea that drugs were prescribed to cure diseases. In the 1960s the full potential of mass health started to become visible, implying exactly what the researcher stated: five or more drugs for life at minimum.[21] This potential was met repeatedly with disbelief, disavowal, denial, and jokes. It became true and absurd at the same time. Yet by the 1990s mass health had become gospel and second nature, part of common sense.

Mass health is both necessary and insufficient. Large-scale clinical trials do distinguish better drugs from worse ones, and the risk they measure produces a kind of truth (chapter 5). The allure of clinical trials is that all successful, well-run ones must have asked relevant questions and therefore reveal treatments that we should follow. The problem is that there are better and worse questions to ask, better and worse ways of framing populations. And good questions for increasing market size do not necessarily translate into a better sense of health and overall well-being.

MAXIMUM TREATMENT

The goal of the launch phase is to influence the physician–patient relationship to maximize the number of new prescriptions. Marketers can generate significant product sales by motivating physicians and patients to take action and by influencing their interaction.
—BOLLING, "DTC: A STRATEGY FOR EVERY STAGE"

This declaration, which appeared in the journal *Pharmaceutical Executive*, aimed at making direct-to-consumer marketing more effective by using "a strategy for every stage"; the goal of such pharmaceutical marketing is explicitly stated: not to cure people or to identify those who should be cured, but to grow the number of new prescriptions as much as possible. The logical extension of risk and its grammatical personalization through biomedical facts combine with marketing here to produce a new regimen of treatment maximization.

On one level the problem can be simply stated: health as a paramount value in our life is defined in part by clinical trials that have to build in assumptions about health, normality, and risk.[22] As there is no logical limit to risk or health, the practical result for pharmaceutical companies is an unlimited imperative. They want to maximize prescriptions by expanding the market of those at risk, defining clinical trials as broadly as possible, and persuading us that all risks are, in fact, conditions that must be treated now with drugs. It is true that, aside from outright fraud, there are limits to what clinical trials can be made to say. Trials do regularly fail and even backfire on the companies that sponsor them. But the point here is that actuarial risks have now been redefined as symptoms. Risk is now a subjunctive present illness: treated as if diseased. Treatment maximization in the era of biomedical clinical trials imposes order where before there was social negotiation and an unstated assumption that illness was defined by patients.[23] For instance, the following type of comment appears quite regularly when new clinical guidelines are published:

> Only a fraction of people with high cholesterol are on statins, despite a barrage of drug-company advertising backed up by guidance from public-health officials. About 11 million Americans currently take one of the statins, while some public health experts say that at least 36 million should probably be on one. Globally, the discrepancy is even more dramatic: About 25 million are taking the pills while an estimated 200 million meet guidelines for treatment.[24]

In this paragraph, taken from a *Wall Street Journal* article published in 2004, a set of population statistics are emphasized that intensify an argument about the dangers of not listening to doctors and clinical trial data. Two hundred million people worldwide, one out of every thirty persons on the planet, is presented as a new target number. Universal screening programs and mass pharmaceutical regimes regularly appear in the news, and the line between good use and abuse is increasingly hard to draw.

The intersection between market logic and the infinite logic of risk is one of incredibly productive tensions. When marketers say their aim is to maximize the number of prescriptions—first, the new prescriptions and, second, the length of time one stays on them—they express a logic of generalized medication. They aim at the maximum number of prescriptions each of us can be made to take. It looks, therefore, like pharmaceutical companies have found a way to grow health via clinical trials, redefining health as treatment, in part by expropriating the means of diagnosing illness through screening tests that tell us and our doctors that we need treatment. Increasingly they use clinical trials to co-produce disease definition, diagnostic test, and treatment as a bundle. The bottom line is that they have exchanged any interest in reducing treatments for the goal of increasing them. No matter how obvious this might seem now, I didn't see the connections right away, even when pharmaceutical researchers said it directly: "No one is thinking about the patients, just market share."[25]

Viewed systemically, this capacity to add medications to our life by lowering the level of risk required to be at risk is what I call surplus health. Surplus health research aims to constantly increase the total number of medicines we consume. A clinical trial designed to *reduce* the amount of medication people take and still save lives sounds like a win-win solution: the company has a better drug to sell that will be more targeted, and people will get better faster. But actually this kind of trial is remarkably rare, even counterintuitive. If successful, such a trial would take a large number of people out of a risk category, essentially telling them they had less risk than they thought. The drugs they were taking to gain health would no longer be seen to do so. In the joke for this scenario, the doctor would tell the patient, "Good news, you haven't changed, but the guidelines have!"

I have talked with doctors as part of my fieldwork, and they, too, have been struck by this oddness. Most trials are set up so that either they are successful and a new, more intensive treatment regimen is indicated, or they fail, and the status quo prevails. Only the trials that backfire and find excessive side effects result in reduced treatment. My doctors are troubled by how easy it is to put people on medication because they meet guideline criteria, but how difficult it is to get them off. Often no studies are conducted to determine when it would be better or safer to stop giving a medication to a patient, even while there are very few studies of the long-term effectiveness or safety of those medications.[26] None of these studies interest drug companies because, again, they would shrink the market for treatments. The general trend is that the only trials conducted by the industry are those that would grow the market by increasing the amount of medication in our collective lives. The health facts we have and the empirical data for pharmaceutical consumption in the United States bear this out. It might seem that publicly funded trials can easily correct this problem, but the economy of such trials and the way even public trials subscribe to the logic of health as risk reduction suggest it is not clear how to do this. By unraveling the dysfunctions within our emergent health systems I want to take a crucial step in that direction.

THE ELEPHANT IN THE ROOM

The pharmaceutical industry is a massive elephant. Like the blind men of the famous parable, we each catch hold of a tiny piece of it—leg, tail, trunk—and think we have a handle on it: it is strong and solid, it is hairy, it moves like a snake. From about $880 billion dollars of sales for 2011, the industry is expected to grow approximately 5 percent a year in the future. Its top ten companies employed 960,000 people in 2009. More than 32,000 clinical trials actively recruited volunteers across 167 countries as of April 2012. More than 2.4 million Americans participated in clinical trials in 2006.[27] While these numbers may seem large, within the health industry they represent a crisis. Four out of every five clinical trials are delayed because of problems in enrolling enough people. In the United States, the problem is that Americans are already on too many drugs and therefore their bodies are not clean (or "treatment naïve") enough to be proper test subjects.[28] As a report by the consulting firm Ernst & Young indicated, "The number of trials has doubled in the past 10 years, forcing companies to seek trial participants in emerging markets outside of the saturated areas in the United States and Western Europe. . . . Emerging markets such as India, China, and Russia offer drug companies a volume of potential subjects, and trials can often be executed at reduced costs."[29]

There are entire literatures devoted to studying the pharmaceutical industry and clinical trials, including reports by economists, critics, and now ethnographers and science studies scholars. These studies include Andrew Lakoff's *Pharmaceutical Reason*, as observed in Argentina; Jeremy Greene's *Prescribing by Numbers*, a history of midcentury pharmaceutical studies and marketing; Anne Pollock's *Medicating Race*, on heart disease and normal treatment; Steven Epstein's *Inclusion*, a history of the practices of clinical trial activism in the United States; Kristin Peterson's work on clinical trials in Nigeria and wider anticlinical trial activism; and Stephen Ecks's and Cori Hayden's studies of the practices of the generics industry and logics in India and Mexico, respectively.[30]

Adriana Petryna's anthropology of the global clinical trials industry and Jill Fisher's study of doctor-run clinical research organizations attend to the phenomenally large outsourcing by the pharmaceutical industry itself, resulting in what Petryna calls "ethical variability." She writes, "There has been little or no public discussion of how outsourcing and offshoring generate novel strategies of evidence making: providing new opportunities for manufacturers to create the data they want and to arbitrage it in the context of regulatory drug approval."[31] As ethnographies, these works detail the ways in which the people caught up in disaggregated industries come to have incentives and worldviews that keep them from understanding the collective effects of their work. They are able to substitute regulatory compliance for ethics and local legality for collective health. Kaushik Sunder Rajan has been studying sites in India where deindustrialization has forced millworkers into situations in which they are being recruited in large numbers as presumed volunteers into clinical trials. Crucially, they are valuable only to the extent that they are anonymous, individualized, healthy, and relatively unmedicated. As Sunder Rajan puts it, their informed consent, even if conducted in the most ethical mode possible, must be understood structurally: "Ethics does not just legitimate experimental subjectivity, it actively depoliticizes it."[32]

Together, these ethnographies capture portions of the elephant. The phenomenal size and continued growth of the pharmaceutical industry depend on these global processes. At the same time, growth depends on the ability to continually change and enlarge the definition of health so that more and more drugs can be prescribed to those who can pay. In this book I try to get a handle on the changing nature of health, given that clinical trials are almost entirely run by drug companies.

My book studies these naturalized logics of clinical trials and risk treatment in American culture. Using a combination of ethnography, interviewing, and media analysis, I focus on how these logics are produced, maintained, and embodied in speech and text. Here I follow Marilyn Strathern in defining culture as "the way analogies are drawn between things, in the way certain thoughts are used to think others. Culture consists in the images which make imagination possible, in the media with which we mediate experience."[33]

I began this study with a survey of the mass media, constructing a database of newspaper and magazine articles about clinical trial results and medical risk guidelines and collecting television and print advertisements for pharmaceuticals. I analyzed these for how notions of risk and evidence were presented and how the activeness or passivity of patients were portrayed. In order to observe how people talk about drugs, risks, and evidence, I analyzed online patient newsgroup discussions. I then conducted a series of interviews with persons taking pharmaceuticals and with doctors, focusing on how exactly they learned new medical facts and how they incorporated these facts into their daily practice. Using the methods of grounded theory to analyze these datasets, I identified logical structures of their arguments, grammatical forms of identification and justification, and regimens of lived practices.[34]

The second part of my research focused on the explicit production of pharmaceutical marketing strategies. I attended a pharmaceutical marketing conference and conducted three workshops with pharma marketers at the Massachusetts Institute of Technology. I analyzed major marketing journals, websites, and business press coverage of pharma marketing. My aim was to document the forms of pharmaceutical companies' explicit attention to creating and maintaining mass notions of health and to formulate a series of hypotheses regarding the ways in which facts, risks, and pharmaceuticals are talked about and incorporated as taken-for-granted parts of everyday life.[35]

I have presented my preliminary findings in a series of talks over the past several years at academic conferences, but also, importantly, I have engaged in a form of constant ethnographic engagement. This has included sharing my talks with marketers, including one who designed a pharmaceutical campaign I write about in this book. I consulted with two marketing firms in which my contribution was to present my ongoing research and discuss with them the changing nature of pharmaceutical consumption. In addition, I was invited to present to a number of groups of doctors in forums, including in grand rounds; in each case a lively debate followed my presentation, a discussion in which we collectively critiqued and sharpened my analyses.[36]

Together, the *logic*, *grammar*, and *regimen* of pharmaceuticals form the results of my research. Logic names the ways in which concepts make sense together. The grammar of biomedical facts tells us about ourselves—who we really are, our personal levels of risk, our symptoms, our future—it helps narrate ourselves as being responsible for ourselves, for our choices, our past, our genes, and our visits to the doctor. It constitutes a moral grammar. Biomedical facts identify risks and induce fear, anxiety, hope, and occasionally denial. Through a personalizing grammar, they create a relationship between us and truth that in most cases we must learn to live with, counter with other facts, or try to forget. These ways of talking about ourselves and becoming persuaded of the truth of our illnesses and treatments I call objective self-fashioning. Because we have invented ways of living with facts, facts in turn become instruments through which marketers manipulate our lives. In addition to logic and grammar we must add an analysis of a pharmaceutical regimen in which prescription maximization replaces health as the force driving treatment innovation and our healthcare behaviors in seeking information and taking medications.

The book is thus an ethnography of the cultural work being done in the name of risk, screens, drugs, and clinical trials. I trace how our ideas of health and illness have transformed in such a way that it has become thinkable that every adult should be taking a preventive cholesterol-lowering drug and every troubled adolescent an antidepressant. By *our* and *we* in this paragraph and throughout this text, I do not claim to speak for all patients or Americans. Instead, following Strathern's approach, I want "simply to identify myself with those who are exposed—whether they wish for it or not—to a range of ideas and images now in cultural currency." These ideas and images are the medical facts, and marketing specifically addresses us as patients or would-be patients.[37]

The methods of media analysis, interviews, fieldwork, and ethnographic engagement have enabled me to create a thick description of how it comes to be common sense for the mass media, doctors, and patients to talk about planet-sized markets and everyone being on five or more drugs for life. We may dispute these claims, but, more important, we do not find them, as many people did before 1990, absurd or unthinkable. We can see how they might make sense to others, and we can imagine that, if presented with the right data, we would come to accept and even advocate them. We share, in other words, the sense that fact-questions about clinical trial data, risky foods, and preventive pharmaceuticals are good questions. Anthropologically speaking, this sense of what makes a good question is a good basis for understanding culture.

The aim of this book is to make our common sense about health seem a bit strange—through seeing the process as a whole, including how it comes to inhabit us, how it is promoted, and how it undergirds the very possibility of a health industry based on a need to grow. The book works to touch and to comprehend a very small piece of the drug industry elephant: corporate health research. Small as it is, I think it is a crucial piece to understand, because if I am right in my analysis of it we will need more than regulatory change. The very idea of corporate health research is a problem we are grappling with. So in this book I isolate that issue and temporarily pass over the many other problems, including corruption, price, bioethics, and poverty, so that we may clearly see just how natural and embedded the notion of health as growth has become.

THE STRUCTURE OF THIS BOOK

Understanding how the continual growth in pharmaceutical consumption has become common sense requires tacking back and forth between a patient–citizen point of view and a pharmaceutical company point of view. Part of my aim in doing this is to show that there are many things on which we all agree, including processes and trends that are not good for either our health or our wallets. Therefore each chapter works out the logics of these two points of view, how they come to make sense and serve as the basis upon which we make decisions. Each chapter can be read separately, but together they show that our healthcare is in need of systemic change.

Chapter 1, "Responding to Facts," examines the ideal smart consumer who encounters a medical fact, like a test result, that forces him or her to make a decision. This protopatient immediately becomes an intense researcher, critically examining the clinical trials available, interviewing doctors, scanning the internet, and weighing options, only to find that despite a large number of studies there are not enough appropriate facts to make a proper decision. The person has become an expert patient and yet something seems wrong with the world of medicine. There is not enough time, however, to get to the bottom of it because a decision has to be made.

Chapter 2, "Pharmaceutical Witnessing and Direct-to-Consumer Advertising," takes the next step and looks at how marketers see us as patients-in-waiting who need education and advertising in order to be brought up to speed on the risks and conditions we should be treating. This chapter details the incredibly fine-grained stages that are used to manage how we come to learn that we *may* be ill and at risk. Clinical trials are part of marketing. They are designed to produce the largest markets, and they are run to yield the types of facts that will motivate the largest population possible to consider treatment. Newspaper articles, awareness campaigns, pamphlets in doctors' offices, patients groups, and advertisements are all part of coordinated campaigns to gain our attention and stoke our anxieties. I repeat again that this is not in itself wrong; it is the logic of our mass health to be extensible. Yet the dilemma is that these are the only facts we have.

Chapter 3, "Having to Grow Medicine," steps back by realizing that a pivotal question is not where to draw the line, but who draws the line. The fact that most clinical trials need to be designed and run by pharmaceutical companies as investments is the assumed condition of the world right now; everyone, including the companies' critics, seems to agree that they are the only ones who can afford to study mass illnesses. Corruption aside, the real issue is that clinical trials are driven by the need to grow the market in medicine and that this is a very different goal for a clinical trial than arriving at the best therapy for people. Pharmaceutical companies are not shy about admitting this impulse—making money is their livelihood—and, as we shall see, they feel this pressure as being inexorable and blame us for putting them in this position. In a guidebook for pharmaceutical employees, for example, two analysts complain that "one of the significant problems for the pharma industry is that of the 400 disease entities identified, only 50 are commercially attractive by today's requirements of return on investment (ROI). Society needs to find a way to make more diseases commercially attractive if it wants Pharma investment in treating any of the other 350 diseases affecting hundreds of millions of people."[38] The analysts are explaining that, as companies who need to grow in order to survive, pharma can afford to do research only on treatments that have a chance of becoming massively huge markets. This has led to the expanding role of marketing in designing clinical trials within pharma companies, allowing those in marketing to make decisions that formerly were in the hands of scientists and clinicians. It is not that companies don't want to eliminate suffering, but they must attend first of all to the bottom line. As another analyst put it, "Pharmaceutical companies tend not to invest in tropical medicines because they are unlikely to recoup their investments."[39]

Chapter 4, "Mass Health: Illness Is a Line You Cross," investigates how clinical trials came to occupy such a critical role in how we think about health. Since the 1950s statistical medicine has slowly transformed health to the point where most of the drugs we take are not to address symptoms we suffer but to reduce our chances of having symptoms in the future. Understanding the notion of risk reduction is incredibly confounding because it is essentially infinite: no matter how much risk we reduce, we still have the 100 percent risk of dying. Where to draw the line thus becomes an ethical and social question, not just a technical and clinical one. This chapter considers the logic of health as risk reduction and how medical professionals have grappled with it over the past half century and more.

Chapter 5, "Moving the Lines, Deciding on Thresholds," looks at how pharmaceutical companies decide how much risk we should treat. It examines their creative strategies for using clinical trials to extend medicine to more and more of our life, under the banner of making us healthier, but only if we can become so by taking more medicine. Treating us earlier, treating us longer, turning risks into treatable conditions, and finding more and more risks to treat are explicit strategies they discuss in their journals and at conferences. Their facts are the most prevalent and sometimes the only facts about our health that are available, and this is why it is hard to find the answers we are often looking for, for example, when to get off of a drug or whether a drug will really help us.

Chapter 6, "Knowing Your Numbers: Pharmaceutical Lifestyles," returns to the expert consumer in all of us and asks what we can do in the face of this marketed field of facts. It looks at how consumers and patients have taken at least three different rational ways of responding to the increasing facts about more and more risks and drugs. One mode of response is to live in constant struggle between one's desires and one's fear of unhealthy consequences, that is, to live against health. Another mode is to change one's lifestyle entirely with the goal of being healthy, that is, to live for health. A third response is to take drugs in order to enjoy one's lifestyle, to take statins in order to continue eating steak, a personal variant of DuPont's slogan, "better living through chemistry." Each mode involves negotiating a constant stream of intense, often worrying health facts. And we all oscillate among these modes and experiment with practices of resisting health.

My hope is that each chapter in this book will challenge readers' ways of seeing health, risk, facts, and clinical trials. Each is designed to show how much these concepts have become the very tools used by pharmaceutical companies to grow markets, to the point that there is no simple way to imagine how to live life without drugs. Early readers have told me that it often seems like an anti-self-help book, emphasizing how hard it is to act and how little we know about the drugs we take because we haven't, as a society, prioritized the right questions. Policy recommendations are beyond the scope of the book, but in the conclusion I outline how clarifying the way health has been transformed into mass risk reduction and working through the way in which facts themselves have come to be managed might allow us as a society to figure out a way to reverse this spiral and head in a better direction.

ONE

Responding to Facts

"Oh, my God," Andy Grove invokes his deity in "Taking on Prostate Cancer," a cover article for the business magazine *Fortune* that narrates his arduous odyssey through the deeply troubled waters of prostate cancer research. Grove's freaked-out reaction is that of a rich businessman, the chief executive officer of the computer chip giant Intel and someone used to operating with facts in order to make decisions, who has found out that medical facts are very elusive and tricky creatures. Grove had just had his first test for prostate specific antigen (PSA), a screen that tracked this bodily substance and returned a number. In his case the result was 5 when "the acceptable range, according to the lab computer, was 0 to 4." In every description of a fact in his story Grove carefully attends to its context and its specificity: who says it, where, how, and with what degree of certainty. Here he notices that it is the lab computer that defines *acceptable*. Grove had not heard of the test, and he next records his doctor's new description of this result: "It's slightly elevated. It's probably nothing to worry about, but I think you should see a urologist."[1]

I have chosen Grove's account in this article as exemplary of the expert patient.[2] He is a smart, careful, resourceful, compliant, and eminently rational patient. He is fully empowered by patient and consumer movements to take charge of his health. In the end, though, he is also the ideal consumer from the point of view of treatment marketers. I analyze Grove's account for how it reveals the gaps in medical facts and in the circulation of knowledge that frustrate his attempt to find the best course of action. The ambiguity of medical facts is accentuated even more by another article in the same issue, in which one of *Fortune's* editors, Tom Alexander, describes facing a similar prognosis and choosing a diametrically opposite response: whereas Grove chooses aggressive radiation treatment, Alexander chooses to wait and see. Both men invoke mass health facts to justify their actions, seeing those same facts through different logics of action and different valences of risk. The openness of mass health to multiple interpretations is precisely the opening through which pharmaceutical companies step in and help shape the way in which we encounter these facts. And since the facts we encounter are the ones upon which we base our judgment as expert patients, controlling the circulation of facts turns out to be a marketing strategy.

Grove's article is a biography of how a fact becomes personally adopted and embodied. In reading Grove this way, I adopt a mode of analysis employed by the anthropologists Arjun Appadurai and Igor Kopytoff, who observed that a thing, say, a car, can be seen to go through many status changes, sometimes being a commodity, then a useful article, a priceless member of the family, then scrap metal. Using the analogy of a biography, Appadurai and Kopytoff proposed that analytic attention be paid to the social life of a thing.[3] Grove, I suggest, offers a detailed account of the social life of a medical fact in the process of being incorporated into a person's life and of the person, in turn, coming to understand himself differently, objectively, and as a patient object of that fact. This dual process I have called objective self-fashioning to highlight the active participation of a person in incorporating this external redefinition of him- or herself.[4]

An ambivalent directive often accompanies the first appearance of medical facts to a patient: be concerned but not worried. Grove is unprepared at this point, uninformed even as to the meaning of PSA. The thorny problem for the doctor, especially the primary care doctor, is one of introducing a possibility to a patient. In multiple ways he needs to inform his patient, which is more than just passing on information. Because of the test, Grove is possibly at risk for cancer, though his doctor avoids saying this. The doctor has a grammatical dilemma: he cannot state the fact of the test without erring emotionally too much or too little; he wants to alert Grove without alarming him and yet without implying he should ignore the alert. Technically, this doctor needs to produce in Grove just enough urgency to see another doctor. It is a question of emotional management: "It's probably nothing to worry about, but . . ."[5]

The patient is always in the position of trying to see past all of this indirection to the hidden truth of this management, asking himself, What does the doctor really think is wrong with me? Grove studies his doctor's comportment, makes a judgment, and relaxes: "He did not seem too concerned, so I didn't get anxious either. I put off the whole issue without too much thought." The doctor failed in alerting Grove, as his attempt at stating the fact was unsuccessful.[6] This exchange of half hints and possible winks reveals the nightmare of doctors.[7] No matter how neutral they try to be, in the face of presenting biomedical facts they will always be interpreted as advocating one action over another. Every statement of fact will be seen as an exercitive, a decision that compels other decisions.[8] As much as they are supposed to allow patients to make decisions, doctors are the experts who know what the facts really mean. They know this dilemma all too well. One doctor I interviewed discussed the difficulty of "truly giving patients informed consent because of the complexity of decision making. . . . You have to inform the patient of what the risks are . . . [but] you have to make sure that you don't allow the way you explain those risks to make the patient lean away from what you feel is a more appropriate therapy choice."[9]

Medical anthropologists have defined this process of communicating what should be done through interpretive flexibility as therapeutic emplotment.[10] The doctor puts the facts into a story that enables the patient to make sense of the facts, their significance, and the action that should be taken next. Grove's doctor seems to have decided to communicate nonchalance, and Grove got the message that he didn't really need to see an oncologist.

Biomedical facts are tipped toward action. While an elevated or unacceptable score may be nothing to worry about, it may also be something to worry about. Grove cannot leave this possibility alone. He "happened to tell one of [his] daughters, who is a healthcare professional" and who happened to know someone who happened to be writing an article on "the pros and cons of screening people with this very same PSA test." Biomedical narratives often have this serendipitous structure in which somebody encounters others who know more or finds a book or website with meaningful information.[11] If one does not deny the connection, one is drawn into learning more. Grove cannot help wanting to learn more about his test result:

> Would I want to talk to him about it? I would, I did.
>
> Oh, my God.
>
> With that conversation, I parachuted into the middle of one of the raging controversies of contemporary medicine.[12]

God appears to mark the switch from the typical medical narrative of being tested, retested, diagnosed, and treated. Instead he was dropped into a war of interpretations. The foundation of Grove's knowledge shifts, and his picture of the medical world is changed. Though he does not explicitly continue either the war analogy or the world-changing one, he structures his entire narrative around them. As a person who has been screened, he is a soldier, a grunt who is parachuted into what increasingly appear to be the front lines of a battle over the production and dissemination of medical knowledge. The reason that even from the beginning he is so attentive to facts as specific material objects is that they turn out to be bullets shot by various parties at each other even while still being medical facts. These facts say something about how a person's symptoms and treatments bear on his chances for illness and recovery. Grove the patient was not supposed to be a soldier, and he does not see the point of being in a war at all.

A PSA test measures a bodily substance whose increase has been correlated with the occurrence and recurrence of prostate cancer. While many screens have false positives—that is, the test is positive, but the person does not have the disease—the main problem with the PSA test is that while it reliably helps identify prostate cancers (by indicating biopsies), the cancers it identifies may not be problems. Strange as it may sound, Grove learns from his daughter's friend that "autopsies show that half of all men who die of other causes have some cancerous tissue in their prostate." Whereas having cancer is normally connected with an image of suffering and dying from it, the implication of the autopsy findings is that 50 percent of the elderly male population has cancer but do not know it, and it does not matter. Perhaps it could be said that for these men cancer is not a disease.[13]

Two separate measures here redefine disease at the same time. PSA tests individually inform more people, people who do not feel any symptoms, that they may have prostate cancer, and autopsy studies inform us, in general, that having prostate cancer may not be so bad. These two maybes do not cancel each other but collide and produce controversy. The person with a high PSA test embodies this controversy in multiple ways. As Grove writes, "Telling a person with an elevated PSA that he might have cancer leads him into a system of increasingly complex and uncomfortable diagnostic tests to ascertain whether it is so. If it is, the patient has to make some choices about what, if anything, to do."

Grove distinguishes here between his doctor, who told him only that his PSA was elevated, and his serendipitous friend, who informed him of the fact that this meant he might have cancer. The difference is not about what Grove has but about what Grove learns he may have. Hearing the personal fact leads him (or anyone) into a system of tests. Narratively, he has been emplotted into a new narrative, one that has reconfigured his possibilities and placed new challenges and goals before him.[14]

Grove also cannot go back to a state of ignorance. Having personalized this biomedical knowledge changes who he is. The factual possibility that he is suffering from cancer has been introduced into him. Was he at risk before the test? Certainly afterward he was. Being at risk is a relation to a fact, an enacted fact.[15] He is at risk; he has been informed. He is led to undergo tests, and, if they are positive, he has to make choices. The researcher who informed him is concerned with this inevitability. He feels that too many men will test positive and be led to tests and treatments that have unpleasant consequences. Men who may have lived with no symptoms at all will now face side effects that are themselves life changing, including impotence and incontinence. (I will investigate the issue of the consequences of screening in chapter 5.) But Grove has already had the test, and the researcher's specific concerns are therefore academic. Faced with his own facts, Grove must continue.

Knowing that one is possibly at risk leads to tests and more tests; answers raise more questions. Knowing that the tests and diagnoses are controversial leads to investigation and more investigation. Each kind of knowledge produces more needs and more action. Having money and free time, Grove conducts internet research. He accesses Compuserve and locates a prostate cancer forum full of discussions of PSA tests, treatments, and side effects. He begins to read technical articles and popular health books. When the facts do not correlate with each other, he forms hypotheses that may explain the apparent discrepancies. In short, he begins to become a lay expert: an expert on prostate cancer as it pertains to himself. He makes the knowledge personal. He learns the possible size of his cancer (if it exists): "I visualized a sugar-cube-sized tumor inside me, and I shuddered."

Controversies are fascinating social processes because they make apparent all of the normally silent and hidden activities that regularly produce our taken-for-granted everyday world. While we usually may be justified in assuming that something called the scientific community has come to conclusions that inform our doctor's assessment of us, a controversy shows us the competing, fractious voices; contradictory facts; and uncertain compromises that are the world of knowledge production. Sociologists of science have looked to controversies as opportunities in which to make manifest the work of maintaining the taken-for-granted everyday by many different groups of people and institutions.[16]

In a controversy, the apparatus of knowledge production also becomes highlighted as concealing assumptions that must now be interrogated for their potential role in helping to settle matters. Grove punctuates his narrative with apparent facts and then wonders if there may be problems with how the data were collected, how the studies were analyzed, and how the instruments were calibrated. In each case he sees these assumptions from his position on the front lines. If, he wonders, the discovery of postmortem prostate cancer is owing to the fact that mostly older men are being screened, then this might explain the high rate, but it would not help him, Grove, who is still "only 58 and otherwise in perfect health." He wonders also about the accuracy of the PSA test: how often does it return a 5 when one's real score may be 4? How many false positive PSA scores does it produce? His future depending on the answer, he wrote, "I decided to test the tests. I had my blood sent to two different labs." Unfortunately for Grove, the tests were precise enough (6.0 and 6.1), and his cancer appeared to be growing. He finally sees a urologist and has a biopsy. He is told he has cancer.

He also has a new relationship to medical facts. All of these investigations took place while he was on sabbatical writing a book that would eventually be called *Only the Paranoid Survive*.[17] While the content of the book refers to keeping a technology business afloat in a rapidly changing information society, the title could equally well refer to how to be a successful patient in biomedical society. In becoming aware of the controversial and unsettled nature of facts about his illness, Grove becomes paranoid in a most rational manner. He will suspect all facts by seeing them as rhetorical phrases aimed at him by specific individuals or institutions, crafted to produce effects in him and on him. While this is paranoid, it is in fact a good description of how scientists regularly understand their field: as competitive, biased, and divided by opposing assumptions and conventions. One good description of scientific method is to suspect everything as a means of discovering what had to be taken for granted before and can now be improved upon. Science is similar to business in that competition and suspicion are good, and monopolies and complacency are bad.[18] Grove must therefore become a lay sociologist of scientific knowledge, understanding not only the basic facts of the field, including current studies and their weaknesses, but also mapping the larger institutional forces that structure what kinds of questions are not asked and what strategies are ignored and why. Again, his status as lay expert becomes a precise job description: whereas a sociologist of scientific knowledge would study a controversy for what it reveals about the ways science works and how knowledge comes into being, Grove needs to know how science works in order to settle the controversy for himself. His clock ticking, he needs to make decisions based, at the very least, on an accurate assessment of the true kinds of uncertainty and bias that inhabit his facts.

Having discussed his diagnosis and his reaction to it, Grove heads the next section of his article "R&D," underscoring how sensitized he has become to the uncertainty of his facts and of the answers given by his urologist. Once he has read online accounts of bad side effects and other problems with treatments, expertise and emotional management backfire: "He walked me through the complications of surgery, but reassured me: 'Don't worry, we can do something about each of those.' The examining room walls were covered with posters of contraptions like penile implants and vacuum pumps. I knew that they were devices meant to restore potency, but they evoked images of medieval torture."

Grove is equally suspicious of the sensitivity of scanning tests. He no longer accepts facts; he must learn what they mean for him by learning how they are used: "I wanted to know more." Having ample resources and time at his disposal, this is possible. He becomes a complete lay sociologist of scientific knowledge: "I also decided to dust off my research background and go directly to the original literature. . . . My wife got copies of these articles from Stanford. My life entered a new routine. . . .

By day, I set up appointments. . . . By night, I read scientific papers, plotting and cross-plotting the data from one paper with the results from another. . . . This whole exercise reminded me of my younger days, when I did the same thing in the field of semiconductor devices."

Grove embarks on an odyssey akin to an investment strategy. A sociologist is never satisfied with claims made, no matter how objective they appear. He is interested in how a claim was crafted and how the appearance of objectivity was staged. Attending closely to the materiality of facts, Grove discovers three central aspects that I summarize as follows: facts are contextual, facts are changeable, and facts are maintained. Stated so baldly, these discoveries are obvious; their power lies in the details of how these aspects change Grove's way of looking at the world. Having become suspicious of facts in the world, he nonetheless clings to truth, to the idea that with proper collection, assessment, and analysis of facts in the world he can come to the best decision for himself.

FACTS ARE CONTEXTUAL

A fact is defined in the dictionary as "something that has real and demonstrable existence," and as such should be as true in one place as in other places, within reason, or with qualifications. Water may boil at less than one hundred degrees in Denver, but that is because the air pressure is less. A more complicated expression of the fact would explain the variance.[19] This simple dictionary definition hints at a deeper problem, though, suggesting that real existence is not enough to secure a fact; it must also be capable of demonstration.

Demonstrations are social events. They insist on performers, audiences, or judges, on rules for proper conduct and success, and on apparatus. If a fact requires demonstrability and institutions for demonstration are lacking, is there no fact? What if the rules here for success are different from the rules there? Who is to decide?[20]

When we compare contexts for their differences, we attempt to penetrate the discrepancies to see how different data are being collected, how different senses are deployed in judging, and how different institutions are organizing discovery. Grove has a more immediate problem. He has to choose between different views that inhabit the same space. Starting from the premise that he is investigating facts within one field, one locale, he assumes there will be some kind of consensus as to the facts, even if there are disagreements over their implications. "The field was hopping," he writes, "not just with new work and discoveries but with controversy." What he finds, to his dismay, is that "each medical specialty—surgery, cryosurgery, different branches of radiology—favored its own approach." Again, this is not surprising; it is even expected, except that favoring turns out to penetrate all the way down to the roots of the tree of knowledge production.

Especially during a controversy, Grove expected that each specialty and each practitioner would constantly be comparing her or his approach with those of others in head-to-head trials in an attempt to figure out which method was best. This was how he had learned research on semiconductor devices should be done. What he found instead was patchy, incomplete, and self-interested research: "Medical practitioners primarily tended to publish their own data; they often didn't compare their data with the data of other practitioners, even in their own field, let alone with the results of other types of treatments for the same condition."

The effect of these publishing practices was that comparisons were very hard to make, as each specialty might start with a different patient demographic, with a different measure of effectiveness, and with different time points. Even though the field was hopping with new work, questions of the type Grove had—which treatment is best *for me?*—were not being asked, let alone answered. When he became convinced that too many people crucial to his research were talking past each other, his solution was to take responsibility for generating proper medical knowledge. "As a patient whose life and well-being depended on a meeting of minds," he says, "I realized I would have to do some cross-disciplinary work on my own."

Grove's easy acceptance of this role and this responsibility suggests there was already an existing subject-position he could assume, the expert patient. Here he implicitly draws upon decades of activist work pioneered by the movements on AIDS, breast cancer, and women's and consumer health. Each of these social movements contributed to public awareness that health cannot be left to experts and that it is often up to individuals to become informed.[21]

Local facts are also built into the common sense of medicine in the concept of the second opinion. The phrase itself assumes that one's doctor does not so much make an objective diagnosis as offer an opinion, subjective and perhaps biased, in any case, as in need of further verification. But it also implies that doctors as a whole make up the field of knowledge and together approximate objectivity.

The expert patient assumes that doctors are just one, limited source of information. As expert patients have evolved and learned from each other, through social movements and online research, they have come to adopt a paranoid approach to facts similar to the one I am ascribing to Grove. I continue to use *paranoia* in the same seriously playful sense Grove does, that is, as a form of wariness that risks taking oneself and one's own collected facts too seriously in order to combat one's given picture of the world.

The philosopher Ludwig Wittgenstein offers an analogy for knowledge and its foundations: a river and its banks. Ever respectful of the complexity of the lived everyday, he notes that while we learn as children "an inherited background against which [we] distinguish true and false," even this can change.[22] The water in a river moves swiftly compared to its banks, but the distinction is not sharp. The banks are also slowly shifting.

Grove works to counter his initial trust in local facts, what a doctor says or a journal article reports, by aggressively soliciting numerous opinions, plowing through a stack of journal articles, and conducting his own meta-analysis. Essentially he poses two questions to the literature: given the variability of subjects studied, which data are relevant to me? And given the heterogeneity of study designs, what dimensions can be compared head to head? He eventually plots a number of studies on a series of charts in order to visually compare disparate therapies. In his charts Grove compares studies that had not been compared by those making the studies. He also parses the data in ways that do not compare one treatment with another, as if only one study could win, but in order to see which is better for his specific PSA scores and the size and age of his tumor.

For instance, he maps nine studies with diverse endpoints to get a sense of both the variability in outcomes across studies and to see how hard it is to simply compare studies (fig. 5). He adds small arrows downgrading the risk of some of the "seed therapy" studies because he notes that these focused on a population with more advanced cancers than his. In this way he reverse engineers the study design in order to answer the question, What data are relevant to me?

The charts enabled Grove to reduce the literature to a series of numbers, basically odds on how bad his condition might be and then how

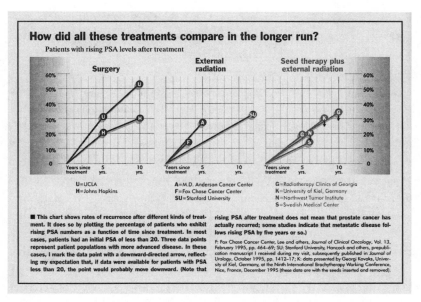

How did all these treatments compare in the longer run?

Patients with rising PSA levels after treatment

Surgery / External radiation / Seed therapy plus external radiation

U=UCLA
H=Johns Hopkins

A=M.D. Anderson Cancer Center
F=Fox Chase Cancer Center
SU=Stanford University

G=Radiotherapy Clinics of Georgia
K=University of Kiel, Germany
N=Northwest Tumor Institute
S=Swedish Medical Center

■ This chart shows rates of recurrence after different kinds of treatment. It does so by plotting the percentage of patients who exhibit rising PSA numbers as a function of time since treatment. In most cases, patients had an initial PSA of less than 20. Three data points represent patient populations with more advanced disease. In these cases, I mark the data point with a downward-directed arrow, reflecting my expectation that, if data were available for patients with PSA less than 20, the point would probably move downward. (Note that rising PSA after treatment does not mean that prostate cancer has actually recurred; some studies indicate that metastatic disease follows rising PSA by five years or so.)

F: Fox Chase Cancer Center, Lee and others, *Journal of Clinical Oncology*, Vol. 13, February 1995, pp. 464–69; SU: Stanford University, Hancock and others, prepublication manuscript I received during my visit, subsequently published in *Journal of Urology*, October 1995, pp. 1412–17; K: data presented by Georg Kovaks, University of Kiel, Germany, at the Ninth International Brachytherapy Working Conference, Nice, France, December 1995 (these data are with the seeds inserted and removed).

FIGURE 5 "How did all these treatments compare in the longer run?" *Source*: Meta-analytic chart from Grove 1996b.

risky each treatment option would be in turn. They did not reduce the magnitude of his decision—every choice was a gamble—but they made the gamble rational: "I decided to bet on my own charts."

Through this process of lay meta-analysis Grove attempted to eliminate the controversy by acting as if all the data were generated as part of a collective enterprise and had simply not been cross-tabulated. He assumed, and felt he had to assume, that with a sufficiently wide search of the literature he would have found almost all of the relevant studies.

Yet even this assumption about the usefulness of the literature must itself be held up to scrutiny. Another part of the riverbank may be shifting. The past few years have seen a large-scale challenge to the very concept of meta-analysis with the revelations that a significant proportion of clinical trials, especially negative ones or those that find high side-effect rates, are systematically suppressed or ignored. In its general form this problem has been known and studied for a long time, and almost all of science is complicit in it: negative findings and studies that show no interesting results are uninteresting, and, in that they require labor to write, edit, and publish and garner no status, they usually end up in the round file cabinet (i.e., trash bin). The net effect of this would be to bias the literature itself, but the reaction of the scientific community in aggregate was to assume that in the long run spurious positive findings would be weeded out by better positive findings.[23]

A small amount of riverbank erosion, however, can be magnified into a full-fledged bend in the river if enough water pressure is trained upon one area or the bank is weakened. In the case of pharmaceutical clinical trials this apparently has happened. Regulatory design at the FDA required that pharma companies submit at least two positive clinical trials of their candidate drug's effectiveness in order to win approval. They also must submit unsuccessful clinical trials of the drugs, but these findings are not made public. The result is that a literature search for most pharmaceuticals turns up only trials in which the drug is found to be effective, even if fewer than half of them found it to be so. Dr. Robert Temple of the FDA was therefore able to state at a hearing in 2002, "We know that studies of antidepressants, even the effective antidepressants that we all know and love, fail a significant fraction of the time. We have looked over several years, and in about almost 50 percent of well-done trials [of effective antidepressants], or apparently well-done trials, [researchers] can't tell drug from placebo."[24]

Another FDA doctor at an earlier 1999 hearing stated that "one of the problems pervading the entire discussion is that, it seems that folks from the FDA see a different set of trials than folks who are not from the FDA." This was also considered "apparent with the depression example."[25] The response from non-FDA doctors to this admission is incredulity at the localness of facts. Facts as material objects can be restricted to certain eyes, and even their existence can be hidden from others who make decisions as if the facts they can find are the only ones there are. Facts do not necessarily travel; they are not facts for everyone.

A marked social and regulatory shift on precisely this problem is taking place. The FDA, medical journals, lawsuits, and fearful companies are all attempting to imagine how a database of clinical trials can be set up so as to reveal a truer picture of the facts. This is not a new solution. Calls for public databases of trials have a history, including an explicit discussion during the hearings at the FDA in 1999:

> DR. WOODCOCK: But, Tom, are you saying also that you can't reliably distinguish active, good treatment from placebo, is that what you are saying? In a trial.

DR. LAUGHREN: You cannot reliably do it. Again, as Bob pointed out, about, you know, a third of trials, maybe 40% of trials, fail to distinguish drugs, standard drugs that we know work, from placebo.

DR. WOODCOCK: Even in that setting.

DR. LAUGHREN: Even in that setting. And again, it's an issue of those data not being available more widely. But we see them, because they come in as part of an NDA [new drug application]. You don't see them, because they're not published.

DR. WOODCOCK: Well, I would like to find some way to make these data available. That's one of my missions.[26]

What the pharmaceutical companies have done is to take a tendency or bias in the scientific field and amplify it to the point of breaking. In the process they turned the assumption that the literature was representative of the state of scientific knowledge (though not perfectly so) into a strategy for manipulating the field of facts itself. The sheer scale of resources available to pharma marketers enables them to turn everyday assumptions about facts into strategies.

When the British government held a series of hearings and decided that antidepressants like Paxil and Zoloft caused, rather than prevented, suicides, especially in children, they banned the use of selective serotonin reuptake inhibitors (SSRIs) (except Prozac) for children. In the United States, however, the same facts were evaluated differently, or rather the institutions conducting the investigations were structured so that the evidence was not treated as fact, and even today a warning but not a ban has been made.[27]

MANIPULATING THE FACTS THROUGH STRATEGIC UBIQUITY

Explanations come to an end somewhere.

—WITTGENSTEIN, *ON CERTAINTY*

Grove, in 1997, was an early adopter of the internet as a means of conducting health research. He used Compuserve (a competitor of America Online at the time) to locate medical references and access newsgroup discussions of patients. Over 115 million Americans have gone online, according to a Pew Institute survey of 2002. Some "45 million people said they had helped another person dealing with a major illness in the past two years."[28] One in five say they have gone online to diagnose or treat a medical condition on their own without consulting doctors. Of those, 26 percent said their use of the internet played a crucial or important role in aiding them. Most people go online alone and find the research process quite easy.[29]

The extent of online health seeking has not escaped marketers, who have turned to their own research in an attempt to shape the results that people like Grove would end up with today. Contrary to fears about gullible internet users believing what they read, researchers determined that most of us take a smart, actively skeptical approach to online facts. Two marketers working at the Medical Broadcasting Company wrote an article for *Pharmaceutical Executive* to teach other marketers how to understand and respond:

> Health information seekers don't use search engines to locate the best website; instead, they use them to locate multiple sites and consonant information—the information most frequently repeated across sites. They use that approach to ensure that what they read is accurate and complete.
>
> "It's clear that consumers who look for health information do so in a number of different places to figure out the common thread," says [Elizabeth] Boehm [of Forrester Research]. "What do they consistently see? That's the piece of which they can be fairly certain."[30]

This lay-expert strategy seems sound. Sociologists of medicine have found that when information is sought online, often to confirm or sort out controversial facts, "repetition was a sufficient indicator of validity [for some women]."[31] Grove determined he had reached a saturation point when he saw no new information. Then he felt he could and must make an informed decision on as-good-as-possible data. Wittgenstein summed up the necessity of this approach with this insight: "Explanations come to an end somewhere." Certainty was a theme Wittgenstein explored in a number of ways, and he concluded that even though in principle we could doubt everything, in practice we are unable to. Grove's paranoia is rational because it has its limits. Wittgenstein referred to these limits, these assumptions regarding when we have explanation enough and stop asking questions, as defining our "form of life." He used this phrase to help us see that our social practices are intertwined with our cognitive ones, and therefore we should not be misled by the apparent certitude of logic. Wittgenstein was pointing out that even logic has its habits.[32]

Once a form of life can be formalized, however, it can also be exploited. In pharmaceutical marketing, our very form of skepticism can be managed into a certainty through the noneuphemistic "strategic ubiquity." The medical marketers continue:

> Online health information seekers don't look for a single website. They investigate many. Therefore, pharma brands need to create an online universe that includes syndicated and sponsored content, alliances with advocacy sites, and partnerships with other influential third-party venues, as well as their own websites, to serve consumers seeking product and disease information.
>
> Through "strategic ubiquity," marketing managers can influence the accuracy and completeness of information about their therapies and targeted diseases. They can also give consumers who browse through disease management sites the most accurate, consistent information about the brand—and a clear path back to the product website.[33]

"To serve consumers" becomes a version of the old joke about the title of a Martian cookbook: "To serve man." Marketing is serving consumers to pharma. The internet is treated as a medium that appears to consumers to be democratic and comprehensive because it encompasses such a diversity of opinions. It may require some sleuthing, but that very effort guarantees that one is not being manipulated. No one could control the whole world. But, like most media, the internet can be bought.

The unsettling implication of strategic ubiquity is that Grove would not be paranoid enough today. In the marketers' ideal, we might all be Jim Carrey in *The Truman Show*, where everything we read and everyone we talk to is being employed to direct our actions for the benefit of a company. Another marketer emphasizes that such an elaborate production of the fact field is not achieved easily, it requires the following:

> syndicating content to patient advocacy, disease management, and similar sites in need of authoritative general information
> creating sponsorship packages with portals, such as WebMD and Healthology
> co-branding sites with third parties, such as HealthandAge.com between Novartis' Foundation for Gerontology and Geriatrics
> conducting PR [public relations] outreach to online news organizations and the online arms of traditional media.[34]

Essentially, the goal of this kind of marketing is to entangle as many websites and other outlets for facts as possible, especially those that have an aura of neutrality. In their exposé of the PR industry, *Trust Us, We're Experts*, Sheldon Rampton and John Stauber call this the "third man" approach: creating an effect of objectivity for a message by articulating it through an apparently neutral third party. As the earlier quotes indicate, pharmaceutical companies are very upfront about their need to derive legitimacy and persuasive power from these alliances. They identify the third man technique as a crucial tool of PR that needs to derive legitimacy and persuasive power through apparently neutral and objective groups.

Partnering with advocacy groups is another facet of strategic ubiquity. An article entitled "Thriving amid Uncertainty" has a section called "Advocacy" because it highlights the growing importance of social movements in public discourse and biomedical politics. "As advocates develop louder voices, pharma companies must forge alliances and win allies": "Third-party messages are an essential means of communication for validating scientific credibility, for legitimizing products, for building brand and disease awareness, and for building defenses against crises."[35]

Another article in *Pharmaceutical Executive*, "Forging Alliances," outlines a history of pharma's relationships with patient groups. It emphasizes the benefits that advocacy developments bring, including "diffusing industry critics" and providing "credible people for journalists to interview."[36] The AIDS activism of the 1980s was a turning point, as activists were able to massively change the regulatory structure in a way that pharmaceutical companies appreciated and could align with. The article notes, "They've been at the table ever since." Breast cancer organizations had opened the path, and other groups followed on this model, with occasional alliances between advocates and pharma.[37] "Forging Alliances" then charts the large change that happened later in the 1980s, when Schering Plough created a campaign, the National Prostate Cancer Awareness Week, to support its therapy Elexin:

> Partners in that program included Cancer Care, the National Cancer Institute, AARP, the American Foundation for Urologic Disease, the Association of Community Cancer Centers, and the National Association of Community Health Centers. At a time when diseases of the male sexual anatomy were not discussed publicly, their common objective was to inform men age 40 and older—and their families—

about the importance of annual testing for prostate cancer, one of the most curable cancers when detected early. During the campaign's three-year run, awareness spread. The topic was no longer taboo, and more than 250,000 men received well-publicized free screenings at clinics across the country.[38]

Ironically, this campaign failed to reach Grove, who had to create his awareness of the disease and tests through his own research. His article, in turn, can be seen as part of another wave of publicity. In addition to Grove's and Alexander's articles, a third article in the same issue of *Fortune* reports on a new campaign to raise prostate cancer awareness in the public and among researchers. The science journalist David Stipp discusses the growing attempt by advocates to address the "gender gap" in cancer research. Citing a disproportionate amount of research money devoted to breast cancer versus prostate cancer, the prostate cancer group members used the appropriative tactic of not just modeling their campaign on the breast cancer movement, but hiring breast cancer activists for theirs. Such mobility illustrates a level of institutions where skills including activism are rendered instrumental, divorcing implementation from the passion that would seem to be its source. Thus, consider the example of Catherine Cantone, a senior manager of PR and advocacy development at Pharmacia, who

> has a special appreciation for the sensitivity needed to work well with advocacy groups and the patients they represent. Prior to joining Pharmacia, she served on the staff of the Leukemia and Lymphoma Society.
>
> That experience is helpful when marketers feel under pressure to "get a group to do something" for marketing support without knowing much about how those organizations operate. "It is important to find the middle ground between what the marketing people want for results and what a group finds acceptable according to its objectives and limitations," says Cantone. "Having been on both sides, I try to explain that perspective to marketing, so they can better understand what's realistic."[39]

The evolution of advocacy has reached the point where many groups "are run like successful corporations," which means they cannot be easily manipulated. "They have become increasingly sophisticated," comments one marketer. As a result, Kristen Williams, the senior manager of ally development for AstraZeneca, says she has to "treat them as customers, not vendors."[40] In business speak, this means that groups have to be cultivated with give and take and not simply managed.

In cases where advocacy groups have not sprung up from the grass roots, marketers must create them, in a process called Astroturfing. The term comes from American politics but equally applies to such groups as the Hepatitis C coalitions, which were created by Schering Plough in order to increase the market for its drug Rebatron.[41]

The intense attention to using "advocacy development as an important business tool" has been identified by Edward Grefe and Martin Linsky as a shift toward new corporate activism, the title of their book. Veterans of the PR industry — Grefe is the former PR director for Phillip Morris — they describe a transition from an older model of influence through lobbying to a newer one in which the public emerges as a force businesses need to reckon with. Subtitling their book *Harnessing the Power of Grassroots Tactics for Your Organization*, Grefe and Linsky describe how messages can be formed, individuals and groups recruited, and databases employed in order to influence but not control issues. The underlying rationale of their approach is simple: corporations can be thought of as the biggest stakeholders in many communities, and therefore community activism should begin with and benefit the companies. Pharmaceutical companies, starting with the rationale that their drug is the best for a given condition, similarly argue that everyone will benefit if all messages about that condition point back to the product.[42]

FACTS ARE MAINTAINED

A corollary of the discovery that facts demand effort to be transported into places is that facts can also disappear if they are not maintained. This problem affected my wife and me directly in 1992, when she was pregnant. In an article we cowrote, we described how she had been exposed to the drug DES (diethylstilbestrol) while in her mother's womb. DES was a synthetic estrogen, a hormone that had been ubiquitously promoted by over one hundred companies for thirty years as being helpful for preventing miscarriages and as safe as vitamins. Over five million pregnant women were given DES between 1940 and 1970, many being told it was in fact just a vitamin, until it was discovered to cause many terrible problems in daughters born to these women. Some of the daughters developed cancers as teenagers; many of them had severely mal-formed uteruses, rendering them infertile or at increased risk of miscar-riage and ectopic pregnancies. When the first cancer cluster was proven, a national registry of DES effects was set up, massive class action lawsuits were launched, and DES was headline news. Doctors were intensely aware of the problems, many were being sued, and women's health groups were galvanized. Nonetheless, twenty years later, when my wife was pregnant and knew to write "DES exposed" on her medical form, three doctors who saw her at a women's ob/gyn clinic knew nothing about the effects of DES. They missed an ectopic pregnancy on ultrasound twice and denied that DES could have had anything to do with it when it happened.[43]

These doctors were not alone in their ignorance. As we discovered and wrote about, when we looked at the literature our doctors might have en-countered, that is, the field of facts they existed in, we found a startling gap *within* the medical literature. Whereas every current textbook we located in a medical library and bookstore included full coverage of DES effects (the need for a special exam, increased risk for miscarriage and ec-topic pregnancies) and often a special section on uterine abnormalities, the same was not true either of obstetric and gynecological handbooks or of most popular guides written for pregnant women. Fewer than half of these include even basic risk information. The issue of physician hand-books is particularly troublesome, as in some cases versions of the same brand, edited by the same doctors, have the information in the textbook but not in the handbook. As the textbooks are all extremely cumbersome, thousands of pages in length and weighing over five pounds, compared to the easily used and accessed handbooks, it becomes understandable, if not forgivable, that a doctor might conscientiously look up possible risks but miss them because they are not in her handbook. As we wrote then, "Despite the history of DES, despite the 'facts' known about DES, one can too easily live in the present as if DES has neither history nor truth."[44] The problem is thus one of the maintenance of facts.

Most critics, when they comment on flaws in the medical treatment system, usually focus on the ambiguity or absence of substantial and sub-stantiated knowledge. The implicit assumption is that once a fact can be firmly established by and among professionals, it is then a real fact and will be treated as such. The finality implied by the notion of an estab-lished fact belies the work of facts. Precisely who hears or reads the ac-counts of the facts? How exactly are they perpetuated from year to year through repetitions in print, in reference manuals, in classes, and online? The case of DES highlights the material and social nature of facts: they do not simply persist and disseminate once discovered; their circulation is uneven and fragile. Another way to put this insight is that in order for facts to function as facts in the world, many kinds of effort are required, and controlling those efforts is one way of controlling facts.

Grove learned this lesson firsthand. His faith in the power of progress in science is most severely tested as he is talking to a doctor who is developing a cutting-edge treatment. Grove is impressed with the man, his reported results, and the entire treatment analogy—which could be describing chip fabrication: "There was a logic to the high-dose-rate radiation therapy that really appealed to me. . . . It's a programmable technique, customizable to an individual case." In the felt appeal of the new technology, Grove experiences what Mary-Jo Delvecchio Good has called the "biotechnical embrace."[45] Fascinating theories are especially tricky in medicine, where their ideal role in suggesting new avenues for research slides effortlessly into marketing: from the sense that if this theory is true, then maybe the following treatment will work, to the sense that this treatment will work because of this theory. In the face of such elegance, Grove's text for once loses its tight grip on situated facts and begins to report them: "The doctor described high-dose-rate radiation as 'smart bombs,' while external radiation or even the implanted seeds were more like carpet bombing. This was important because . . . if one could irradiate the tumor heavily while minimizing the exposure of the other organs, theoretically one should get good results with minimal side effects. In fact, this was consistent with this doctor's results. I sat in his office absorbing the elegance of this technique."

Making sense, being logical, can also mislead. As part of its requirements for new drug applications, the FDA demands that each proposed drug come with a theory of its efficacy. The theory does not need to be demonstrated, merely plausible. David Healy, interviewing pharmacologists of the past half century, was alarmed to discover that time and again theories that had been effectively disproved were nonetheless trotted out and attached to new drugs in order to submit them to the FDA. He cites a case in which a theory of drug response, of forms of depression to monoamine oxidase inhibitor (MAOI) drugs, was suggested but never proven. Nonetheless, "these concepts flourished during the 1960s and 1970s, at least in part because it was in the interests of certain companies for them to survive." Large dissemination campaigns produce what many physicians take to be the scientific literature. "In this manner," Healy writes, "many concepts that might otherwise be retired early to inhabit the back shelves of libraries are given an extended lease on life."[46]

Relating Healy's discovery in terms of Wittgenstein's river of knowledge analogy, we could say that old, discarded theories are never completely washed out but persist in the literature as a reservoir, remaining available in the archive for return to the river of explanation to aid a troubling fact's passage. Healy notes that these cases are not about bad drugs getting free passes—the clinical trials still make the case—but that elegant yet incorrect theories get back in through the rear door. So what? Marketing. Healy worries that doctors will listen to theories and be absorbed by their elegance rather than attending to the data: "The idea that depression was 'known' to involve low levels of biogenic amines was something that fitted neatly into the snappy format in which truths have to be conveyed on advertisements to physicians. Indeed, a feature of many sciences, but certainly psychiatry, is that at a certain point key terms succeed in pulling the field together by virtue of combining the right measure of simplicity and ambiguity."[47] I will return to marketing's effect on doctors in the next chapter but note here that a series of studies on doctors' prescribing habits have confirmed Healy's concerns.[48]

Even as Grove sat mesmerized, optimistically playing with the future of his illness, his story confronted him with a devastating twist: "I sat in his office absorbing the elegance of this technique, and then I turned to [the cutting-edge doctor]. 'If you had what I have, what would you do?' He hesitated. Then he said, 'I would probably have surgery.' I left, utterly confused—but with some more unpublished data from the two seed doctors that I could add to my charts."

Stunned by this admission, Grove learns to make sense of a new contradiction. How could a doctor-researcher who both generates compelling data and makes compelling arguments in its favor not listen to these very same facts himself? Which should Grove be more suspicious of: facts claimed by persons who will not follow them, or by persons who won't believe their own admitted irrationality? Finally, Grove returned to the contradictory researcher to confront him: "It sounded good, but I had one last question. 'Why,' I asked, 'would you have surgery done to yourself then?' He thought about it. Finally, he said, 'You know, all through medical training, they drummed into us that the gold standard for prostate cancer is surgery. I guess that still shapes my thinking.'"

For this doctor the correctness of radiation therapy confronts the learned rightness of surgery. One reader of a draft of this book who was an MD was reminded of other Kuhnian paradigm shifts in medicine, such as Barry Marshall's discovery that stomach ulcers are caused by *Helicobacter* infections rather than by stress or oversecretion of acid. He wrote, "It can be hard for docs (and other people) to let go of old theories or mental models and adopt new and 'strange' ones." Evidence confronting one's common sense is a timid but profound reflection of Wittgenstein's point that at some point explanations can pass into mere description, and what was once disputed becomes the very scaffolding of thought. Wittgenstein's investigations into this slippery business of knowledge and learning focused on the difficulty of apportioning feeling and cognition. This difficulty is described, but not by any means solved, in the analogy of the river and its banks. The doctor's ego, the *I* in his statement, lies in the blurred zone between one and the other.

LIVING WITH AN UNCERTAIN PRESENT

Grove's first encounter with the researcher who opposed the PSA screen led him to ask: "Why submit unsuspecting men indiscriminately to this test, which only leads to more tests, which then lead to a series of choices, none of which are very good?" The adjective "unsuspecting" denotes the troubling relationship between the almost invisible application of the test and the cascade of consequences and entanglements it engenders. The anthropologist Rayna Rapp found that all forms of prenatal testing force the question of abortion into discussion, sometimes springing it on couples who do not know how to imagine deciding whether a defect is severe enough to warrant such action. Facts in the form of tests thus come to inhabit the bodies and identities of those tested.[49]

A second aspect of "unsuspecting" is that the mere fact of being tested, of being selected for a screening test, implicates one as being at risk and arouses the consequent anxiety and potential desire to do something proactive in response. Pharmaceutical marketers deploy screening tests precisely to produce and direct this anxiety toward consumptive ends (see chapter 2).

Grove is unapologetically proactive in his case—his PSA test was positive, and he came to believe, on the basis of his research, that some action was preferable to no action. He ends his article by writing, "Conclusions: First, tumors grow. Sometimes they grow quickly, sometimes very slowly, but they do grow. I think you should hit a tumor with what you believe is your best shot, early and hard. . . . If my best friend had this disease, my advice to him would be, 'Investigate, choose, and do—and do it quickly. Be aggressive now. Don't save the best for later.'"

Grove's aggressive attitude toward tumors contrasts baldly with the wait-and-see attitude toward wily tumors that Tom Alexander described in his article. Grove conducted a meta-analysis that compared treatments and did not even include nontreatment as a choice, excluding it from consideration. When he does mention nontreatment in passing he derides it: "And, finally, doing nothing and playing the odds. This is euphemistically called 'watchful waiting.'" His entire series of expressions—"doing nothing," "playing the odds," "euphemistically"—imply that watchful waiting is nothing but a form of denial of a situation that demands treatment action.

Alexander, surveying his own literature and doctors, refused to conduct a meta-analysis in Grove's fashion but attended to the uncertainty of the field as a crucial part of the cancer itself:

> My waiting strategy relies on PSA as a surrogate [substitute] for changes in tumor volume and malignancy, which in turn are supposed to warn when my cancer may start to grow rapidly. A normal PSA is usually considered anything below 4 nanograms per milliliter of blood. At diagnosis my level was 5.9, but it has since soared as high as 10.9, possibly because of an infection, and dipped as low as 5.8. Besides PSA fluctuations, another difficulty . . . is that by the time we've seen a PSA move convincing enough to act upon, it may be too late.[50]

Given the variability inherent in the disease and the treatments, playing the odds and waiting might be the best rational strategy. Alexander arrived at this position in part because he saw the contradictory medical literature as constitutive of the prostate cancer field: "As I wound my way through the contradictory medical literature and interviewed experts, I became aware that, in fact, there was dispute over whether any of the known treatments was likely to prolong my life."[51] Alexander starts from the assumption that there may not be a treatment for his cancer. Grove evaluates the literature for the best current treatment. Grove and Alexander look at the same facts but evaluate them with different logics. The controversy over PSA testing teaches them different lessons.

Another way to think of different relationalities of risk is through gambling: the correlations discovered through the clinical trials that lend predictions to PSA scores are odds. Despite the appearance of rational gambling, many analysts have pointed out that odds alone do not make a good bet. A 60 percent chance to double your money is good, if you can afford to lose 40 percent of the time. At one hundred dollars it may be worth it, especially if you can do it multiple times. But if you have to put your whole life savings at stake, then even a 95 percent chance to double it may not be rational.[52] Moreover, there are different types of gamblers, conservative ones and risk takers, and neither is inherently better or more rational than the other. Each has a logic that allows him, like Alexander and Grove, to make a clear but different choice.

Grove's conclusion is axiomatic, paranoid, and appropriate given the contradictory advice he encountered:

> There is no good gatekeeper in this business. Your general internist is not; the field of prostate cancer is a complex and changing specialty. Neither is a urologist; urologists have a natural preference toward surgery, perhaps because urologists are surgeons and surgery is what they know best. Any other treatment is deemed experimental even if it has just as much data associated with it.
>
> The whole thing reminds me of the uncomfortable feeling I experienced when I first sought out investment advice. After a while, it dawned on me that financial advisers, well intentioned and competent as they might have been, were all favoring their own financial instruments. I concluded that I had to undertake the generalist's job myself; I had to take the high-level management of my investments into my own hands. Similarly, given the structure of the medical practice associated with prostate cancer, that's the only viable choice any patient has.

The responsible person must exercise executive control over expert advice. All such advice, financial and medical, must be understood as relative facts suggested by interested parties. Accept only those facts you can corroborate yourself from other sources. Grove suggests what may be the unfortunate, pessimistic conclusion of seeing factual controversy firsthand: "If you look after your investments, I think you should look after your life as well. Investigate things, come to your own conclusions, don't take any one recommendation as gospel."

Grove and Alexander both accept this utter outsourcing of the medical system onto individuals like themselves, a generalization of medicine onto life. Sociologists have called this the medicalization of the everyday.[53] Grove's approach uses resources—financial, educational, social—that he believes the readers of his article in *Fortune* may share, but they are not ones that can be extended very far. I will argue in the next chapters that there is a broader trend of outsourcing health education that mirrors Grove's personal odyssey. What to him appears to be the proper rational response to a disorganized medical industry is a form of cost cutting for medical providers and of marketing for pharmaceutical companies.

ANTICIPATING THE FUTURE

Facts change through progress. New findings, new tests, new drugs surpass the old and make them obsolete. Newness is a temporal frame that organizes how we understand truth and its surprises. Grove writes, "The most important thing I learned was that the use of the PSA test reset the entire field of prostate cancer studies. PSA tests went into use only about ten years ago [around 1986]. Their use moved everything forward in time. Typically, a PSA test can indicate the presence of prostate cancer as much as five years earlier than diagnosis by other means, like digital rectal exam."

PSA tests allowed not only advanced detection of prostate cancer over other diagnostic technologies, but also studies of recurrence and thus the acceleration of treatment effectiveness. Given an equation of speed and the future with goodness, no harm can come from fast-forwarding diagnosis, and yet it is precisely the social context within which this technological process occurs that must be detailed if we are to understand its lived implications.

Rapp studied how technologies like ultrasound and amniocentesis changed the experience and meaning of pregnancy for women. In each case the change eventually required a complete shift in how pregnancy was conceived, how birth defects were defined, how education and counseling were conducted, and how decisions were made. These changes were not uniform, but they were pervasive and profound, as each technology fast-forwarded not only the abstract probability of a problem but also the reality of the pregnancy and the anxiety of the uncertainty.[54]

In Grove's case, the sense of accelerated newness and radically good change is foundational to his worldview, grounded as it is in the computer-business age of Moore's law, which says the speed of information processing doubles every eighteen months. Grove understands progress as being disruptive: new inventions constantly interrupt what had been best practices and replace them with new ones. This understanding of disruptive time enables Grove to hedge his medical bets by trusting the market.

Grove and Alexander share the business sense that accelerated time equals accelerated novelty. Both chose their strategies in part on the assumption that ten years is a long time. Grove states the axiom of change revolution: "I have a rule in my business: To see what can happen in the next ten years, look at what has happened in the last ten years. PSA happened in the last ten years, and it is transforming the diagnosis and treatment of prostate cancer. Big things, I reasoned, could happen in the next ten years."

Such change enables him to gamble on the newer treatment that does not have data on long-term effectiveness. Similarly, Alexander chose watchful waiting precisely because he could hope there would be better science in the future: "Meanwhile, I hope for ten or 15 years untroubled by the negative effects of either cancer or its treatments, during which time maybe some of the promising current research on genes and immunity may finally pay off with real answers to this weird disease of ours."[55]

Grove and Alexander incorporate radically distinct relations to both science and the future. Alexander found the controversy to signal that science did not know enough yet to take action, and he says he "probably wouldn't even think much about prostate cancer were it not for those calls and letters"[56] from readers of his first article. Both men continued to get regular tests, but Alexander sees any rises first as regular variability, while Grove anticipates the worst. Enacting his paranoia, Grove continues to live with a shadow: "Even though the results were good, it was a reminder that at least emotionally, things would never be altogether 'normal' again. Half a year and three PSA tests have since passed. My life has been the same as before: my energy, well-being, physical functions (including sex). Still, periodically I have to face the dread of a PSA test.

And although the results of the first three tests were very good, I know I will be stuck with this fear for the rest of my life."

OBJECTIVE SELF-FASHIONING FOR THE RATIONALLY PARANOID

Grove learns that his body is unknown via experience, but knowable through facts. He does not know himself through his body, but he knows his body through medicine (even through statistics when he imagines the size of his tumor). He knows his risk, his disease, his odds, and so forth. He sees the tension at first as lack of control over this knowledge: he didn't know he should be screened and then, when screened, he wasn't able to get the information he should have. To him, that constitutes the failure of the medical system.

He assumes that knowledge about his body is his, that he has a right to it and to control it. He sees that he has to take an active role in generating and acting on this knowledge. He personalizes facts and risk. They do not stay abstract. They are not subjective either. They are objective facts about himself that require work to produce. This is one form of objective self-fashioning.

Grove evaluates facts according to his own position, his positioned body, demographics, and so on. These produce not his decision, but the best odds at the time. He arrives not at a truth of decision, but at the true gamble he can now assume responsibility for. Grove tries to see through persuasion to truth. Given the best current knowledge, he can, like a businessman, make a rational gamble. It will still be a gamble, and he acknowledges that others might face the exact same odds and gamble differently. This gamble is based on his personal reasons, including an evaluation of preferences for risking side effects versus risking remission. This is an informed decision of the personal-objective subject. He sets this apart from the urologist, who is subject to his training. Grove has succeeded in the end (and at the end of his article) in settling what is his (fears, life, gambles) and what is objective. The urologist fails.

What Grove cannot abide are those who do not get as much information as possible and who stick their heads in the sand through ignorance, denial, or fear. These are irresponsible people, they refuse responsibility for knowledge, and they cannot act at all.

I have used Grove's exemplary reflexivity to make visible the logic of patients accepting responsibility for their health in an age of mass screening and mass treatment. To Grove, this duty to be healthy, to know, and to act on that knowledge is assumed to be absolutely natural, logical, and justified. As a reflexive, responsible patient, he notices the contradictory situations he is put in when facts disagree, and he valiantly attempts to resolve them and make good and right decisions. Alexander examined similar contrary facts and also made his own good and right decision. In the final chapter of this book I distinguish between three ways of accepting responsibility for one's health, three relationships to risks, tests, and treatments. In that set of distinctions, Grove's specific decision-making style, that is, his willingness to change his lifestyle in order to live more healthily, takes on additional significance as it is opposed to two other ways of being a rational, responsible patient.

TWO

Pharmaceutical Witnessing and Direct-to-Consumer Advertising

People come into my office, throw down an ad, and say, "That's me."
—A PSYCHIATRIST

It's a disease that often has no symptoms.
—FROM A TV COMMERCIAL TO ENCOURAGE GENERAL AWARENESS OF
PERIPHERAL ARTERY DISEASE

If you answered 7 or less for question 10, you probably aren't feeling like yourself.
—A QUIZ RESULT ON A WEBSITE FOR DEPRESSION AWARENESS
(WWW.GOONANDLIVE.COM, NOW DEFUNCT)

The statements in these epigraphs share a relatively new grammar of illness, risk, experience, and treatment, one in which the body is inherently disordered and in which health is no longer the silence of the organs; it is the illness that is silent, often with no symptoms. I want to interrogate this grammar, examining how it involves an image of health as risk reduction and an image of information as full of partial facts. Together, these images underpin a logic of accumulation of pharmaceuticals in the United States such that it becomes natural and imperative to treat one's body with more and more drugs for the duration of one's life. This situation has become so commonsensical that even critics of the pharmaceutical industry and advocates of alternative medicine share in this logical growth.

The ads one sees on TV and in magazines promoting prescription-only medicine are relatively new, with most analysts dating the big shift to 1999, when the FDA outlined requirements for TV ads. The challenge was to allow marketers to raise awareness about a condition or a treatment without taking over the doctor's role as the proper gatekeeper. Making overly broad claims for efficacy or overly simple claims for symptoms or not warning enough about side effects are lines still being negotiated today.[1] Pharmaceutical marketers know exactly what their endpoint is: profit in the form of ongoing mass pharmaceutical consumption. Profit ultimately boils down to prescription maximization, which can be achieved through growing the absolute number of new prescriptions, extending the time a patient stays on a prescription, or shortening the time between having a condition and getting a prescription for it.[2]

The challenge in studying pharmaceutical marketing is that the commercials do not usually work this easily. In fact, they don't work well at all; most people ignore them. But the marketers feel they work well enough to justify their repeatedly spending money on them. Both the number of prescriptions and the amount of drugs per prescription are projected to continue to grow at 5–15 percent per year for almost all classes of drugs for chronic conditions.[3] For marketers, some people responding some of the time is all they need: their processes of persuasion are designed to work in percentages, or market share. If they can get even a small additional percentage of Americans to consider that they might be depressed or have high cholesterol, and a small percentage of those people go to a doctor and request a prescription, the profits on these tens to hundreds of thousands of additional patients are more than enough to cover the advertising costs.[4] It does not matter whether those people believe they are sick, only that they act in accordance with that belief as delineated by the marketing campaigns. In a fascinating set of studies by Richard Kravitz and colleagues, actors posing as patients visited doctors, presented symptoms of depression, and in some cases mentioned seeing a direct-to-consumer (DTC) commercial and asked for a drug by name. The troubling result by these "standardized" patients was a profound increase in prescription rates for antidepressants.[5] This suggests that the very act of asking your doctor if a drug is right for you influences whether or not she or he will give it to you.

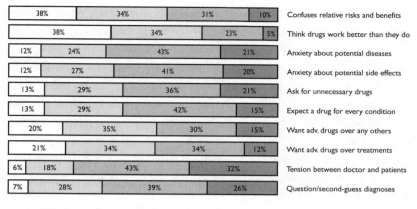

38%	34%	31%	10%	Confuses relative risks and benefits
38%	34%	23%	5%	Think drugs work better than they do
12%	24%	43%	21%	Anxiety about potential diseases
12%	27%	41%	20%	Anxiety about potential side effects
13%	29%	36%	21%	Ask for unnecessary drugs
13%	29%	42%	15%	Expect a drug for every condition
20%	35%	30%	15%	Want adv. drugs over any others
21%	34%	34%	12%	Want adv. drugs over treatments
6%	18%	43%	32%	Tension between doctor and patients
7%	28%	39%	26%	Question/second-guess diagnoses

☐ Not at all   ☐ A little   ☐ Somewhat   ■ A great deal

FIGURE 6 "Problems DTC [Direct-to-Consumer] Advertising Creates for My Patients and Practice." *Source*: Aikin 2002.

Studies of DTC advertising suggest that the commercials are successful in generating concern and anxiety (fig. 6) and that they drive pharmaceutical sales just enough to justify continuing to invest in them.[6] My challenge is therefore to account for this aggregate growth. I am thinking of this as an ethnography of the aggregate. So I begin with a study of how marketers imagine people to be manipulable enough.

My discussions here are based on my research into mass-market medicine as the advertising of mass health to the public. Mass-market medicine refers to blockbuster pharmaceuticals whose yearly sales exceed $1 billion and whose customers are measured in the millions. I analyzed hundreds of pharmaceutical TV commercials as well as magazine ads and internet sites; tracked patient discussion groups online; and interviewed pharmaceutical marketers, doctors, and patients' groups as well as holding workshops with them. Here I examine advertisements for their grammar of facts and health. I also analyze the so-called gray literature written by pharmaceutical marketers for each other to improve their practices. I aim to show how our ways of talking articulate with theirs in such a manner that we may get what we want, but it may not be what we need. *Pharmaceutical Executive* is one journal that concentrates on marketing strategies that target doctors and the public. I trace a major shift in marketing toward what I call factual persuasion and what *Pharmaceutical Executive*, in its first branding seminar in April 2002, termed "Pharma's challenge to convert science into marketing."[7]

Most pharmaceutical marketing overviews start with the product cycle. A drug in the United States must go through an extensive regulatory protocol in order to be approved for use. The process includes testing the drug for safety, first on animals, then on humans. Its potential efficacy is then assessed, and, finally, its actual efficacy is tested in a clinical population for a specific illness through clinical trials. When all of these requirements have been successfully accomplished, the pharmaceutical company applies to the FDA for approval. If approval is granted, the company enjoys the exclusive right to market that drug for a certain number of years to doctors and to the public for that illness.[8] Marketers therefore divide their strategies into stages: prelaunch, launch, market exclusivity, and transition to generic competition. Embedded in their articles about DTC marketing, however, is a complex theory of the mass market as being full of potential patients who do not know they are ill and must be led, step by step, toward a prescription.

REMAKING THE BODY AT RISK

Using tools from many disciplines, pharmaceutical marketers are building on a long tradition of public relations aimed at calibrating emotions for maximum effect in concert with the authoritative discourses of science and medicine that dissociate viewers from their own bodies and experience.[9] I begin with an early pharmaceutical commercial. Figure 7 shows screen captures from a DTC television commercial for a "depression kit" manufactured by Lilly, which provides a "personal checklist" in the form of an interrogation. The commercial features simple, highly general questions such as, Are you sleeping too much or too little? But the seriousness of these questions is transmitted in the follow-up: "These can be signs of clinical depression."

This conclusion converts the questions into a medical algorithm, a logical process of following a series of steps. But the grammar arrests: "These can be signs" is a peculiar phrase. It is retroactively transformative: aspects of one's life are inscribed as symptoms. What you had previously thought of, if at all, as personal variation is brought into heightened awareness. The first implication is that you are possibly suffering from a serious disease and do not know it. Your body, in other words, is potentially deceptive, concealing its own decline. This is not a presymptomatic form of awareness. Unlike the situation in Dorothy Nelkin and Laurence

Have you stopped doing things you used to enjoy? Are you sleeping too much, are you sleeping too little? Have you noticed a change in your appetite? Is it hard to concentrate? Do you feel sad almost every day? Do you sometimes feel that life may not be worth living?

These can be signs of clinical depression, a real illness, with real causes. But there is hope. You can get your life back. Treatment that has worked for millions is available from your doctor.

This is the number to call for a free confidential information kit, including a personal symptoms checklist, that can make it easier to talk with a doctor about how you're feeling. Make the call now, for yourself or someone you care about.

FIGURE 7 Depression awareness commercial, DTC advertisement by Lilly. *Source*: Screen captures, demo reel, 2002.

Tancredi's *Dangerous Diagnostics*, in which a brain scan or genetic test reveals a disease before it manifests symptoms, here you find out that you have been suffering from symptoms without feeling them.[10]

The phrases "These can be signs of X" and "You could be suffering from X" are also not simple performatives. They do not assert that you *have* depression; they do not diagnose.[11] For legal, marketing, and health reasons, the grammar is explicitly modalized as possibility: These can be, You could be, You might be. But they are giving you a new possibility. They market uncertainty as worry.

Information about the possibility of pathology transforms modalization into mobilization.[12] You can't ignore the possibility morally because your status has changed.[13] This can produce a very strong duty to be healthy (now that you know you are not) and a rational "having to try" (since you know there is something you can do) that is as deeply moral as the imperative to be tested identified by Nelkin and Tancredi.[14] You are now at risk, you now know that you have been at risk, and you have to try to do something about it. Since treatments are available, there is hope.

From a marketer's point of view, once you are aware of the disease in general, the question is how to get you to add depression, breast cancer, cholesterol to your lived anxieties, to your personal agenda, enough so that you attend to the possible condition, find more information, and talk to your doctor about it. This is termed personalization. The marketers' problem is how to get their facts into your head as facts that you come to depend on. This practice recalls and builds on an older generation of advertisements that teaches you that you might be suffering from bad breath or be overweight and not realize it but now this personalizing effect is amplified by passing it through tests and diagnostic algorithms.[15]

For instance, another commercial (see fig. 8) begins with a scene of middle-aged people on exercise bikes in a gym, working out but looking tired. The only sound is a ball rolling around, and superimposed above them is a spinning set of numbers. Finally the ball is heard dropping into place; the number is 265. The cholesterol roulette is over. The text on the screen reads, "Like your odds? Get checked for cholesterol. Pfizer."

The challenge of thinking through how these commercials work dialogically lies in the fact that they aim for a retroactive status change. Rather than illness punctuating ordinary life, the everyday conceals illness. Once this is identified, once you identify with it, then your true, real life can be returned to you. The process here is a counterpart to inter-

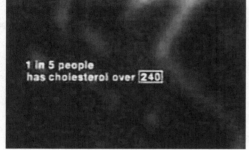

FIGURE 8 Cholesterol awareness commercial, DTC advertisement by Pfizer. *Source*: Screen captures, Court TV, November 20, 2001.

pellation. Louis Althusser's process of interpellation involved the always already self-recognition of the subject, where the teacher or policeman hails you or asks you a question, and your response confirms the self-evidence of your being a subject: "I am I."[16] Here your self-evidence is directly assaulted. Your self-identity is called into question via the algorithm. You are not who you think you are. Your body is not what you think it is. Your feelings are not what you think they are. The algorithm offers, in turn, to identify your objective self for you, so instead of the interpellated response, "Yes, it's me," we say, "Oh! So that's who I am."

I begin with this close grammatical reading of how some DTC commercials are constructed in order to argue in effect that we as viewers are vulnerable to redescriptions or reclassifications of our everyday variability into symptoms and that we can be led to identify with the possibility of disease and treatment through rhetorical persuasion. I want to attend now to the logics and grammars of pharmaceutical marketing as they are circulated and analyze these in accordance with the explicit strategies outlined by marketers. Marketers have a highly developed language for articulating the steps of conversion through which nonpatients come to see themselves as undiagnosed patients, then actively visit and persuade their doctor to give them a prescription. Using their terms but focusing on how marketers approach a person as someone who does not even know they require a drug, I have mapped their implicit strategy onto five distinct steps:

1. Awareness through education
2. Personalizing the risk
3. Motivation to self-diagnose
4. Seeing and convincing a doctor
5. Branded compliance

Most DTC commercials are aimed broadly at addressing people in any step, at reinforcing this stepwise progression as logical and natural, and at helping people move on to the next step. This process involves much more than just advertisements; it includes designing clinical trials, arranging screening programs, constructing databases, and monitoring compliance. As we, patients and potential patients, try to learn facts about our risks and illnesses and come to incorporate these into our identities and bodies, almost every aspect of the medical world we encounter is being modulated (not constructed, but adjusted) in accordance with profit motives. Marketers are capitalizing on our suffering bodies and our biomedical identities. This is therefore a troubling opportunity to understand how, in our capitalist culture, facts, risks, and illnesses work in and on us, transforming how we experience, understand, measure, and value both our health and the health of others.

ADVERTORIALS: AWARENESS AND ALERTNESS THROUGH EDUCATION

Health information can be manipulated through selection and amplification, privileging one form of explanation over others. The idea that information empowers can be turned into a structured or controlled empowerment, what the sociologist Dixon Woods has called "information for compliance" in contrast to "information for choice."[17] One strategy for producing a market is direct education of doctors and the public. According to one *Pharmaceutical Executive* article, "Companies realize that an effective way to reach commercial goals is to cultivate long-term patients through education rather than acquiring new consumers through brand awareness advertising."[18]

Even before the launch of a new drug, time is spent crafting messages about the disease that shape it toward market ends. In the United States, *advertorials* is a technical term for this process: quasi-educational spots whose function is to teach about specific disease symptoms and mechanisms. Advertorials are ads "designed to deliver the experience of reading an article."[19] They are used increasingly in the United States to build awareness of disease, to "create an urgency to treat diseases earlier and more aggressively,"[20] and to draw attention to underserved populations.

The assumption behind the idea of education as patient cultivation is that the public, doctors, and medical institutions are ignorant. The status quo is harming people in a most dangerous way because they are not even aware of the harm they are doing to themselves. Ignorance about medical issues justifies an emergency public health response: explicit manipulation or "facilitated awareness." There are two main approaches to awareness through education: preparing the market and health literacy. At different levels of generality, each aims at changing the status quo of common knowledge through critical presentation: redefining what health is, what treatment is, what a smart person does to be healthy, and so on. They aim, in other words, to reframe how we see the world working and what we take for granted. In this manner fact-based marketing creates a receptive climate.

In an article in *Pharmaceutical Executive* Sibyl Shalo and Joanna Breitstein write, "Ilyssa Levins, chairman of GCI Healthcare Public Relations, underscored how public relations supports the 'science and marketing connection' by creating a receptive climate through advocacy and issue-oriented media relations. She said PR can facilitate awareness and adoption among regulators, payers, medical influencers, and patients alike by conditioning the market for acceptance of new concepts such as overactive bladder."[21] The premise of health literacy is that a large segment of the population cannot handle complicated information. As Pfizer's president, Patrick Kelly, implied in a 2003 article, they must be managed like children: "Limit the content. Make it easy to read. Make it look easy to read. Select visuals that clarify and motivate."[22] This kind of handholding "conditions the market"; medical information is streamlined so that it becomes more efficient in producing more prescriptions.

The aims of health literacy campaigns as envisioned by marketers are to cement the relationship between knowing and doing. Targeting a sixth-grade reading level allows marketers to imagine a market of 110 million people who could be addressed with health information. The health-aware individual is thus presented as one who can and will act on medical facts. Whereas facts are typically seen as descriptive, health facts are seen as being meaningful and successful only if their knowledge induces action. Noncompliance with facts is framed as a problem of literacy: if they aren't acting on the facts, it must be because they don't understand them. Health literacy grammatically frames the public as being well intentioned but ignorant, illiterate, uneducated, and disempowered. Kelly continued, "When health information is offered, people cannot understand or act upon it. When that happens, [often] low health literacy may be at fault. Health literacy is defined as the ability to read, understand, and act on health information, and it becomes more important as patients are asked to take a more active role in their own healthcare."[23] The moral grammar of health information is that facts will be acted upon. This grammar precludes resistance: if you do not act on what you know, you must be doing so for social and psychological reasons. You are confused, embarrassed, intimidated, or ignorant. In turn, each of these reasons offers an opportunity for strategic intervention by marketers to fix the problem of those of us who have encountered the information but are not acting on it.

In Europe this challenge is acute because brand-name pharmaceutical advertising to consumers is not allowed, though advertorials are. Sandoz (Novartis), which had an antifungal agent, Lamisil, to promote, needed to find another way "to encourage patients to talk with their doctors about onychomycosis and its treatment options. So the company renamed the condition the more consumer-friendly 'fungal infection' and took out newspaper ads asking readers to call or write to 'Step Wise' for a free brochure on foot care."[24]

Besides capturing future patients through the informational relationship, the phrase "fungal infection" became an indirect brand, an illness fused with Lamisil as its treatment. The challenge for pharmaceutical companies is managing education that is not directly branded without giving too much away to competitors. Their goals are similar to those outlined by Jay Bolling in "DTC: A Strategy for Every Stage," to "employ prelaunch promotion to prepare potential customers for future product use, without generating new prescriptions for the competition."[25] Mechanisms include quasi-branded cues that will later be branded explicitly when the drug that works on just that mechanism is launched. Even the color schemes and typography are tied into this process of managing awareness in anticipation of a future market.[26]

PERSONALIZING THE RISK

Once a prospect is aware of a risk and therefore accepts that it is possible, he or she must then be made to personalize the risk. Having been introduced to a fact, one needs to enter into a relationship with it. Personalizing is an explicit tactic in marketing literature and involves having the risk become part of an existing internal and external dialogue. It has to become part of your story, how you talk about and represent yourself to others. Personalizing requires that the possibility of risk in general now becomes your possible risk. What is needed is that you worry about this possibility, that it go from being an object of your attention (awareness) to becoming an object of your concern (worry). Bolling explains:

> When its efforts to market to physicians had reached the saturation point, the manufacturer of a prescription health product for women

decided to launch a DTC campaign to expand product sales. The company's goal was to pull through new prescriptions by increasing the target audience's awareness of the need for treatment to prevent the onset of osteoporosis. The first communication objective was to get patients to "personalize" the risk so they regarded the disease state as important enough to warrant taking further action. If the company introduced the brand too early in the relationship, before the target woman considered herself to be at risk for the disease state, she would quickly dismiss the therapy as not appropriate for her.[27]

Medicalization is a term used by sociologists to describe the historical process through which conditions, complaints, normal variation, and socially undesirable traits are turned into medical conditions and interventions.[28] Analyzed as power conflicts, medicalization can be a coercive force turning people into patients in order to control and manage them. Alternately, medicalization can be a tactic by sufferers to become objects of attention and care through becoming patients.[29] In DTC advertising, these problems of "my status" and "my bodily state" are offered as explanations for what you are and should be now concerned about. It appears noncoercive, even empowering. You are offered a gift to freely evaluate. But, as medical anthropologists have noted, characterizing the process of medicalization is fraught with narrative and conceptual difficulties for everyone involved.[30]

How does medical identification happen? How can we ethnographically describe an encounter with an advertisement that is effective as documented in increased prescription demands, yet does not reduce the viewer to a judgmental dope, to use a phrase from the sociologist Harold Garfinkel, that is, someone who is passively duped by the media?[31] In order to investigate processes of identification, I want to make a detour into the anthropology of religion and personhood and draw on the work of Susan Harding, who studied Christian fundamentalist followers of Jerry Falwell.[32] She analyzed the techniques of evangelical witnessing, the explicit process of attempting to convert nonbelievers into believers through dialogue and actions. Her study offers a framework for understanding the active, participatory process of identification and persuasion that unfolds in pharmaceutical advertising.

Harding approaches conversion and status change from the inside, so to speak, as one who is involved in the situation, in the dialogue, struggling to understand. Harding notices her involvement as she is driving home after interviewing a minister. She almost gets into an accident. In that moment of danger, she finds herself asking, "What is the holy spirit trying to tell me?" Finding herself asking this question begins a key insight. She began "to appropriate in her inner speech the evangelical language and its attendant view of the world." Her modes of embodied attention, cognitive and emotional, were drawn to the near accident as a gap in the ordinary, an event within the everyday in which "the seams split."[33]

Harding argues that one moves from being an unbeliever to a believer through a "process of acquiring a specifically religious language. . . . If you are seriously willing to listen, and struggle to understand, you are susceptible to conversion." It is the unwitting, basic desire to understand that aids this process. The listener gets "caught up in certain kinds of stories" in which the personal referents, the pronouns, "Christ died for *you*," slip up and slip into one's own language. Her description is deeply processual: the listener struggles to make sense of stories with uncertain references, stories that force attention onto events, past, present, and future, which disrupt the normal flow of life, leaving those disruptions open and vulnerable and making sense only through a religious grammar.

Harding shows that the worlds of the believers and the unbelievers regarding fundamentalism are each clear and logical, but that evangelicals want to convert and save others. While it appears that from the unbeliever position there is no middle ground, that you either believe or you don't, Harding insists there is a substantial in-between position, which evangelicals describe as "being under conviction." Harding describes "coming under conviction" as a kind of individualized dialogic approach to status change.

Similarly, the suggestion "These may be signs of a serious illness" and the question, "Is this a symptom?" can be thought of as part of coming under a biomedical conviction. This "inner rite of passage," Harding suggests, works subliminally in that she and others who are witnessed to often have no idea what is happening. They are not changing status within a culture, however that is to be defined, but are instead switching cultures or worldviews.[34] Finding oneself asking, "Is my cholesterol too high?" is already such a switch. One has begun to personalize, acquiring a specifically pharmaceutical language and worldview.

In pharmaceutical marketing, this switch often turns on some sort of bodily hook. This is a facilitated recognition in which you come to understand that what you had previously taken for granted or overlooked in your body is in fact an object of concern. In this manner your attention to a risk possibility and your self-concern become linked, and the temporal fact that you had overlooked this before adds an emotional surprise and worry to the mix. The archetypal form of this identification is the "ouch test," as described by the virtual contributing editor Vern Realto in *Pharmaceutical Executive*: "Of course, in the world of DTC, it helps to have a product indication in which patients can point to a spot on their bodies and say, 'Ouch!' Prilosec [for acid indigestion] has such luck. And its DTC creative makes full use of the fact. Patient self-selection is the point. For a heartburn sufferer, looking at the campaign's ever-present cartoon figures is like looking in the mirror. Does it hurt? Yes. Would you like 24-hour relief with a single pill? Yes!"[35]

The grammar of this concise description conceals the interpellation at work. Patient self-selection is the retroactive effect of the campaign when it is successful. A person who does not consider herself a patient or even necessarily a sufferer comes to recognize a complaint as suffering and as treatable and therefore recognizes herself as a patient. Althusser called this process of coming to see oneself as having already been a patient a "subject effect." As noted in chapter 1, I call this process, when it happens through a scientific fact, objective self-fashioning because one's new identity appears to have been verified as one's real and objectively true identity.[36]

The retroactive effect can also happen at a bodily level, within a subject's body, when an ache or complaint is reframed as a symptom. In the following description by a patient compliance expert the headache is always already a symptom that the unaware consumer has mistakenly ignored: "DTC ads can make consumers aware that symptoms they have tried to ignore, believing that nothing could be done, are actually the result of a treatable condition. For instance, a person who suffers from frequent headaches may learn from a DTC ad that those may be the symptoms of a migraine and that there is treatment available. Those ads can give us hope. They can help us identify positive steps to take. They can motivate us to talk with the doctor about subjects we find embarrassing."[37]

Furthermore, one recognizes that a third-party expert enabled this objective redescription of one's so-called symptom as the truth of one's experience. In addition to a subject-effect here, there is a truth-effect. At this point in the DTC process, the target is common sense. First, in the awareness step, you will recognize not only that heartburn is a treatable medical condition but also that you should have known this. As a fact, it should have been part of your taken-for-granted background against which you examine the world. The compliance expert continues, "If we think there is no treatment available for our symptoms, we may decide it's not worth spending the money on an office visit."[38] Now, with personalization, you can see that you may be suffering from this treatable medical condition. You may possibly be a patient.

Realto's account of Prilosec notes that one is lucky to have this built-in auto-identification ouch test. Then the problem is only one of medicalizing a portion of experience. The bigger challenge for marketers is producing identification with an asymptomatic condition, making patients recognizing themselves as in need of treatment despite feeling healthy. Medical sociologists and anthropologists have long used a distinction between illness as lived experience framed by lay notions of suffering and disease as biomedical knowledge.[39] The aim of risk and symptom personalization is precisely to conflate these understandings of illness and disease so that one talks in terms of medical facts, risk factors, and biomarkers, so that one literally experiences risk factors as symptoms. Realto asks, "Will the same approach work for a cholesterol-lowering medicine? No. But if a way exists to make patients recognize themselves through any DTC communication, therein lies the first lesson in consumer health care marketing. You can take it to the bank."[40]

The lived body must be reframed as no longer giving forth symptoms, but instead as naturally concealing them. One's body itself, as marked or measured, then takes the place of a bodily symptom. Even a basic demographic attribute like sex, race, or age can become the basis for risk personalization and marketing. In a commercial for the osteoporosis-prevention drug Fosamax, women are urged to recognize themselves first positively as being healthy, active, successful, and empowered and therefore as being at risk (fig. 9). The ad presents a number of such vibrant women saying, "I'm not taking any chances. I'm not putting it off any longer. . . . A quick and painless bone density test can tell if your bones are thinning. If they are, this is the age of Fosamax." The commer-

I'm not taking any chances. I'm not putting it off any longer. Fifty-eight percent of women in their fifties have thinning bones, and risk increases with age.

But a quick and painless bone density test can tell if your bones are thinning. If they are, this is the age of Fosamax. Fosamax once weekly is for post-menopausal women at risk for or with osteoporosis. It's proven to help reverse bone loss.

You should not use Fosamax if you have certain disorders of the esophagus, are unable to stand or sit upright for thirty minutes, have severe kidney disease, or low blood calcium. Before use, talk to your doctor if you have stomach or digestive problems. Stop taking Fosamax and tell your doctor if you develop new or worsening heartburn, difficult or painful swallowing, or chest pain, as these may be signs of serious upper-digestive problems.

Bone density test? Bone density test. Sounds like a good idea to me. Ask your doctor about a bone density test and if Fosamax is right for you. This is the age of Fosamax. Helping REVERSE bone loss.

FIGURE 9 Fosamax bone-density test commercial, DTC advertisement by Merck. *Source*: Screen captures, CBS, February 2, 2003.

cial concludes with multiple female voices: "Bone density test?"; "Bone density test"; "Sounds like a good idea to me"; "Ask your doctor about a bone density test and if Fosamax is right for you."

For a viewer, identifying as a positive, healthy woman becomes identifying with the risk, which must be tested since it cannot be experienced. A successful advertising encounter is one which accepts and internalizes this uncertainty under a biomedical conviction: that one might need Fosamax, and only the bone density test can tell.

Targeting a slightly older demographic, a series of commercials for Zocor feature grandmothers and grandfathers, including the football coach Dan Reeves, discussing how much they enjoy their time but how much they want to see the future, their grandchildren's graduations, and so on. They relate that they have had a heart attack and that diet and exercise weren't enough to lower their cholesterol: "I could dance all night back there. So I was thrilled when my grandson wanted to follow in my footsteps. But before our first lesson, I had a heart attack. I needed to lower my cholesterol. How will you take care of your high cholesterol and heart disease?"

Their doctors' information about Zocor gives them a salvational solution: "Be good to yourself. It's your future. BE THERE." This mode of storytelling provides an image of a responsible, rational actor who, upon hearing a new fact, incorporates it first by becoming concerned and then by taking action. The very act of reciting this tale repeats this process, passing on the informational possibility of risk to the listener and the personalized possibility of taking it up responsibly.

Rhetorically repeating a tale about a fact is a mode of passing on the grammar through witnessing. The tale is told in the exact words that viewers can in turn state for themselves, to others, and to their doctors: "Because I want to be there." At the same time, the risk information is translated from an odds sense of possibility to a powerfully imperative one of probability. If you, too, are a woman or middle aged, how can you not be ready, get checked, and so on. You may have been fearful of death before, but now you have a precise plan of action for dealing with that fear. Putting these tactics together requires a precise effort at timing the market, that is, coordinating public relations campaigns, including mass media articles and doctor awareness, so that biomedical identification and pharmaceutical conviction successfully take place.

MOTIVATING SELF-DIAGNOSIS

Once identification has taken place and viewers accept a possible risk as their own, marketers see the next step as converting the possible into actual risk or, in the case of symptoms, getting the patients to self-diagnose. The next step of motivation then confirms this personal possibility as a probability through some kind of objective self-assessment: a self-diagnosis through a checklist or another external tool. Self-help is promoted as a free activity: it does not cost anything to see if you fit the criteria; you don't risk anything; you just take this simple quiz. Ambiguities of language in ads and teaser articles aim to induce curiosity and concern about one's apparently neutral and healthy status. As Bolling writes, "The goal during this pre-launch stage is not to motivate patients to see their doctors but to motivate them to respond for more information."[41]

Checklists and risk-factor charts are provided in DTC commercials, ads, and news articles, on websites, and in direct-mail pieces. The personalized patient is still a patient-in-potential, and these self-help techniques aim to create empowered self-identified patients whose next task will be visiting their doctors and convincing them of their condition and need for treatment. Checklists empower and disempower at the same time. The paradox of checklists is that while they appear to be a form of self-help they take the question of diagnosis, Am I sick? out of the subject's hands. Even if feelings and experience are used to fill out the checklist, the algorithm then decides whether or not these count as objective symptoms. The score one receives takes the place of a lived experience of illness; the score can even become its own experience. In this way one comes to verify that, indeed, the possible risk or symptom is a true risk or symptom. One has gained not just a fact about oneself but also a vocabulary, rationale, and moral judgment about the unfinished process.

Checklists therefore function as a kind of rite of passage. The anthropologist Victor Turner described rites of passage as liminal processes in which a person is socially unmade and then remade into a different person, for example, a boy into a man. In DTC campaigns nominally healthy persons, or prospects, become secretly sick persons, or patients-in-waiting, who are oriented toward becoming healthy again.[42] In the DTC rite of passage, one gives up one's sense of self and health as the body becomes a silent traitor that has concealed its condition. One then submits to the ritual of questions in order to discover that the body really is disordered. If one is sick, the promise is that one will then be treated and reunited with one's true self and true community. The process is enacted explicitly in many DTC commercials. For example, a Zoloft commercial about depression provides a story about the disease's progression (fig. 10).

The story in the Zoloft commercial enacts the classic anthropological rite of passage. The subject, you, is at first separated, alienated by a series of descriptions that are aligned into accusations. The biomedical facts are then introduced in a reflexive, subjunctive voice, the voice of liminality. These may not be your fault: they may be symptoms of a biology. You, at this point in the story, are in the liminal state of being both this and that, both mental and physical, accused and sick. You know you don't feel right, but you need the commercial to tell you that the feeling is a real symptom. And the grammatical voice, as Victor Turner observed, can then shift from the subjunctive to the optative, from hypothesis and possibility into emotion, wish, and desire.[43] "There is hope," a narrator explains, "treatments are available." The conclusion of the story is reaggregation, a return to society with a new status, a new, true you (fig. 11).

These stories are sanctioning themselves through the model of the rite of passage. They have appropriated the frame of the rite and packaged it for consumption. From the point of view of Harding's conversion, the viewer is first called on to attend to interpersonal tensions as patterned problems requiring solutions and is then offered a narrative grammar that makes sense of them. Within the story, the shifts in status function as what the rhetorician Kenneth Burke called a "conversion downward," in which the complex social situation of the distressed, struggling you is given a much simpler rationality of motivation.[44]

Harding characterizes the way in which one who is confronted by an evangelical who witnesses can "gradually come to respond, interpret, act, as if believing [in Jesus], with or without turmoil and anxiety." This process is not a social ritual, but "a kind of inner rite of passage" that involves acquiring a new form of "inner speech," a process in which one is gradually alienated from one's old voices because they no longer satisfy the gaps one experiences. One is cast into limbo, "somehow in a liminal state," she says, "a state of confusion and speechlessness, and begin to hear a new voice."[45] A number of commercials explicitly elaborate this concept: a voice-over offers a diagnosis and treatment, and the patient says, "I feel like *me* again" or a loved one states, "I remember you!"

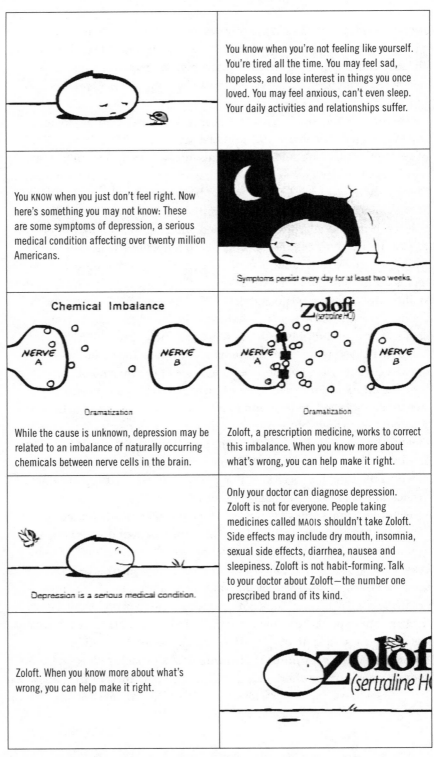

FIGURE 10 Zoloft commercial, DTC advertisement by Pfizer. *Source*: Screen captures, CBS, November 28, 2004.

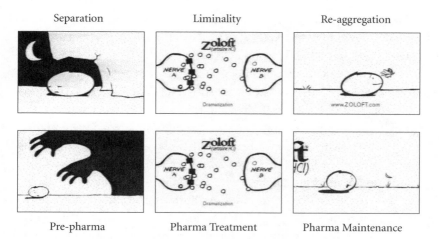

FIGURE 11 Zoloft commercial exemplifying liminality.

These commercials and hundreds like them engage in a form of biomedical informing that one might call pharmaceutical witnessing. Through the passing on of facts embedded in stories in which the subject of the story is potentially you, the viewer is put in a position of having to make sense of the story or ignore the risk it portrays altogether.

The sociologist Steve Kroll-Smith uses the self-test as an example in which the voice of experience and the voice of medicine are "beginning to converse outside of the once solid container of institutionalized medicine."[46] Kroll-Smith has studied the development, deployment, and use of excessive daytime sleepiness (EDS) as a definite illness defined publicly through a self-reported measure of excessive sleepiness (based on seven-point scales). He suggests that "a person who self-diagnoses with EDS after taking [a self-test] . . . is exercising, if only momentarily, an alternative authority [to that of modern medicine]."[47] Calling for a "both-and" approach to (culturally defined) illness and (biologically defined) disease, he suggests that popular media play a crucial role in fashioning medicine and bodily knowledge.

Stigma and social approbation are intimately associated with how persons come to think of themselves. Whereas Kroll-Smith uses contested diseases as examples, marketers see the same media empowerment as being useful for emphasizing outsider conditions and amplifying the power of the checklist over the consumer and of the consumer over the doctor. Marketers do not like stigma because they fear it will inhibit self-recognition of patient status and therefore reduce prescription demand. Writing to marketers, a director of behavioral sciences, Lynn Edlen-Nezin, called these stigmatized diseases "diseases of denial," implying that individual psychology is at the heart of the marketing problem. "Diseases of denial can be broadly categorized as medical conditions that make patients feel excluded, rejected, devalued, inadequate, or guilty. . . . That's one reason pharma marketers should facilitate undiagnosed or untreated patients' self-identification and encourage them to communicate with healthcare providers about treatment options."[48]

Marketers are here aligned with sufferers who struggle to understand, accept, and communicate their suffering as illnesses. Sufferers often form their own communities online in discussion groups and offline in mutual-help groups. In these sites they actively invent ways of living with their conditions.[49] Often there are many groups with varying approaches to the same condition. Marketers with treatments to sell actively court those groups whose interests align with their needs. They accelerate the circulation of these social innovations in ways that also help sell products. The result is often a public service educational advertising campaign that draws attention to an illness by reifying it as treatable and by destigmatizing it.

The marketers I have talked with regularly monitor online discussions of pharmaceuticals and hold focus groups with patients, and some of them have hired anthropologists to conduct ethnographies of diseases. They consider one of their greatest strengths to be finding a patient who eloquently expresses a private insight about an illness that accords with their mission to increase prescriptions. Their job is then to greatly amplify that insight so that others may come to identify with it. Cutting and pasting is a fitting description of the general circulation and mediation of pharmaceutical experiences and practices. Communicational media, mass media, everyday discussions, and research techniques feed back on one another.[50]

Turning worry into incipient action and navigating between hope and stigma require precise attention to the live language of consumers as potential patients who are struggling with a concern. Perhaps more than at any other step, grammar matters when the personalized risk must become incorporated into consumers' identity as patients. Individual differences among persons require careful scripting in order to produce a mass market. One marketer explained that the level of attention is increasingly precise: "HealthMedia uses a combination of Healthcare technology and behavioral science to design 'action plans' that give patients tips, advice, and strategies to obtain a healthcare 'goal.' In essence, the action plans are the front end of a highly sophisticated customer relationship management program that can segment at the individual level so that each fragment of every sentence in the plan is customized and corresponds to how patients answer a constellation of questions."[51]

Michel Pêcheux, in his study of language, ideology, and discourse, found that motivation and identification were mediated by specific word choices.[52] As the above passage reveals, marketers manage these processes through empirically verified texts. Questionnaires are meticulously designed through extensive market research. Each question on surveys and checklists is a psychological tool. At the conclusion of this step, concerned consumers have become worried, self-diagnosed potential patients who know what they have and want treatment for it. From a marketing point of view, they are empowered patients ready and motivated to see their doctor.

THE CRITICAL MOMENT: CONVINCING THE DOCTOR

With self-diagnosis accomplished, the goal of pharmaceutical promotion is still only halfway done. The potential patient must now get to the doctor, convince the doctor to diagnose and prescribe treatment, and then take the drug and continue taking it. Marketing must now aim at "pass-through persuasion," giving the patients the tools to convince their doctors. Doctors, in turn, are seen as obligatory obstacles to be overcome and as lacking authority to make a diagnosis. Any resistance on the doctor's part is seen as a lack of knowledge, of interest, or of time. Though this reading may seem harsh, DTC campaigns constantly reinforce it, in spite of the required acknowledgment they must make that "only your doctor can make the diagnosis." Bolling explains:

> Marketers can generate significant product sales by motivating physicians and patients to take action and by influencing their interaction. On the consumer side, that means providing enough information to patients so they can convince a busy, uninformed, or disinterested physician to prescribe the brand; getting more patients to fill their

initial prescriptions; [and] motivating patients to comply with their medication regimen.[53]

Some campaigns make incompetence of doctors a direct theme, wherein the patient has to diagnose herself by seeing a commercial and then filling out an online checklist in order to convince the doctor of her true condition. A Lilly commercial about bipolar misdiagnosis is an idealized example of this (fig. 12).

In this commercial viewers see a patient who has dutifully watched tv in order to recognize her own misdiagnosis and misprescription, then used the internet to prepare an objective reidentification of herself as manic-depressive and in need of Lilly's drug Zyprexa instead. Her doctor happily accepts the checklist, verifying his incompetence or perhaps impotence.

The doctor, in other words, is directed by the checklist, and the checklist in turn can become the measure of an illness and of effectiveness of treatment that otherwise is not perceptible to her. In many cases like this, checklists developed in order to conduct clinical research have become both a marketing and a self-diagnostic tool. The result is described by David Healy: "Increasingly . . . in the 1980s and 1990s, clinical freedom became constrained by algorithms, and [primary care] practitioners were encouraged to use instruments (checklists) such as the Hamilton Depression Rating Scale . . . in their daily practice. Far from these epitomizing a 'scientific' approach to psychiatry, however, these new practices enjoin clinicians to fly blind or to immerse themselves in a virtual world. The behavior of clinicians is now progressively less likely to be based on knowledge derived from direct clinical encounters."[54]

Another aim of this campaign is to further a "depsychiatrization" (to use Robert Castel's word),[55] a pseudodemocratization of diagnosis and a generalization of medication. The demotion of all specialists in consumer campaigns is explicit because the campaigns are trying to empower the prospective patient over doctors in favor of prescriptions. General practitioners are understood by marketers as "busy, uninformed, and disinterested" and therefore more amenable to persuasion than specialists. In 2007, nonpsychiatrists wrote 79 percent of all prescriptions for antidepressants and 51 percent of all prescriptions for antipsychotics (up from 16 percent in 2001 and 30 percent in 2004, respectively).[56]

Furthermore, marketing directly to nurse practitioners and physician

Your doctor probably never sees you when you feel like this.

THIS is usually who your doctor sees. That deeply depressed you who BARELY dragged yourself in for treatment . . .

That's why so many people with bipolar disorder are being treated for depression and not getting any better. Because depression is only half the story. That fast-talking, energetic, over-doing-it, up-all-night you . . . probably never shows up in the doctor's office. Right?

Log on to BipolarAwareness.com sponsored by Lilly on WebMD, the place for healthcare answers. Take the test you can TAKE to your doctor. You can CHANGE your life.

Let your doctor in on it. In order to make a correct diagnosis, your doctor has to know about your ups as well as your downs. Getting a correct diagnosis is the first step in treating bipolar disorder. Help your doctor help YOU.

FIGURE 12 Bipolar awareness commercial, DTC advertisement by Lilly. *Source*: Screen captures, CBS, November 14, 2004.

assistants, cutting out the doctor, is encouraged: these two lower-status groups have gained increasing power to write prescriptions in the last ten years. In 2005, nurse practitioners were estimated to have written 125 million prescriptions per year and physician assistants 75 million more. In 2007 the two groups wrote 6 percent of all psychotropic prescriptions (more than 28 million prescriptions for each group).[57] And it has been justly noted that although physicians are required to oversee and countersign nurse practitioners' and physician assistants' prescriptions, "their influence as practitioners is paramount for pharmaceutical companies looking to offer education to today's key prescribers." Pharma companies have described these billion-dollar "invisible prescribers" as "today's primary-care clinicians" who are "very approachable and very interested in working with the pharma industry."[58]

In other words, neither the patient nor most prescribers can do anything but depend on these checklists as the only measure of an illness and of treatment effectiveness. In self-diagnosing via ads and commercials as well as by researching their conditions and risks online, patients exploit this blindness by reversing the traditional manner in which doctors convince patients. Patients often discuss in support groups and online the possibilities of taking this increasingly mechanical form of diagnosis and using it to emplot their doctors, telling them exactly what needs to be said to get what they want.[59] DTC commercials actively encourage such behavior. In this counter-emplotment, then, both patient and doctor become dominated by the code of the marketers. In the language of sociologists, this is termed symbolic domination.[60]

As members of what Ulrich Beck calls "risk society," we are prepared for the fact that many dangers are imperceptible to us, below our conscious perception, and that we cannot trust our senses but must trust instruments and other technologies of identification.[61] The virtual world for the clinician is precisely the self-identified world of the advertisement grammar.

Much DTC marketing, therefore, offers a consumer the precise language with which to accomplish this counter-emplotment. Through the focus groups, interviews, and fieldwork, marketers attempt to fuse personal stories with the rules of diagnosis. Calibrated for maximum effectiveness, the scripts simultaneously dumb down and reify the patient's experience into generic, branded stories of suffering and, in so doing, empower them to translate these stories into effective action in their doc-

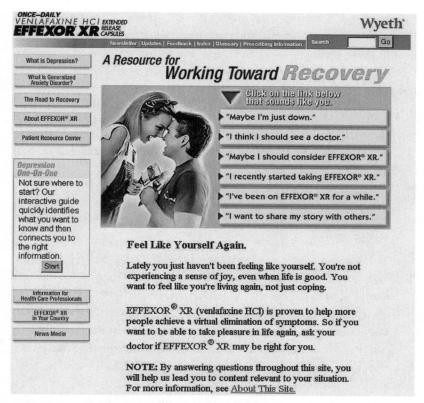

FIGURE 13 Effexor XR website, by Wyeth, retrieved October 22, 2002.

tors' offices—in order to get what they now know they want. The doctors, in the end, are even more dumbed down and reified. For if a patient should arrive at the doctor's office saying these words, the doctor will have little choice but to observe that the patient has stated all the right things in the right way.[62] In a section called "Critical Moment," Realto's article describes how important this scripting is: "All of the DTC communications for Prilosec aim at this crucial intersection of physician and patient. The campaign primes potential gastric reflux patients to report symptoms accurately and ask about treatment with Prilosec."[63]

This situation of doctor-emplotment through witnessing was also illustrated by the Effexor XR antidepressant website (in its 2002 format; see fig. 13). It was designed so that the first thing the viewer saw was a list of statements and was told to "Click on the link that sounds like you." The choices were, among others, "Maybe I'm just down," "I think I should see a doctor," and "I want to share my story with others." Clicking on one of these brought up a page that did nothing other than offer the words that best fit these feelings. There were no further instructions. For example, by clicking on "Maybe I'm just down" the patient would come across the following:

Maybe I'm just down

Does this sound like your situation?

Please note: The following story is fictitious and describes a general situation.

"After a few weeks, I knew something was wrong. Nothing really bad happened, but I was having more and more negative thoughts. At first, I figured it was normal to feel sad and empty (even hopeless) for a few days, maybe even a week. After all, I wondered, don't most people feel down every once in a while? But I couldn't snap out of it. I started to get concerned that something was seriously wrong. Why was this happening to me? I decided to look for some answers.

"I learned that I was experiencing the symptoms of a medical condition—depression—and that my doctor could help me feel like 'me' again. I also learned that I should not feel ashamed or embarrassed because it was beyond my control. That's when I called my doctor.

"It didn't happen overnight, but I really have come a long way. Recognizing that I was experiencing the symptoms of a medical condition and understanding that help was available was the best thing I could have done for myself."

Do you feel sad and empty? Do you no longer feel like "you" anymore? Perhaps you are suffering from symptoms of depression. You may find some helpful information in What Is Depression? or What Is Generalized Anxiety Disorder? and Symptoms of Depression or Symptoms of Generalized Anxiety Disorder. You might also want to use the Success Scale or see Evaluation and Treatments for Depression.[64]

These pages are written in a nonreflexive manner. They are posed as fictional stories that tell your story better than you could tell it yourself. The situations are described in the past tense as personal testimony, but they are grammatically precise, such that in repeating them you would obtain from your doctor exactly what you think you want. The isomorphism of marketing is here aligned with that of patients' groups against a healthcare system that, for good or ill, is attempting to resist the costs of increasing pharmaceutical interventions and maintenance. The net result is the aggregate increase in patients asking for and receiving prescriptions for daily medicines. And it works. As I noted earlier, in a series of brilliant studies involving actors playing patients, medical researchers showed that referencing an ad or asking for a prescription by name greatly influenced the likelihood of a doctor diagnosing and prescribing treatments.[65]

BRANDED COMPLIANCE

The final stage of marketing is to have patients complete the purchase and continue to refill their prescriptions for as long as possible. This is the payoff: one prescription purchased now and hopefully many more in the future. *Compliance* refers to patients staying on the prescriptions they are given and refilling them. As some marketers have found, compliance also refers to the gap between those who should be on lifelong medicines but are not:

> Companies are increasingly using physician-supplied patient starter packs containing user leaflets, tips, FAQ advice, and patient diaries at the initial prescribing consultation to help ensure the right patient/ brand compliance from the start. Those packs create the basis of initial patient expectations with resulting patient treatment outcomes fostering repeat brand loyalty in terms of prescribing decision making and user preference.[66]

The aim at this point is to cement a relationship between self-assessment, diagnosis, and branded treatment, to integrate the pharmaceutical into the everyday and reinforce a notion of dependent normality. The notion of a so-called healthstyle requires support from many directions. The initial one is through community with other patients. Second, brands are proposed as anchoring a patient's healing to future purchases. With brand loyalty comes product advocacy. Bolling advises, "Addressing those needs by providing valuable, customized information will not only foster product loyalty among patients, but also generate product advocacy. And there's nothing more powerful than patient-to-patient endorsements. Although a physician's recommendation may be highly credible, it doesn't carry the power of empathy and understanding that a fellow sufferer typically conveys. Great brands not only become part of patients' health and perception of well-being, they become part of their lives."[67]

Achieving this integration, says Bolling, starts with knowing as much about patients as possible and making patients understand "the need to take medication daily," "how to convert education to action," and to "associate their medication with being sick or well." Above all, marketers need to determine answers to the following: "Do patients accept that they have a chronic disease or condition and need to continue to take medication for it, or are they in denial that they need to do that?"[68] Contrary to writing on chronic illnesses that stem from pain or fatigue or suffering, none of these issues are taken for granted with these lifelong pharmaceuticals aimed at asymptomatic conditions.

The explicit manipulation of unfounded fears offers insight into the single-mindedness of marketing. The war here is between companies, branded versus generic multinationals, in which patients are the means, their minds the instruments used in waging the battle. Bolling goes to recommend: "Overall, the key is to increase consumers' comfort level so they're resistant to change if faced with the option to switch."[69]

CONCLUSION

In liminal situations, Turner argues, we develop our grammar, "ways of talking about indicative ways of communicating. . . . We take ourselves for our subject matter."[70] Perhaps even in subliminal marketing experiences, we develop and refine our modes of expressivity, changing our minds in order to change our bodies. In addition to his careful attention to the grammar and creativity of process, Turner constantly attended to the role of the anthropological writer who must always make choices about where to locate agency in process: in the individual, in the social structure, or in some sort of balance. Here I have portrayed the pharmaceutical marketing encounters with an emphasis on how they can bring some people under conviction some of the time. In other work, I have stepped back behind the focus groups to see how activists and everyday acts of creativity and resistance have shaped the terrain of the doctor–patient encounter and invented most of the forms of informing that marketing has in turn taken up and amplified.[71]

Health activist groups today are often in a dilemma as to whether or not to accept funding from commercial, especially pharmaceutical, sources. Roddey Reid has described how even antismoking activists have been caught off-guard when they are offered money by a drug company, who considers them to be helping to grow the market for nicotine patches and smoking prevention pills.

Many drugs work much of the time and for most of the people they are intended to help. The issue at stake for marketers in DTC is how to continue to grow the market big enough and fast enough to keep up with investors' expectations, which they often do by stretching the evidence from clinical trials. Many pills currently in use work to modulate our bodies in ways that we may not be able to completely describe but that we nonetheless desire for curative, preventive, experiential, or experimental reasons. However, we have far too little data and are not, in fact, collecting data as to the long-term effects and side effects of most drugs, the interactions between chronic drugs, or the positive dimensional effects like enhanced school performance, mood brightening, and so on. Especially disturbing is the increasing tendency to add drugs in treatment algorithms for the side effects of a previous drug.[72]

The expressivity of the commercials, websites, and marketing efforts remains my central concern. To the extent that they do posit objective self-identification of feelings and possible risks as symptoms, I wonder where, when, and how self-talk adopts and deploys this new grammar within and alongside other modes. The topic of my ongoing work is the invention of ways of living within this pharmaceutical world. As much as marketing provides potential patients with the exact words with which to emplot their doctors into providing them with their pills of choice, people also share and disseminate counterstrategies to avoid certain drugs, to calibrate their own doses by splitting pills, and to explore alternative treatments, alternative diagnoses, and alternative explanations.

For the moment, though, the average patient, by which I mean the marketer's average patient, comes to experience his or her body under pharmaceutical conviction. This body is silently disordered, counter-experiential, waiting to be evaluated and measured in order to speak. This body is always under construction. For more and more Americans, health is a sign of concern, something they must see a doctor for in order to ward off the invisible risk they have been taught to worry about. Treatment is neither an imposition nor a choice: it is increasingly ordinary and the action one must take.

THREE

Having to Grow Medicine

Almost three times as many people, most of them in tropical countries of the Third World, die of preventable, curable diseases as die of AIDS. Malaria, tuberculosis, acute lower-respiratory infections—in 1998, these claimed 6.1 million lives. People died because the drugs to treat those illnesses are nonexistent or are no longer effective. They died because it doesn't pay to keep them alive.

Only 1 percent of all new medicines brought to market by multinational pharmaceutical companies between 1975 and 1997 were designed specifically to treat tropical diseases plaguing the Third World. In numbers, that means thirteen out of 1,223 medications.

—SILVERSTEIN, "MILLIONS FOR VIAGRA, PENNIES FOR DISEASES OF THE POOR"

The journalist Ken Silverstein's devastating critique of contemporary drug research—that it is directed toward diseases of rich people in rich countries while poor people suffer—shows the callousness of pharmaceutical companies. When I teach this article in my undergraduate classes the students' response is one of horror. Similar critiques have been leveled by medical anthropologists who have analyzed this "values gap" between countries where people are able to pay for medicine and those where people are not.[1] Yet the very same critique appears within pharmaceutical textbooks, where authors make the same points but for different reasons. In the introduction I quoted pharmaceutical consultants who stated that only forty of four hundred diseases are "commercially attractive by today's requirements of return on investment." Whereas Silverstein begins from a position of social critique—it is horrible that companies are not allocating scarce research resources in equitable ways—pharmaceutical companies pose society itself as the problem: as described in the introduction, two analysts claim, "Society needs to find a way to make more diseases commercially attractive,"[2] so presumably the research dollars would flow in a more humane direction. Other pharma analysts put the blame on shareholders: "Pharmaceutical companies tend not to invest in tropical medicines because they are unlikely to recoup their investments. . . . Given the pressure on pharmaceutical companies to maximize their return on investment, this attitude is unlikely to change without a major change in shareholders' attitudes."[3]

What many see as a critique is declared baldly to be "best practices" in texts written by pharmaceutical researchers for new people entering the field. Either society or shareholders or the fact that companies need to profit explains the problems. It seems straightforward to hold drug companies responsible for the choices they make about which diseases to research, but, as these textbooks indicate, this critique is a part of corporate logic. Almost every pharmaceutical industry textbook I found narrates an ongoing debate over precisely this issue of whether a pharmaceutical company can afford to care about medicine and people rather than profits. By framing the ethics of clinical trial choices in this manner to future industry scientists, the industry can teach them the proper answer. Thus, the biomedical consultant Bernice Schacter asks her readers, "Should they develop for this specific use and that one, but not the one unlikely to succeed or unlikely to generate a sufficiently large market?"[4]

I reexamine here the purpose of clinical trials, not, as in chapter 1, from the point of view of patients but from the point of view of pharmaceutical companies. The companies are quite explicit that the issue is not health but profit and market growth; not research toward cures but research that grows the number of prescriptions. In practice, they cannot imagine making more efficient drugs if that would mean making a market smaller. Ultimately, they see no end in sight for the number of drugs people might be indicated to take, as there is no end to risk identification and prescription generation. Patients and doctors may not want this outcome, but, unfortunately, it is marketers, not scientists or clinicians, who decide what information, knowledge, and facts are worthy as opposed to worthless. And, again unfortunately, the companies, as I will show, are doing an amazing job of growing the markets for prescriptions.

In brief, marketers want to maximize the number of prescriptions in order to maximize profits. They see clinical trials as investments whose purpose is to increase sales of medicines. Statements like "Important clinical studies to conduct from a scientific or medical perspective are sometimes not important studies to conduct from a drug development perspective" are found in pharmaceutical industry textbooks and journals, and they are not new. As historians of medicine have pointed out, from its beginning in the 1950s the pharmaceutical industry has seen health as an investment to grow, and they have slowly perfected this growth and its justification.[5] I will unravel how clinical trials became the growth engine of pharmaceutical companies and how our illnesses, treatments, and health keep growing. The increasing number of drugs in our bodies and the state of biochemical accumulation in the bodies of Americans continue at a rate that seems unbelievable, absurd, and unsustainable. At the center of the growth of prescriptions in the United States are clinical trials as the dominant form of facts about health and treatment and of the guidelines that use those trials to redefine illness as a threshold. In this manner, health is reframed as being virtually limitless.

According to books written by those inside the pharmaceutical industry, one seems to feel that one's company is at stake, but so is one's life. These books include *Drug Discovery: From Bedside to Wall Street* (2006), written by Tamas Bartfai, a longtime pharmaceutical researcher at Hoffmann-La Roche and now chair and professor of neuropharmacology at Scripps Research Institute. The book is coauthored by Graham V. Lees, a scientific editor and publisher. Other books are *The New Medicines: How Drugs Are Created, Approved, Marketed and Sold* (2006) by the researcher and consultant Bernice Schacter, and *A Healthy Business: A Guide to the Global Pharmaceutical Industry* (2001) by Mark Greener. These books are concerned, above all, with helping scientists and laypersons understand how it matters that pharmaceutical research and sales are always a business. The very fact that disease research is an economic investment establishes equivalence between investments, such that they become comparable along one dimension and often only one dimension: quantitative health in the form of treatments. Increasing the size of the treatment market becomes the most important factor in clinical trial research.

"VENTURE SCIENCE" NEEDS TO GROW

> *WIRED*: Why is it important to be a lot bigger than you are now? Maybe it's obvious, but why does that matter?
>
> ANDY GROVE: Growth is kinda built into everyone's genes. . . . People expect companies to grow. Management measures its performance by growth. Employees measure their opportunities by potential to grow. Growth is the fertilizer for the tree that a company becomes. Why do you get up in the morning if all you do is serve exactly the same market with the same customers and the same products? It's not a healthy state not to grow—from the investment, employee, or strategic standpoint.
>
> —HEILEMANN, "ANDY GROVE'S RATIONAL EXUBERANCE"

Though it may seem blindingly obvious, public companies need to grow, not just in size but also in shareholder value. Why? Because shareholders expect growth. The value of the company stock will fall if these expectations are not met. This accumulation sentiment pervades pharmaceutical industry discussion: "In order for Pharma and biotech companies to maintain double-digit growth rates through 2005, they need to multiply their productivity by a factor of five."[6] Similarly, Greener, a former research pharmacologist and the editor of *Pharmaceutical Times*, notes,

> Increasingly, large companies need the mature sales . . . generated by several blockbusters—drugs that achieve sales of more than $1b annually—to fund R&D programmes and meet shareholders' expectations of growth. . . The stock market expects the pharmaceutical sector to grow at a healthy rate. A survey of 15 analysts in 2000 found that they expected the large pharmaceutical companies to grow between 12% and 15% per year between 2000 and 2005. They also expected sales to increase by between 8% and 10% each year, with the market increasing between 6% and 8% annually. However the US market—the last unfettered, free pharmaceutical market—accounts for some 75% of growth worldwide, reflecting in part the impact of pricing controls.[7]

Not only is profit an unavoidable priority for large pharmaceutical companies, but massive growth is, too. Especially today, under the pressure to maintain growth, apparently vile decisions like ignoring diseases of the poor are driven by a clear perception of waste. One is literally throwing money away if one is not making as much as one could, compared with other investments.

Inside a pharmaceutical company this comparison is a source of continual negotiation. Clinical research directed at healthiness can clash with market research, leading to struggles over who should really be deciding clinical directions. Bert Spilker, the head of project coordination at Burroughs Wellcome and an author of many pharmaceutical textbooks, writes of this struggle in his six-hundred-page *Multinational Drug Companies: Issues in Drug Discovery and Development* (1989). Note how, in the following passage from this book, "medical . . . value" retains only a ghost of its apparent persuasiveness: "The cooperation of research and development and marketing groups may be severely tested when an investigational drug has a high medical and low commercial value and the project draws resources (or would draw resources) away from projects that the marketing group believes have greater commercial value and are of high or medium medical value."[8]

There is a defensiveness in the qualifier "of high or medium medical value," as if a "me-too" drug with low medical value would not be chosen no matter how commercially valuable it was. Me-too drugs are variants on existing blockbuster drugs, different enough to count as new drugs for the FDA but often no better than existing treatments. They are pursued relentlessly by the pharma industry because their market has already been identified and the FDA approval path is much simpler and cheaper than for a new category of drug. Hidden (and assumed) within these debates over medical and commercial value is the fact that clinical trials seen from the point of view of investments become a diverse sort of beast from those seen from a medical point of view. The highly innovative power of science and technology, productivity, and intensity comes to be transformed, mutated into profit-and-growth monsters.[9]

The problem of comparing possible treatment research within pharmaceutical companies is that saving one set of lives through R&D, marketing and sales must be compared on the grounds of return-on-investment profit with saving other lives that may return more net revenue, that is, total prescriptions times price per prescription. One pharmaceutical marketing textbook explains that "products that are not able to limp along must be eliminated. They are a drain on a business unit's financial and managerial resources, which can be used more profitably elsewhere."[10] Most critics do not begrudge pharmaceutical companies this attitude because they understand and have naturalized corporate funding of research. Bartfai and Lees suggest that because drug development is capital intensive, economic value comes naturally to supplant scientific or health value: "Pharmacoeconomics plays a pivotal role. Drug development is very capital intensive and even big indications such as malaria and tuberculosis are affected. The cost means that small indications suffer, regardless of how good the science is. If drug discovery were a science-driven activity, one would expect scientists to be running drug companies. However, since Roy Vagelos of Merck retired [in 1995], no Big Pharma has been run by a scientist; they are all run by people who were trained in economics."[11]

Here is the twist so peculiar in capitalism and biomedicine: the company that one loves because it makes healing medicines becomes secondary (logically) to the money it returns. The disease one wants to cure becomes secondary to its market size. It comes to appear that it has to be this way. Once diseases come to be defined as existing on a continuum with health, the only meaningful diagnosis is that which indicates treatment. Treatment therefore equates with diagnosis, and the market indicated by a diagnostic threshold is both a measure of profit and the very definition of *health*. As health is an a priori good, comparisons of two possible clinical trials turn on their relative profitability. Health is thereby structurally subordinate to profit.

At the same time, the ever-increasing scale of clinical trials, the sheer number of them and the size of each one, has put them more or less out of reach even of governments. Across the board, the pharmaceutical industry, government officials, and critics agree that companies and only companies have the resources to conduct most clinical trials. For example, in examining the discussions that took place at the FDA over Celebrex and Vioxx, two blockbuster drugs with serious heart side effects discovered after they were on the market, one pharmaceutical researcher noted, "Lengthy discussion about what kind of trial or trials are needed to clarify the issue of the relative cardiovascular safety of the NSAIDS [nonsteroidal anti-inflammatory drugs], triggered both by the FDA's question and a suggestion by Dr. Robert Temple, Director of CDER's [Center for Drug Evaluation and Research] Office of Medical Policy, that what he called an ALLHAT trial be done to compare the cardiovascular effects of NSAIDS using naproxen and diclofenac as controls. Whether such a megatrial could be done and who would fund it remained unclear, though the enthusiasm among the members of the committee was high."[12]

In other words, the proper questions that needed to be asked of the drugs were ones that probably could not be asked since the clinical trials would cost the government too much. The remaining usable funds for research are tied to companies and the question of direct comparison. Testing one drug head to head against another turns out to be too risky a question for a pharmaceutical company to ask.[13] The dilemma at this point is precisely that pharmaceutical companies are expected to run clinical trials, and even critics like Jerome Kassirer, a former editor of the *Journal of the American Medical Association* (*JAMA*), concede that companies legitimately deserve profits.[14] Drummond Rennie, another *JAMA* editor, agreed that drug companies "are intent on keeping consumers on [new] drugs, which are not as good as older drugs, for the simple requirement of profit . . . and it would be strange if they didn't. They've got to be prevented [from doing this]."[15] For Kassirer, Rennie, and many critics, the answer is better regulation to define ethical bounds on the system to enable profitable pharmaceutical health.

However, such regulations leave untouched the fundamental transformation of health value as measured by treatments. Indeed, better regulations would help curb the scandalous abuses, like lying about and hiding data on side effects, but they do not address a deeper structural concern, which is the dynamic shift that takes place when clinical trials are run by industry in order to grow markets. The result of this shift according to Greener is that "marketing concerns now influence stop-go decisions in research and development (R&D) to a greater extent than ever before."[16] Health economists reinforce this point: "Science and objectivity are of interest to a private, for-profit corporation only insofar as they further the quest for profits."[17] How clinical trials are implemented opens a window on how treatments and illnesses continue to be expanded.

GROW THE NEED

Market demand equals price-times-population.
—BURNS, *THE BUSINESS OF HEALTHCARE INNOVATION*

Given that biomedical companies are, first and foremost, companies that exist to make profits, the unsettling consequence is that they must run clinical trials as investments whose purpose is to grow returns. Therefore, the return on investment (ROI) is calculated not solely on the labor of workers or clinical trial subjects: value is seen to accrue also from the patients via treatment numbers and price per treatment (even speculative ones). Hence clinical trials become machinery for generating evidence for generating prescriptions. In other words, the flipside of an evidence-based marketing strategy is that markets are made through evidence, and potential marketable evidence, gained via clinical trials, is the determining factor in running the trial in the first place.

The pharmaceutical industry agrees that most contemporary clinical trials are too expensive for governments to fund and that the only way to properly fund trials is as speculative investments. This argument for what I call venture science, after venture capital, has a corollary: since clinical trials are investments, they must be not only carefully and ethically run but also designed to produce a good ROI.[18] For a pharmaceutical company this means that if the trial is successful it must result in a product that will generate profit covering a number of failed trials as well, either through taking market share from a competitor or growing the size of the entire market for that drug. Sue Ramspacher, a marketing executive, writes, "In order to meet aggressive growth projections in a shrinking market, ALL brands must do business like first and best in class—and this means growing the market, attracting new patients."[19]

In accounting terms it works this way: the pharmaceutical company sees the clinical trial, the pills, and marketing as sunk costs; the only variable capital is the total number of prescriptions that are filled, which is the number of patients times the number of prescriptions they purchase (fig. 14). The number of projected total treatments, therefore, measures the value of health research.

As the chart in figure 14 makes clear, a pharmaceutical company thinks of health directly in terms of number of prescriptions sold. In other words, prescriptions become the meaning of health; they are what health is used for.[20] Therefore, a patient is valuable to a pharmaceutical company to the extent that she takes treatments and continues to take them. A healthy person who is not on or not likely to be on medicine is, from the perspective of this economy, not valuable. In other words, from the perspective of value, healthiness is antithetical to biomedicine—only health as continual treatment is valuable.[21] Biomedicine thus calls to life the powers of statistical medicine in order to create wellness, but it wants to use treatments as the measuring rod for those giant health forces and confine those forces within the limits of treatment value.[22]

Now we can understand why Western diseases are prioritized over tropical ones. Once you take the perspective that what matters is not

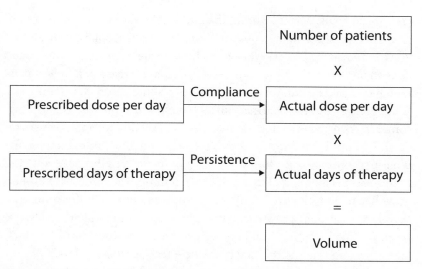

FIGURE 14 "Converting Patients to Volume." *Source*: Cook 2006.

return to health but the growth of prescription sales, it is obvious that patients are valuable only to the extent they can afford to purchase treatments (or have treatments purchased for them). Often, research is directed, as I noted above, at me-too drugs, tiny variations on existing drugs with very little difference in efficacy that can nonetheless be patented and used to take over existing markets. Lest one think I have overstated the logic, here is how Bartfai and Lees put it:

> A significant problem for the FDA is that there are too many me-too drugs submitted. . . . The companies see it as a way of generating profits, through establishing a new market share, and it is also seen as a safe way to introduce a new drug . . . [since the competition] has already validated the target. . . . *But no one is thinking about the patients, just market share.*[23]

Pharmaceutical companies have found a way to grow health via clinical trials by redefining health as treatment. Step by step, the logic is impeccable, and everyone agrees with these basic points and the underlying framework: since medicine is so expensive, pharmaceutical companies are required to fund much of the research, and, as companies, they must be able to earn a return on these investments. This framework is not scandalous. If the analogy holds, then it makes clear a strange dynamic, namely, health as a growth field through treatments, treatment growth via clinical trials. Mickey Smith, the author of a dozen classic works on pharmaceutical marketing, describes this indefinite resource of health as growth: "For as long as everyone is destined to die from some cause, a decline in one can only come at the expense of an increase in another. This is an inescapable truth, yet there seems to be some failure to recognize it. What society, and the pharmaceutical industry to some degree, is doing is making conscious or unconscious decisions about 'tolerable' causes of death."[24] Smith is pointing out that if health is defined as reducing risk, then it is infinite, since for every risk you reduce or eliminate you still have a 100 percent risk of dying from something. The limit to treatment growth is no longer a lived body free of suffering but a risk-free one, and therefore treatment growth is virtually without limits. There is always room for another study and another treatment, perhaps until we can't take any more treatment because of side effects, costs, or effort.[25]

ALIENATED RESEARCH

> The company's order of priorities is extremely clear. The major factors in selection of a clinical candidate in the company's own priority order are: (1) marketing . . . (2) internal economics . . . (3) scientific, technical and legal issues. . . . The regulatory and marketing groups, and then the clinicians, can always override scientific considerations; they "call the shots." . . .
>
> Under current circumstances this is unavoidable. . . . Decisions of this caliber are so expensive and so delicate for the companies' future that they cannot be left to scientists and clinicians alone.
>
> —BARTFAI AND LEES, *DRUG DISCOVERY*

Each clinical trial is evaluated first by whether and by how much profit it will generate for the company. Bartfai and Lees take pains to spell out to their readers these "unavoidable" priorities. Companies are only doing what they have to do in order to survive. Like all capitalists, pharmaceutical executives are possessed by the circumstances. The result, as we shall see, is that each clinical trial must be designed so that it grows the amount of prescriptions purchased. It might seem that a steady state, keeping us healthy and making better drugs to take the place of less safe ones, would be enough to keep an industry alive, but the pressures on biomedicine to grow are enormous, leading to the need to accumulate prescriptions.

The centrality of clinical trials in defining these thresholds as marketing efforts arises from the awareness that doctors, regulators, and consumers all desire evidence-based marketing. Marketers look at how powerful clinical trials can be in convincing and organizing people and in enrolling allies, and they ask whether clinical trials can be shaped as "effective marketing tools," to borrow the section title of a brochure by Cutting Edge Information on cardiovascular marketing.[26] According to an article by the marketers Richard Daly and Mick Kolassa, companies must therefore prioritize market size in designing trials: "Before clinical trials ever begin, companies need to think about what they want to say to the market about a product. . . . With . . . indications in front of you, write the copy for your ideal package insert. What would you like it to say?"[27]

The package insert is the description of the drug you get with a prescription. It is what the FDA approves, and it defines what a pharma company is allowed to market. The article continues:

> This point is counter-intuitive to many companies. Doesn't the science lead the way? Well, yes and no. Without the science there is no product at all. But here's what happens all too often with companies who overemphasize the science at the expense of the messages: they may develop very elegant answers to irrelevant questions. Does the following scenario sound familiar? The R&D team comes up with a product. It develops a research protocol based on the scientific judgments of their clinical professionals. They design the drug trials and execute them, and only then do they turn the product over to the marketing function with the order to be fruitful and multiply. The result, more often than companies will admit, is a product that is not aligned with market perceptions and needs.[28]

This passage appears to be quite contemptuous of clinician-driven research: science is secondary to the message. Clinical science and marketing are narrated as being at odds and on that account an acute problem for pharma companies, leading to this articulation of a technologically reflexive practice: if there is no market for a drug, it will not matter whether it works. Marketers inside pharma companies have therefore extended the bioinvestment argument to direct research; research is valuable only to the extent that it produces profitable results. By placing science within the ethical context of the market, they construct the oppositional categories of worthy and worthless facts, thoroughly confusing moral value with monetary value. Marketers are then critically needed to do what science cannot: determine science's value. Companies would be irrational not to learn, for instance, "how leading cardiovascular drug manufacturers design and run clinical trials to help push drug sales, especially after the initial launch."[29]

Nonetheless, this instability of facts-as-experiments and facts-as-representations is fundamental to science. There is no right description, no final interpretation of the implications, but this instrumental approach to marketing experiments indicates a division of labor within what had been the researcher. The researcher here is alienated from his scientific labor; he is no longer the author of his own results but is framed and reframed by marketing. This social division of the labor of knowledge production and alienation within science is emphasized by Daly and Kolassa:

> Once those essential marketing messages are established, have your dream team bring their respective expertise to bear upon them. Medical and scientific affairs people will tell you whether the science is there to defend the message. Clinical will tell you if trials could be designed to demonstrate it. Regulatory will show you where boundaries may exist. Marketing research will determine what the message is worth in terms of patient value and market share. And the finance department will share what it is worth in terms of the business case. Pricing and reimbursement and pharmacoeconomics will identify key points in the healthcare delivery system that will affect the product and will advise on the need for specific dosage forms and other issues that will affect reimbursement and the product's sales potential.[30]

Facts and drugs are never produced in a linear manner from clinical trials outward into the world. The world, in the form of economy, culture, regulations, and audience, allies and enemies, co-shapes every fact and every product. Each skill of the ideal researcher in managing the clinical trial design is parceled out to a different department. Such careful elaboration of how many considerations go into making a fact illustrates what Sheila Jasanoff, a scholar of science studies, has called co-production, in which each part of a system shapes the other one, and the joint product or knowledge is not reducible to one or the other.[31] The marketer's view of co-production justifies the division of scientific labor by assuming that

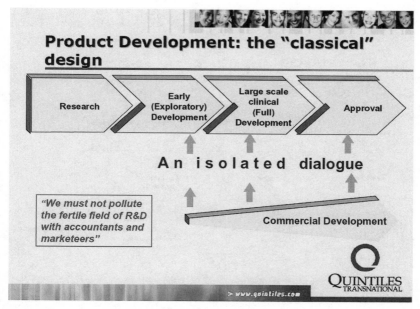

FIGURE 15 "Product Development: The 'Classical' Design." *Source*: Bell 2002.

if evidence-based marketing is not explicitly followed, a drug will be co-produced but in an inefficient, undesirable manner. Scientists and clinicians are, in turn, reduced to figuring out if they can produce results to order.[32]

This alienation of pharmaceutical scientists from the process of choosing what questions to ask is starkly illustrated in two PowerPoint slides from Quintiles, one of the largest contract research organizations. The slides contrast the "classic model" of drug development, in which research and marketing ran on parallel tracks with little dialogue, with the "current model," in which there is a continual framing and evaluation of research by market possibilities (figs. 15 and 16). Even the initial disease choice is determined in this way, reinforcing the comments I cited earlier in which diseases are deemed profitable or unprofitable. Here this determination is decisive.[33]

Once a megamarket can be imagined, the next question is how to produce the facts that will support it. Starting from the perspective of the product, the drug, the question becomes how to produce the right clinical facts. From the point of view of sales, marketing based on estab-

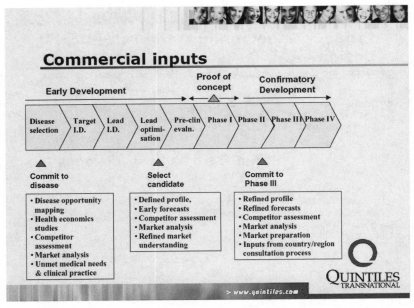

FIGURE 16 "Commercial Inputs." *Source*: Bell 2002.

lished facts is fraught with delays and uncertainties. Clinical trials may need to be spun too much to make the right point and risk counter-attacks by competitors or the medical community. Therefore the right facts must be produced, even if it takes many tries. And pharma companies can take many tries to get a successful clinical trial because the FDA officially turns a blind eye toward failed clinical trials and sets acceptance based on the production of two or three positive trials. As Bartfai and Lees write, "Extensive and extended trials are the norm. In order to prove efficacy in major depression, a company would need to pay for around nine Phase III trials. Even 17 years ago, Prozac had seven, and most of the other SSRI-type antidepressants had nine trials before accumulating three positive trials and receiving drug approval. The recent obesity drugs had many trials, each involving 12 to 18 months and 20,000 people."[34]

For a long time the failed trials disappeared, except for their presence in the pharmaceutical company's investment ledgers. Outrage over this practice has led to the establishment of public registries of clinical trials, but the ability to keep trying until one has enough successful trials remains.[35]

GETTING WHAT YOU PAY FOR: GROWING
TREATMENTS INSTEAD OF REDUCING THEM

"Cholesterol Guidelines: A Gift for Merck, Pfizer"
— *FORBES* MAGAZINE ARTICLE TITLE, DECEMBER 7, 2004

If the combined logics of mass clinical trials and risk-preventive public health already enable the continual growth of medicine in our lives, then the for-profit health research industry, especially pharmaceutical companies, are dedicated to ensuring it happens. The cholesterol guidelines of 2004 were the ones that recommended that one out of every thirty people on the planet should be taking statins.

The attention to cholesterol-reducing statin markets introduced a determinate economic accounting into the otherwise apparently objective picture of medical adjudication. Millions and millions of people, one out of every five American adults, meant billions and billions of statins to be prescribed, purchased, and consumed. Since 2000, yearly sales of the top three statins, Lipitor, Zocor, and Pravachol, were more than $7 billion,[36] and this trebling of the market represented a "potential windfall of nearly $30 billion in additional sales. . . . [Within two weeks] their revenue prospects were boosted, their stock prices shot up."[37]

The guidelines were discussed in both the national and health news and in the business sections of many newspapers. Wonderment and anxiety about the sheer human magnitude of the problem competed uneasily with awe over the market consequences. Criticism was also leveled, in part, at less worthy motives behind the timing, if not the facts: a newspaper reporter found that "the message comes at an opportune time for the makers of cholesterol-lowering drugs known as statins. Sales of Lipitor and other statins have grown by as much as 20 percent a year, reaching $12 billion in 1999 and $14 billion last year. 'Without the recommendations, growth probably would have slowed,' said Stephen Scala, a pharmaceutical analyst with SG Cowen in Boston."[38] To return to the absurdity of ever-increasing medication, it is obvious that pharmaceutical companies cannot, on good business grounds, imagine conducting a clinical trial that resulted in a smaller market, in less medication, or less risk.

We all acknowledge that investments need reasonably safe returns. In order to understand future risk as treatable conditions, health research is needed at an incredibly large scale, involving large numbers of people to detect small decreases in future risk. And that scale makes such research dependent upon and therefore a form of large-scale capital investment. Given that randomized clinical trials are the accepted gold standard, the problem is to decide which definition of illness and improvement a trial should test. This threshold will then become the meaning of diagnosis and treatment. Ideally both the threshold's importance for health definition and the treatment for it should be tested. But, according to pharmacoepidemiologists, this kind of useful answer would require hundreds or more systematic clinical trials — to decide what definition of high cholesterol can be *best* treated — and that is materially impossible because it is too expensive in terms of money and bodies.

Invoking or, rather, assuming the logic of what Kaushik Sunder Rajan calls biocapital,[39] even critics of the clinical trial industry concede that proper health evaluation is both necessary and too expensive for government to take on.[40] Pharma companies are therefore left with the task of ethically conducting clinical trials. But as capital investors, it is therefore understood, for instance, that "industry understandably has concerns about direct comparative trials because of the risk that the answer will be definitive in the wrong direction."[41] What Andy Grove wanted most, direct comparison of two treatment modalities, is precisely what both medical specialties and pharmaceutical companies actively avoid because clinical trials cannot be completely controlled, and if a direct comparison fails, the results can be catastrophic for that treatment.[42] The pharmaco-epidemiologist Robert Califf stated the problem as follows:

> Leaving the direct comparative questions unanswered allows industry to avoid a "winner-take-all" scenario, instead inadequate comparative claims can be used as the basis for marketing efforts that allow segmentation of the market without undue risk of being eliminated by being proven to be inferior. . . . Thus the industry, the regulators, clinicians and patients are left to draw conclusions from *intrinsically inaccurate data.*[43]

The form of this argument is not unique. In "Give Me a Lab And I Will Raise the World" the STS theorist Bruno Latour argued that science in general needs to be understood as dependent on a scale of investment model in which the facts we come to know are dependent on the resources available to pose them. The fissure Califf identifies is that we no longer operate under a scientific model of facts; we now operate under a system in which the best data are biased and inaccurate. Clinical trials are being designed in order to answer the question, What is the largest, safest, and most profitable market that can be produced? We can see in sharp relief the contradictions that today's doctors, patients, and pharmaceutical analysts face. Many of them can no longer imagine how to generate truly accurate and needed clinical information because the problems of scale have alienated research from lived suffering.

Returning to the quotation from Bartfai and Lees, we can see a strange plea in it: "One of the significant problems for the Pharma industry is that of the 400 disease entities identified, only 50 are commercially attractive by today's requirements of return on investment. . . . Society needs to find a way to make more diseases commercially attractive if it wants Pharma investment in treating any of the other 350 diseases affecting hundreds of millions of people."[44] Bartfai and Lees are saying that clinical research is a question not of choices but of structural pressure. Their mode is one of enlightened attack. Society needs to find ways to make health research better, to make unprofitable diseases profitable.[45] Written by a former pharma researcher and a publisher, *Drug Discovery* seems to be a call for regulation to save the pharma industry from its own structural violence.[46]

FOUR

Mass Health

Illness Is a Line You Cross

"So there's a lot to be said strategically for identifying people at risk at the earliest possible point," said Dr. Ronald Goldberg, who runs a cardiovascular disease prevention clinic at the University of Miami.

—S. SMITH, "NEW GUIDELINES SEE MANY MORE AT RISK ON BLOOD PRESSURE"

Although it may be common sense today to extend risk treatments to the earliest possible point as Dr. Goldberg suggests, how did it get to be this way? In this chapter, I trace the history of how general health or well-being began to rely on statistics and changed the very meaning of health, a story that involves shifts in three aspects of the health industries: prevention as public health, randomized clinical trials, and large-scale clinical studies revealing risk factors.

These three elements lay the groundwork for what I call mass health, a definition that puts health and disease on a continuum, with the understanding that the line between them is just that, a line, but one that requires fine collective judgment by experts as to where that line can be drawn. The corollary is that the line is determined not by overt pathology but by clinical trials and can be pushed further and further back to the point where it seems anyone could be considered ill. I also consider the media logics by which public health's message of prevention comes to take the form of an imperative to do anything possible to reduce risk. Patients and doctors are faced with increasingly technical notions of health and risk to *manage*. The logical extension of the problem that continues to be proposed is, Just treat everyone! As reporters regularly find, "The drugs are so effective, in fact, that cardiologists often joke—and only half in jest—'why don't we just put them in the water supply?'"[1]

RECONFIGURING PUBLIC HEALTH THROUGH TOBACCO

From stopping epidemics to vaccinating the masses to putting fluoride in the water supply, public health has been an arm of governmental investigation and enforcement. It has been lauded for its mass action on and mass protection of national populations. The logic of public health is protection through prevention, weighing the costs, including time, money, discomfort, and health risks, of preventive measures against the value of those measures in increasing the health of the population. Such balancing is not easy. Putting fluoride in the water supply to prevent tooth decay is allowed in only about 50 percent of counties in the United States, and every year some ten to twenty counties change their minds. Almost all European countries have banned fluoride, and worldwide fewer than thirty-two countries fluoridate their water.[2] A historian of public health and the author of *The People's Health*, Robin Henig, describes the problem: "The American fluoridation saga captures the struggle in public health to balance benefits to the public against risks to individuals. At what *point* are public health officials justified in intervening on a community-wide basis to protect a group of people who are not all equally at risk and who might not want to be protected? The push and pull of paternalism versus autonomy is a constant refrain in the field."[3]

Public health encapsulates a problem of mass informed consent. When an intervention is being considered, who should make the decision? Should fluoride in the water supply be put to a public vote? Should city councils or mayors or special boards make the decision? There is no simple way to determine how to decide this question, and in the United States every county has a different way of doing things.

Though public health decisions always involve some measure of convincing a public, most are not as easy to implement as pouring a drug into the water supply. And interventions do not depend on the effects of group-biological protection in the way vaccines do, whereby my getting vaccinated helps protect you. Instead, decisions require convincing people individually that they should take action despite the risks of accepting the intervention and despite the high probability that they will not benefit from it. Many contemporary campaigns to reduce hypertension, heart disease, cancer, and so on work on the appearance of a model of informed consent, informing people of their risks and options. The paradox of this type of information campaign is that success is measured not simply by how many people come to know about their risk and options, but by how many people know about them and actually do something about it—like using condoms to prevent HIV/AIDS transmission. Public health campaigns see the purpose of information as propaganda (in the neutral sense of persuasive communication): information that propels actions.

The crucial shift in public health via statistics came about in the fight against tobacco in the 1940s through the 1960s. The relationship between smoking and an increased risk of death by cancer and emphysema, while common sense now, had not been established. In fact, some people smoke all their lives and never get sick, while others get lung cancer without smoking or being around secondhand smoke. It took statistics and the numbers about masses of people to prove the incredibly strong link between smoking and increased disease and ultimately death. To understand this process, we need to turn to the fascinating analysis presented in the book *The Cigarette Century* by the historian of medicine Allan Brandt, a work that centers on the strategies of the tobacco companies in the first half of the twentieth century.

Public health officials had already recognized that some illnesses needed to be treated collectively in order to prevent repeated outbreaks. Using vaccinations as the prototype, debates were waged in the 1950s over whether the surgeon general could make a claim about individual health for noncommunicable diseases based only on nondefinitive statistics.[4] Vaccines are active: they prevent illness in those vaccinated, and their effects are visible to the patient and the doctor. Mass vaccination practices can halt the spread of a disease entirely. Yet intervening in public behavior was not a governmental health activity until the 1970s.[5]

It is now well known that in order to hide the connections between tobacco and lung cancer, tobacco companies manipulated the field of knowledge about cancer for nearly half a century. This was accomplished by hiring scientists to produce counterfacts about the causes of cancer, amplifying minority opinions to the point that it appeared to anyone surveying the field that there was an even controversy over causal factors; by emphasizing at scientific venues and in the media that scientific findings were not completely certain and required more research; and by amplifying dissenting expert voices about statistical illnesses. The dissenters emphasized the many cases of people who smoked all their life and did not get lung cancer and asked, how could there be cause then? These techniques exploited the ambiguity of science (that it is based on skepticism and falsification rather than verification), and they exploited the dissemination of science (that the media are a very imprecise form of information about scientific consensus). The tobacco industry did not skimp on spending money to make these minor points more prevalent and well known and therefore more respectable, even if they are held by very few scientists.[6]

Early attempts, in 1948–49, to study tobacco effects on cancer epidemiologically were easily criticized as statistical, not randomized, and researchers made no headway in convincing the general public of the dangers of smoking. Critics of statistical medicine, including some prominent physicians and scientists, had their own critiques of the assumptions such studies needed to make. And Big Tobacco fought back against evidence of the tobacco–cancer connection by amplifying those critical messages and hiring as consultants those independent researchers who were criticizing statistical medicine. In the end, the epidemiologists faced the problem of proving that statistical trends in health needed to be taken seriously and noted, "Resolving the lung cancer–smoking relationship would require a new and more sophisticated understanding of the very character of medical knowledge."[7]

Over time, medical researchers, epidemiologists, and public health researchers became convinced by the emerging data and joined forces to publicly insist that despite nondirect causality there was a real existing and imperative "statistical causation" requiring a response. As Brandt shows, "These persistent industry denials helped to generate a major innovation in medicine and public health: the consensus report. . . . The development of consensus reports would have long-range implications for establishing public health knowledge, clinical guidelines, and what would eventually come to be known as evidence-based medicine. . . . An independent and definitive assessment of the scientific evidence could not be achieved without state intervention."[8]

Brandt described this process as a new form of procedural science, one in which conflicts of interest, clinical studies and trials, and meta-analysis combine to create a new relation between the state and society. The consensus of a group could potentially silence the paid minority. Brandt writes, "By setting out to determine the true relationship between cigarettes and disease, the government accepted new authority for science and health in the consumer culture. Inherent in the report, therefore, were powerful notions of the possibility of the liberal state."[9]

The state had to assume such power precisely because neither doctors nor patients could assess the type of illness and health that was being detected by the statistical clinical trials. These new statistical mandates fused facts about correlations with obligatory action, *as if* the cause was direct. In retrospect, one can see in the consensus report and procedural science the construction of a kind of Pandora's box, that is, the possibility that statistical medicine could result in a sliver of health benefit turning into a mandate for mass treatment, held in check only by the ethical requirement that the consensus committees be independent and have the interests of society at heart.

ILLNESS AS UNFELT AND IMPERCEPTIBLE

As public health was learning how to target tobacco with large numbers, statistics were entering medicine in other areas, for example, in the invention of clinical trials, in which, as noted earlier, treatments can be compared in ways that don't require doctors to be able to see improvement. This began a shift in the meaning of the term *effective treatment* even as many medical professionals resisted it. The historian Steve Sturdy explains how this shift in power to drug companies took place:

The scene was set for the rapid institutionalization of clinical trials in the postwar years. Drug companies, government agencies and charitable organizations now realized that, by exerting strict controls over the supply of new drugs, they could force clinicians to participate in standardized clinical trials. But at the same time, clinicians came to recognize that they too could benefit from participating in such trials. The development of dramatically effective new drugs, including the antibiotics and subsequently such molecules as cortisone did much to raise public expectations of the power of modern medicine. By acting as gatekeepers to potentially beneficial new therapies, clinicians could do much to enhance their own professional prestige and authority over patients. As a result, large scale clinical trials became one of the defining features of the postwar medical landscape. Drug companies and administrative bodies were now able to conduct large scale clinical experiments to measure the therapeutic effects of a wide range of novel substances. . . . Doctors had now ceded much of their clinical autonomy to the administrative demand for standardized forms of medical practice.[10]

The historical transformation of individually diagnosed illnesses into the acceptance of clinical trials as the gold standard was neither obvious nor easy. During the first half of the twentieth century, communities of physicians evaluated treatments by talking with each other. Doctors were experts whose judgments were based on a self-validation of immense personal experience with patients rather than on their mastery of generalized knowledge. The enforcement powers of the early Food and Drug Administration (FDA), which began in 1906, were extremely limited, and initially the agency could prevent only so-called misbranded products from being sold. After a scandal involving a drug treatment that killed many children, the Food, Drug and Cosmetics Act was passed in 1938 to regulate the safety of drugs, and henceforth the FDA relied on networks of trusted doctors associated with the Council on Pharmacy and Chemistry of the American Medical Association to evaluate the claims made by manufacturers. Groups of doctors created cooperative research programs to evaluate therapies, but few of these were funded by the state, and most relied on the sponsorship of drug firms. In the 1930s, suspicion of corporately sponsored research and the use of such research in marketing created noise in the realm of medical facts.[11]

Only after the Second World War did the contemporary clinical trial emerge. One place it began was in research projects designed by the Veterans Administration in which the primary achievement was discovering how to compare treated populations with untreated ones. This production of control groups allowed the efficacy of the drug to be made visible and was possible only through the organization of participating doctors, who agreed to "subordinate [their] individual judgment to a common purpose."[12] At the time, it was not only strange but also reprehensible to many doctors to imagine that randomized controlled clinical trials were the most objective way to determine the efficacy of a drug. Relying on statistical results meant that participating medical professionals would be forbidden to treat patients to the best of their ability and instead had to stick to a protocol. To many, statistics did not make sense; they directly implied that only some patients would get better. This was gambling with patients and denying them other treatments.[13]

The response by statisticians and therapeutic reformers was to point out that the doctor's experienced judgment, like all inductive judgments, was experimental: good doctors withheld generalizing about a new treatment until they had seen a number of cases. The historian Harry Marks summed up the argument: "The clinician experiments 'continually' on his patients with each new treatment; one simply learns more from the 'deliberate experimentation' of the statistically informed investigator."[14] Statisticians offered a better method of both multiplying the power of individual observations and eliminating the empirical and human biases that result from a variable world full of hype, hope, and hubris. Marks notes emphatically that, at the time, this was seen less as better science than as a more efficient way to learn. It was simply a more effective way of determining what the method of polling trusted doctors already revealed.

Yet conducting a clinical trial did not solve the problem of how to turn its results into policy. Strictly speaking, a clinical trial applies only to the type of population who served as its subjects, and with control for the same variables. Marks notes that in the case of acute diseases, for which endpoints and improvement were easier to define, trials worked quite well. But for chronic diseases there was a host of difficulties:

> In the treatment of chronic diseases, where controversies over the merits of particular therapies ran deepest, the promise of improvements in experimental method to adjudicate differences of opinion about clinical and scientific questions was harder to realize. Here the strategy of collecting more and more data in the course of a study ran the risk of producing more, not less, controversy, as physicians attached different interpretations to voluminous data reported. And the obvious methodological solution to scientific disputes—conduct another, better study—was hardly a routine option in circumstances where hundreds of patients and years of follow-up might be needed to complete an experiment.[15]

One important consequence of the invention of the randomized control trial in the 1950s was to take decision making about new drugs out of individual doctors' hands and heads. The large-scale trial produces supposedly objective evidence of even small differences in effectiveness between new treatments and older ones. This objective finding is often something so small that a single doctor with a small group of patients would never be able to see it. The natural consequence of this type of logic is that doctors not only have to rely on clinical trials to tell them whether a patient might improve—owing to the statistical nature of improvement as defined by the clinical trials—but also must accept the idea that patients should take the drug regardless of whether they seem to improve or not.

The first crucial difference in the definition of illness via epidemiology or clinical trials is the notion of a line or threshold. To use a fictitious example, a clinical trial may be designed to look at whether a new drug, Plotec, treats depression better than not taking the drug. Two hundred people who suffer from depression will be chosen, and they will be randomly assigned to either a group that will get Plotec or a group that will get a placebo. The placebo is used in order to rule out the possibility that thinking one is getting Plotec helps one as much as actually taking it, and the people taking the fake pill are labeled the control group. In a double-blind study neither the researchers nor the patients know whether the pills being taken are real or fake. At the end of the study, the blind will be broken, and statisticians will try to determine whether the pill helped the people it was given to more than the controls and also whether the pill helped enough to justify recommending that doctors prescribe it to their patients with depression. A similar study can be done in which an existing standard treatment is used in place of the placebo.[16]

Why are all these components necessary to figure out if a pill works? Why must a clinical trial have so many patients, a specific procedure, randomization, and secrecy? The briefest answer is that if a pill works quickly and really well, it doesn't need a randomized control trial at all, though it may still need a large trial to determine relatively low-frequency side effects. Many contemporary clinical trials study the effect of a treatment on a large group of people over a period of time (two weeks to ten years), and it is the large scale of the trial that allows a small treatment effect to be multiplied enough to be visible. For example, it might require a trial of ten thousand people over the age of thirty taking a beta blocker over five years to reduce the risk of heart attack. If ten fewer fatal heart attacks are found (that is, forty among the five thousand taking the drug versus fifty among those not), then the study might reach statistical significance and be used to get FDA approval for the drug.

If well designed, this trial then becomes a type of public health fact. If you are over thirty and take the pill every day for five years, you reduce your chances of having a heart attack by 20 percent (this is a big percentage because the chances of the heart attack were 1 percent to start with and are now reduced to 0.8 percent). Another way to look at it is that five hundred people must take the pills every day for five years in order to prevent that one heart attack, and the number of people needed to treat (NNT) to achieve that result is five hundred. Four hundred and ninety-five of those people would not have had heart attacks in any case, and four of them would have heart attacks even though they took the pill. So there is a lot of unneeded treatment going on, which is another way to think of that NNT. This kind of result is known as the prevention paradox, in which "many people must take precautions in order to prevent illness in only a few."[17]

As a consequence, many pills today do not work on most people, and it takes a long time to discover how well they work, especially if their job is to prevent a future medical event; so it takes a lot of people a long time to determine if the pill helps enough people to make it worthwhile, given that even relatively safe pills cause side effects. Both health effects and side effects are thus statistical. For example, in the Plotec trial, let's say twenty on the pill were improved 10 percent versus ten on placebo. A typical conclusion might read as follows: In this study, Plotec helped 20 percent of patients get 10 percent better than the placebo, and 30 percent of patients experienced one or more side effects compared to 15 percent on placebo."

The uncanny thing about describing the trial this way is that it implies that *which* ten out of one hundred patients get helped is up to chance, given our knowledge today; the other ten of the twenty that got better would have gotten better anyway. This is the very point of randomized control trials: randomly choosing which patients get Plotec and which get placebo (or a different treatment) is done to ensure that nothing other than chance and the treatment affect who gets better. This is the type of fact that clinical trials produce. Treating patients in this way also requires ensuring that the patients be, in fact, comparable as patients. That is, they must all have depression in a similar and measurable manner, and their improvement must also be comparable. Therefore all two hundred enrolled in the clinical trial must be treated in a similar manner.

A finding that a new treatment is 2 percent better than a generic, for instance, might mean that the new drug helped ten people in one hundred rather than eight, or that it helped patients on average improve 2 percent more on a scale of symptoms. Either way doctors would have to accept the results of the trial and prescribe accordingly. While many doctors in the 1950s rebelled against such research by statistics, today's doctors are often "flying blind," to use David Healy's metaphor: "The behavior of clinicians is now progressively less likely to be based on knowledge derived from direct clinical encounters."[18] Health and illness have become epistemic, a question of third-party knowledge and measurement in reference to established facts. One might say that both patients and doctors are alienated from illness in that they cannot tell when they need treatment or whether the treatment is working.

RISK EQUALS ILLNESS EQUALS TREATMENT

The third element of statistical health involved large-scale prospective clinical studies. The Framingham Heart Study, begun in the 1950s, involved over five thousand members of an entire small city being carefully monitored over generations. It aimed to discover connections between ongoing behaviors like smoking or biomarkers like cholesterol and future events like heart attacks and death. The study helped produce the notion of risk factors like elevated cholesterol levels, hypertension, and smoking. It, too, approached illnesses collectively, even if they were not spread like infectious diseases.

Indeed, according to the historian Jeremy Greene's research, by 1961 it was evident to the pharmaceutical industry that drugs could be expanded almost indefinitely. An industry executive stated the goal in the case of diabetes: "To uncover more hidden patients among the apparently healthy." Large trials were increasingly needed "to render visible the relatively small improvements provided in less severe forms."[19]

Debates over screening in diabetes concerned how to decide where to set the hard endpoints or thresholds of diagnosis. To many doctors a more troubling shift took place as the definition of *prediabetes* shifted along with its names: "By the early 1960s, however, the territory of prediabetes had shifted, and those formerly diagnosed as prediabetics were now diagnosed as chemical, mild, or early diabetes."[20] The American Diabetes Association's slogan in 1961 was "Be alert—be tested—be sure—check diabetes." Greene points out that the shift toward earlier and earlier diagnosis was driven by the existence of a therapy to test and theories about how the drug worked, especially when the drug could serve as a diagnostic tool. The shift was enabled by a different way of thinking about the disease: "By equating the linear gradient of physiological parameters with the temporal progression of disease, the concept of prediabetes invested borderline test results with a sense of pathophysiological urgency."[21] Today, a similar shift is happening with Ritalin and other stimulants whose prescription is being used to diagnose as well as treat attention-deficit hyperactivity disorder (ADHD): if Ritalin helps a person, then the person must have ADHD.[22]

Described as a "double shift" by Greene, illness began to be seen in an entirely new way.[23] Diseases previously regarded as incurable downward progressions came to be seen as long-term chronic conditions requiring prediction, surveillance, and chronic treatment. Preventing those diseases from manifesting in the first place emphasized prediseases and *their* treatment. Prediseases by definition usually had no felt symptoms, but as they became treatable they came to be viewed as diseases in their own right. Prediseases involved large percentages of the population, and Greene notes that it required the availability of extremely safe drugs that could be given to hundreds of thousands of patients to make the category of predisease diseases clinically meaningful:

> Diuril's launch had taken place in the midst of a fundamental debate on the diagnosis and treatment of hypertension. The emergence of specific therapeutics with demonstrated ability to lower pressure— as well as a significant set of adverse effects—demanded a pragmatic consensus about which patients had a true *disease* that merited treatment and which had merely a blood pressure measurement that was above average. As the question of who to treat began to trump the question of what was normal, Diuril became materially involved in altering the definition of hypertension in America, helping to transform a degenerative and symptomatic condition into a symptomless and treatable category of risk.[24]

Illness was redefined by treatment as risk and health as risk reduction, and the line of treatment was itself determined by the clinical trials and an associated cost-benefit calculation. And the sum of these shifts was as controversial as the establishment of randomized control clinical trials (RCT) in the first place. If the RCT meant that doctors had to give up control during the trial and trust the numbers afterward, the emergent notion of illness as defined by that line was equally troubling precisely because it was both arbitrary and unsatisfying. Why at this number and not a bit higher or lower? Why are the numbers usually so round (everyone over thirty should be on cholesterol-lowering drugs)?[25]

The constructing of illness via mass measures both as continuous with health and as statistical produced two immediate and somewhat troubling dilemmas. First, there was no clear direction as to where to draw the line. And, second, because the illness was statistical and not everyone on the bad side of the line would suffer bad consequences (as Grove discovered—see the discussion in chapter 1), how did one make the line to begin with and with what force could medicine make a claim of illness in a patient? Debates raged over the "fallacy of the dividing line,"[26] and the tobacco model was invoked to provide clarity. In that case, all smoking was a public health risk. Lines represented both clarity and blindness, health became aggregate, a property of populations, not individuals, and clinical trials became the eyes and ears of the doctor and the patient.

Large-scale clinical studies like the Framingham Heart Study later enabled pioneers in epidemiological medicine like Geoffrey Rose to articulate the need for a comprehensive notion of preventive health. Outlined in his now-classic treatise *Strategies for Prevention*, Rose described how large-scale studies slowly transformed our definition of health from the traditional, simple models of disease, in which the suffering patient first calls upon the doctor, to an epidemiological, measured model of diseases like hypertension and high cholesterol. Each of these was "a type of disease not hitherto recognized in medicine in which the defect is quantitative not qualitative."[27] Rose describes the traditional model of diseases as one of felt illness whose treatment aims at removing it. The quantitative model, on the other hand, is one of measured deviance whose treatment aims at reducing the risk of future adverse events.

The most meaningful difference between the two models is in the form of diagnosis, as one move away from Has he got it? to How much of it does he have?[28] Given a continuum of measurements, Rose asks, where should the diagnostic line be drawn? Our current administrative medical system demands definitive decisions, and "this decision taking underlies the process we choose to call 'diagnosis,' but what it really means is that we are diagnosing 'a case for treatment,' and not a disease entity."[29] In other words, given the continuum of scores in which everyone has some blood pressure, the only meaningful reason for drawing a line is that that line makes a difference in what we do about it. Rose's public health perspective allows him to see and state unambiguously the consequence of quantitative disease models, that diagnosis equals treatment.

This notion bridges diseases of physiology like diabetes and diseases of risk like high cholesterol, which is a risk factor for coronary heart disease. Large-scale clinical trials do not determine the need to fix an entity, etiology, or even a state of unwellness or dysfunction. Rather, these trials correlate mass population treatments with statistical population health improvement. The drugs they indicate also mark a shift in the very meaning of chronic diseases. Greene sums up the transition: "A shift in the basic conception of chronic disease from a model of inexorable degeneration to a model of surveillance and early detection. Both drugs [Mevacor and Diuril] fueled a movement to make the screening and treatment of 'hidden patients,' or those unaware of their own pathology, into a public health priority."[30]

SO WHERE *DO* WE DRAW THE LINE?

A risk and continuum image of disease requires close attention to where to draw the line, as each line has its costs and benefits and the prevention paradox becomes ever more visible. More and more treatment is needed to reduce the smallest amount of illness, and the very notion of being healthy is questioned and joked about. Is anyone ever not at risk of being ill? At what point shouldn't a person take precautions against those future illnesses?

Definitions of health and illness vary historically and culturally. Diseases that today are quite commonly understood and diagnosed are discovered and defined through clinical work and made culturally visible through social work. A consequence of defining health as a long-term treatment for population risk reduction is that potentially everyone has some risk that might be detectable. The medical anthropologist Robert

Hahn highlights this in his book *Sickness and Health* (1995) when he describes how high blood pressure requires both recognition and repugnance in order to be a sickness. However, where to draw the line between high blood pressure and near–high blood pressure is not clear. Similarly, cancer could be defined as a tumor that causes suffering in a person or as that which might cause such suffering. Hahn worries that if sickness was left to such devices, there would be a slippery slope in which almost anything could be called a disease: "We would not want to describe a person as 'sick' from the instant of this [cancerous] cell division, since the disease might never follow or might follow only decades later. With a definition including all first events in causal processes as sicknesses themselves, we would all be sick from birth, for it is likely that causal processes of sickness and aging are present from the outset."[31] In this passage Hahn makes a normative claim: "We would not want to describe a person as 'sick' from the instant of [cancerous] cell division." This is a *reductio ad absurdum* argument, implying: because doing so would be silly. He thinks it goes without saying that defining everyone as being sick from birth does not make sense. He also seems to think we should have some say in what sort of definition of disease we want to accept.

Another way of understanding many illnesses is as risks. If I am at a high risk of having a heart attack in the next five years, I may be diagnosed as suffering from a condition defined by this risk and put onto treatment to reduce it. By reducing my risk, I am considered healthier. But, as in Hahn's worry, there is a slippery slope we must negotiate. How much at risk do I have to be in order to be worried, diagnosed, and treated? Risk, after all, is something I cannot feel; I must be informed about it to have any experience of it at all.

H. Gilbert Welch, the author of the provocatively titled book *Should I Be Tested for Cancer?*, answers the question his book poses with "maybe not," and his argument describes just the sort of absurd progression Hahn feared. Cancer, according to Welch, is variously defined as tumors that kill, tumors that cause symptoms, tumors that will cause symptoms, tumors of any size and sort, and, finally, any kind of precancerous cells. The problem, he points out, is that the smaller the tumors and precancerous cells you look for, the more you find and the less likely they are to ever cause symptoms. Ironically, the more carefully and frequently you screen for cancer, the more cancers you find. But very rarely has any study found that the benefits of intensive screening for cancers outweigh the costs of the geometrically increasing numbers of people who receive false positive diagnoses of cancer or who are diagnosed with cancers and treated for them even though they don't need to be. His book is a careful walk-through of the morass of often contradictory information and multiple ways of thinking about screening, whose ever-increasing sensitivity is producing a country in which everyone is sick from birth.[32]

The historian of medicine Georges Canguilhem also worried about this. He understood that, historically, pathology had been grounded in the suffering experience of the patient. But when Canguilhem confronted the notion of risk-defined illnesses, he, too, was reduced to arguing nonsense. Defining health in 1943 as "being able to fall sick and recover," he asserted, "Health is a set of securities and assurances, securities in the present and assurances for the future." He then recognized that, logically, if health is an assurance for the future, unless we will never get traumatically ill we are not actually healthy. At which he joked: "But who isn't in the shadow of a traumatism, barring a return to intrauterine existence? If even then!"[33] To assure the future opens the slippery slope of "for how long?" because everyone is at a 100 percent risk of dying and at some smaller but finite risk of dying in the next five years. Canguilhem jokes about risk before birth without using the term *risk* and even though he lived in a world without prenatal testing, though logical, he finds this consequence of infinitely extended risk absurd.

The slippery, sliding, and expansive notion of illness is present whenever it is defined in terms of a threshold, a numerical measure beyond which a person is ill. Universal screening programs and mass pharmaceutical regimes are regularly appearing in the news, and the line between good use and the absurd is increasingly hard to draw. Once there is a line, in other words, the area just below the line becomes cause for concern. If a doctor medicates someone who is at 5 percent risk for an adverse event in the next five years or who has an LDL cholesterol level of 130, wouldn't it be a safe bet to medicate someone who is at 4.9 percent risk or has an LDL of 129? The logic of health as risk reduction places the burden of proof on not treating someone, which for doctors means they are legally liable in case an adverse event does happen. In many cases, the line just keeps moving.

Therefore doctors like Ronald Goldberg, quoted in the epigraph for this chapter, come to see the same logic identified by Hahn and Canguilhem vis-à-vis diagnosing people at the earliest possible point and do not find it absurd or shocking. Instead, they find it ordinary and common-sensical and run with it. This notion of earliest possible treatment has been formalized in clinical and insurance literature as prospective medicine, in which a personalized health plan is designed from birth and tailored to each individual by a "health coach."[34]

AWARENESS MEANS ACTION: MEDIA LOGICS

Increasingly, patients and doctors are faced with a technical notion of health and risk to manage. Public health messages transmitted through the media in turn transform risks into forms of panic. For example, on May 16, 2001, the facts about cholesterol and heart disease changed massively. Every major newspaper—under headlines like "U.S. Report Raises Cholesterol Fears; Guides Could Put 23 Million More on Medicines," "Check Cholesterol Early and Often, Docs Urge," and "Lower Your Cholesterol by Any Means Necessary"[35]—carried articles explaining that the National Cholesterol Education Program (NCEP) had released a report that redefined who was at risk for heart disease and who should be on medication. The report lowered a number of biomedical thresholds, the net effect of which was that many tens of millions of Americans who had not been at risk before now were. This was not the first time that acceptable cholesterol levels had been changed, even by NCEP. This was, in fact, the third time an official report and accompanying guidelines had been released.

The report itself was deemed an event and a "mass media act"[36] that transformed the social truth of many people. This act was facilitated by the press, even in its somewhat skeptical and objective manner, as the media were the necessary tool for amplifying this newly discovered emergency. As one headline declared, "America gets a red alert on cholesterol level. Heart disease lurks for the complacent."[37] What does it mean to have a report change one's risk? Could millions of Americans really be at higher risk of heart disease and stroke? It would seem that the objective risk would stay the same; what had changed was the awareness of that risk. The grammar used suggested that risk, like facts, required a material embodiment, that it was a function of transmission and recognition. After all, if you ended up never having a heart attack, one could say you were never really at risk for one. Risk, then, required a social analysis of its use and its deployment. In fact, "complacent" was an odd word given the strange, retroactive temporality of the event. Another newspaper headline read, "Government Wants More People to Be Tested, Treated for High Cholesterol: Commonly Accepted Levels Are Not Safe, Report Says."[38]

The tone of nascent emergency sounded by the report was also suspect. National announcements, red alerts, and urgency permeated the news accounts of the report. But the report did take twenty months of effort by twenty-seven experts who evaluated the accumulated evidence of clinical trials spanning fifteen years, debated the results, wrote it up, and then timed the release so that they were all available to be interviewed by the media.

The intensity of the accounts should be seen as an urgency effect, created through the use of explicit demands in the headlines and the text. A combination of imperatives like "Check cholesterol daily" and "Lower your cholesterol" alongside emotional warnings like "raises . . . fears" and "lurks" insists that readers must first read and then respond. These are what Deleuze and Guattari call "order-words," which carry with them social obligations.[39] We are urged, implicated, and commanded to take action. These demands are sent to us through a cascade of referents: the committee, the medical profession ("doctors urge"), the government ("U.S. report"), science ("clinical trials"), biology ("cholesterol levels"), and life ("risk"). All of these actors have been enrolled in agreement that we are in imminent danger. A newspaper article warns, "Most of all, the medical profession wants people to find out their cholesterol levels and use that knowledge to keep them from dying of heart disease and stroke, says Dr. Jerome D. Cohen, a professor in cardiology at St. Louis University School of Medicine and director of its preventive cardiology programs."[40]

The announcements about the guidelines thus introduce a normative tripling: in addition to changing who has acceptable risk and who does not, they insist that if one is at risk one must be treated, and that everyone even possibly at risk must get checked. The third of these social obligations justifies the warning bells: we must be engaged and even scared into becoming responsible for our health and motivated enough to learn our true risk. Knowledge that can keep us from dying is crucial knowledge, and death is regularly invoked as part of getting the message out:

"More than 100,000 deaths from heart disease could be prevented if the guidelines are fully implemented," said James Cleeman, coordinator of the . . . NCEP, which issued the guidelines.

"This is directed at every adult . . . to know their cholesterol levels," he said. "These guidelines apply to high-risk people and low-risk people."[41]

Because the guidelines are themselves media interventions, every article presupposed that the new facts required action and that the articles themselves were the first step in raising awareness about the facts and making the facts emotionally salient through reporting fear and surprise. In her survey of advertorials used by pharmaceutical companies to promote awareness of disease categories, Charlene Prounis, analyzed the "urgency to treat" tactic of instilling "an immediate sense of hurry" through reporting of unexpected deaths and dramatic, alarming statistical data.[42] Such alarming facts are staples of news reporting that can be shaped by news sources in order to drive news in desired directions.

What distinguished the NCEP guidelines of 2001 from previous ones was that they were excessively detailed and technical, comprising a two-hundred-page report full of definitions, redefinitions, thresholds, and formulae. In addition to the published volume, a summary of the guidelines appeared in an article in the *Journal of the American Medical Association (JAMA)*. The guidelines implied that neither patients nor doctors could be trusted to be able to diagnose on their own; the process was replaced with calculations based on laboratory tests and risk scores. The resulting instructions for determining risk and treatment were complicated enough that many experts were quoted as saying they were worried that primary care doctors might be "overwhelmed with the volume and detail . . . and not be able to act."[43] One doctor, in a harried response, longingly imagined a future in which he would be able to plug "cholesterol values into handheld computers that would instantly spit out a risk profile."[44] Even so, the complicated guidelines were boiled down in each newspaper article to four fairly straightforward changes.

First, cholesterol as a biomarker of risk of heart disease was split into good cholesterol (HDL) and bad cholesterol (LDL). Each of these was given revised thresholds for action compared to the NCEP's guidelines of 1993, which emphasized the distinction between good and bad instead of a single cholesterol number. LDL now had to be below 130 instead of 160, and anyone at high risk needed an LDL below 100. HDL needed to be above 40 instead of the previous 35. The effect was to redefine normal health in a highly categorical manner. As one reporter put it, "By broadening the definition of high cholesterol, the new guidelines instantly reclassified millions of Americans once considered healthy, as borderline risk cases."[45] This description does not simply refer to the world, it intervenes. In this case, the redefinition of high cholesterol effects an instantaneous transformation of millions of Americans, who upon being so designated go from being healthy to being at risk.[46]

The understood acceptance of this "reclassification" should give us pause to consider how health is utterly decoupled from anything experiential. Canguilhem's insistence that "the doctor is called by the patient," that "one does not scientifically dictate norms to life"[47] is rendered quaint by the use of the past perfect tense in newspaper articles, such as "had once considered healthy" and "with levels they may have thought acceptable." Health is now opposed to risk, even to borderline risk, so that being at risk at all becomes a substantial state of unhealth. One no longer says, "I'm healthy but at some risk for heart disease," but substitutes instead, "I thought I was healthy, but I have high cholesterol." This is objective self-fashioning, changing who we objectively are by changing how we think and talk about our scientifically defined bodies and futures.

Facts, in the form of biomedical theories and illustrations of how cholesterol works, are often provided by the media, reinforcing just how bad bad cholesterol truly is. In one article, cholesterol itself became the cause of the disease, substituting in the statistics for heart disease: "You can't see high cholesterol nor does it have any symptoms, but more than 98 million Americans have it. This hidden danger kills an estimated 500,000 Americans each year."[48] This example illustrates a more general point, namely, that correlations discovered in clinical trials and epidemiological studies can become risk factors, and risk factors can become diagnoses. Cholesterol is a measure that for many years was very controversial throughout the medical profession, often accused of being a fad.[49]

The second major change discussed in the news of May 2001 was the broad reformulation of high risk, rendering it highly technical: one was at high risk if one was calculated to be at 20 percent or greater risk for a heart attack over the next ten years, or if one had diabetes or a newly promulgated condition: metabolic syndrome (see chapter 5 for a discussion of the production of this syndrome). Estimated to afflict one in every four Americans, metabolic syndrome is itself a combination of more general risk factors. In news reports, metabolic syndrome appeared as a joke that nonetheless needed to be taken seriously:

> Syndromes we tend to shrug off as part of a middle-aged couch-potato lifestyle now would be viewed as death-dealing disease symptoms.
>
> Perhaps the most significant example is so-called metabolic syndrome, characterized by abdominal obesity.
>
> "That's medicalese for the guy with the big potbelly," Lauer said, noting that the syndrome amounts to a recipe for disaster, including high blood sugar, insulin resistance, low HDL, high triglycerides and high blood pressure.
>
> The guidelines for the first time recognize metabolic syndrome as a specific disorder that deserves serious medical attention.[50]

Almost all the members of the committee on cholesterol were available for interviews by the media and spoke in identical populist terms as part of the report launch. Aiming at one-quarter of all Americans is a tall order, logically demanding this sort of mass media attention and the non-medicalese, dumbed-down descriptions used by Dr. Michael Lauer. In this case, he uses a typical caricature, "the guy with the big potbelly," that maps onto the technical description because the target group is so large. This helped spread the understanding of risk and also trained people in what kind of language they should use.

Subsequently, technical discussions appeared regularly in newsgroups and in question sections of the same newspapers that carried the simplified versions. For example, the following description would seem to exceed any sense of newspaper literacy:

> Q: MY recent blood test report shows that my Total Cholesterol Level is at 5.7 mmol/L, Triglyceride Level at 2.6 mmol/L, and Coronary Risk Ratio (CRR) at 5.1. However, my HDL is at 1.11 mmol/L and LDL at 3.4 mmol/L—both within the healthy range. Why then is my cholesterol considered high? What does CRR at 5.1 mean? What is triglyceride level? What is the critical total cholesterol level before a person is struck with a heart attack or stroke? What sort of diet would help reduce the total cholesterol level? Please advise.
>
> A: YOUR HDL cholesterol is 1.1mmol/l, which is still low. The accept-

able ranges are above 1.5. The total cholesterol is the sum of HDL, LDL cholesterol and total triglycerides divided by 2.2. Most of the triglycerides is carried by VLDL [very low-density lipoprotein]. Your HDL and LDL cholesterol may not be high but the VLDL is and therefore the total cholesterol may be elevated. The low HDL cholesterol and high total cholesterol cause an elevation in your CRR.[51]

The level of technical detail here fits with an acceptance of lay-expertise, do-it-yourself health, and patient self-help. It also increases the seriousness of the risk by increasing its technicality. Knowing your number becomes having to know all of your numbers. The combination of the general interest article and technical help emphasizes the true level of responsibility for one's health knowledge one should aspire to. These first two changes are both in the realm of awareness and fear: your health status may be mistaken; please see your doctor now.

The third key point of the mass media message was aimed at transforming awareness into change. The NCEP guidelines insisted that doctors start screening everyone at age twenty, rather than the 1993 recommendation of forty, and every five years thereafter, "even if they show no signs of the disease." This message was targeted at doctors, many of whom had shown a reluctance to suspect risk everywhere, yet enforced suspicion was now becoming the norm.

Universal worry was produced, in part, by success stories of people who had flirted with death but were now stabilized on statins and enjoying healthy cholesterol levels and by stories of sudden deaths and dire statistics. One doctor who screens younger patients states, "I've seen 25-year-old women with heart attacks. Heart disease kills 500,000 men and women every year."[52] The implication is that if people get screened and know their cholesterol numbers, these specific personal facts will motivate them to start and maintain their treatments. Dissemination of guidelines and thresholds involves first instructing readers how to assess themselves directly or how to assess their uncertainty as a spur to screening. One reporter talked to both the coordinator of the NCEP report and a local doctor:

"This is directed at every adult . . . to know their cholesterol levels," he [coordinator Cleeman] said. "These guidelines apply to high-risk people and low-risk people." And it is a message to be heeded especially in Wisconsin, which has a high number of people who have risk factors for heart disease, such as obesity and smoking, said cholesterol expert Tom Ansfield, a clinical professor of medicine at the University of Wisconsin-Madison.

"Unfortunately, living in Wisconsin may be an independent risk factor for heart disease," Ansfield said. "Have you ever walked through the parking lot at Lambeau Field an hour before the game and looked at what people are eating and smoking?"

[The panel recommended] that every five years all adults aged 20 and older receive a cholesterol profile that looks at total cholesterol, LDL cholesterol, HDL cholesterol and triglycerides.[53]

The goal was to try to catch as many people as possible as soon as they crossed the risk threshold and get them on treatments. The NCEP estimated that thirty-six million Americans should have been on statins, up from the thirteen million that would have been recommended by the old guidelines. Yet fewer than half of them were taking the drugs.[54]

These numbers were repeated in almost every article, spoken identically out of the mouths of members of the committee, of leading cardiologists, and of foundation spokespersons. Cleeman and others were insistent that every person found to be at high risk should be "treated as aggressively as patients who had just had a heart attack."[55] This meant starting the statins immediately and continuing to take them probably for the rest of one's life. Aggression was a constant theme in news coverage.[56] This zero-tolerance approach to risk signaled that risk was now to be seen and felt as immediate, not as something that happens in the future.

Do everything possible: the determination of a threshold of treatable risk is also a threshold for action. Knowing that one is at risk is not enough, one must "take control."[57] The language here reinforces the notion of diagnosis: one must act as if one is ill. Yet because it is not in fact a diagnosis, the language insists on obligation and responsibility: "When it comes to fighting incipient heart disease in young people, just watching cholesterol levels is not enough."[58]

The fourth and final message of the report was the most innovative and controversial: everyone at high risk needs to go on medication; specifically, they need to be treated with statins. For the first time in any of the NCEP reports, statin drugs were named and tied directly into the screening apparatus:

The old way of thinking was, "Yes, wait three months and try the diet and only start on the medications if you need to," said Margo Denke of the University of Texas-Southwestern in Dallas, who helped draft the guidelines. "The new way is . . . we're just going to start medication right away to lower immediate risk. We're not chucking the diet, but we're saying we need to pair it with medication."[59]

In Denke's formulation, risk is no longer even a neutral state of not being healthy. It is a condition that is isomorphic with a disease. If a risk is present, it needs to be treated immediately. Certainly the language used to describe cholesterol transforms it from a risk factor into a disease. One headline reads, "The Cholesterol Cure."[60] The FDA approves treatments in some cases solely on the basis of reducing a risk factor. Doctors are regularly quoted as treating a patient's cholesterol. Similarly, other risk factors and biomarkers like bone density, obesity, breast cancer genes, and so forth are recommended to be treated. Risk no longer has any sense of probability about it, nor does it depend on the future; rather, risk is a measurably bad condition that one has now.

In a theme that I will return to again, changes in lifestyle such as exercising more and watching one's diet are rendered secondary. The nuance between risk and diagnosis is managed by the phrase, "treatable range."[61] If one is treatable, then one has the obligation to do everything possible, starting with pharmaceutical treatment.[62] In a spectacular inversion, perhaps diet and exercise will follow: "And once someone has been identified at risk, 'it's important to bite the bullet and take the statins,' Denke says. 'Besides, maybe paying for the drug will get you to get your rear end out there and move and do something about losing weight.'"[63]

By defining thresholds of diagnosis through treatments, risk has essentially been collapsed. If one is at risk, then one should be on treatment. And pretty much everyone is at risk. As the alerts quoted above indicate—"Check Cholesterol Early and Often, Docs Urge," "Lower Your Cholesterol by Any Means Necessary"—dealing with the panic is more than individuals can reasonably be expected to follow or tolerate.

AS LOW AS POSSIBLE? WHY NOT GIVE THE DRUGS TO EVERYONE?

So maybe they really should put statin drugs in the water supply as some heart doctors only half-jokingly suggest. The put-it-in-the-water quip inevitably surfaces whenever

There are two principal ways of understanding chronic diseases: through management and through risk. In the first case, as with diabetes, one has symptoms of the illness that interfere with one's life, and constant treatment is needed to monitor and respond to changes in order to prevent the symptoms from turning worse. In the case of risk, one is assessed as being in danger of a future adverse event. The risk itself is then treated as if it were a present problem. Almost everyone and all of the media, including doctors, patients, health studies, news articles, and business reports, then connect treating risk with treatment, for everyone is at risk. If there is a risk that can be reduced with a drug treatment, then that treatment should be used, now, on everyone at risk, for as long as they are at risk, which is for the rest of their life. If the whole globe is at risk and the treatment benefits outweigh the risk, then why not treat the planet?

For over a decade cardiologists and other doctors have considered treating everyone; they have been "half-jokingly" suggesting that we put statins in our drinking water. As the joke goes, more than half the country has high cholesterol, studies show that statins work, and these drugs are as safe as aspirin. All of these facts have been verified and reverified. The facts imply action as *is* implies *ought*. And in fact the growth in statin consumption is phenomenal: virtually a straight line increase in the number of diagnoses, prescriptions, pills, and sales. Everything does seem to be running smoothly, and yet the joke has remained constant for ten years and it is always a half joke. Here is a sample (emphasis added):

> Dr. Pearson said in an interview that since there seemed to be so many who could potentially benefit from statins, "some of my more exuberant colleagues are talking of putting this in the water supply." *Facetiousness aside*, he added, the drugs cost a great deal—$900 to $1,800 a year for each patient, depending on the dose—and many must take them in order for a few to realize the actual benefit. (*New York Times*, May 19, 1998)

But the most interesting study is one of about 6,000 individuals that shows that even if you have a completely normal cholesterol level, it [statins] can decrease your risk of having a heart attack by 37 percent. And that's led some cardiologists, *half-jokingly*, to say this is something that ought to be in the water supply. (*Today*, December 8, 2000)

"Some of my colleagues feel [statins] should be put in the water supply," said David A. Drachman, a neurologist at the University of Massachusetts Medical School. He was *joking, of course—but not entirely*. (*Washington Post*, May 19, 2002)

Cholesterol-lowering statin drugs are so ubiquitous, top doctors now *only half-jokingly* suggest putting them in the drinking water. (*Wall Street Journal*, January 26, 2004)

There's a history of such water-supply jokes, including ones about Ritalin and hormone replacement therapy.[64] In each case clinical trials and other facts are enrolled to ground a taken-for-granted truth that drugs are good and necessary.

If *half-joking* means partly joking and partly serious, then one implication is that cardiologists think that neither patients nor doctors can be trusted. So the experts inform reporters, "Doctors fail to offer statins to people who need them; people who need them fail to take them." The reasons offered for this include high expense, overworked and out-of-touch doctors, pill-phobic patients, and "Then there's the fact that the medical system often emphasizes treating disease rather than preventing it."[65]

These numbers of how many people who should be on the drug but are not are formulated as problems of noncompliance. Noncompliance in medicine usually refers to patients who do not follow directions and take the medicines their doctor prescribes for them. When almost everyone is indicated for a drug, then everyone becomes a protopatient, and those who do not take care are noncompliant. Noncompliance is seen as a problem of informational and emotional management that is consistent with both an ethics of care and an ethics of informed consent.

Such management is another example of therapeutic emplotment in which doctors consciously frame facts for patients to get them to do the right thing with knowledge. In the case of statins, the risk, as defined by the pharma company and cardiologists, is that patients must be properly informed of just how good the pills are and how truly low the side effects are. And the patients must be taught how to accept this data calmly and without suspicion. Putting it into the water supply would take care of choice altogether. The half jokes make it clear that there really isn't any choice here but to choose to consume the statin.

But treating everyone as noncompliant would be true if doctors were fully joking rather than half-joking when they suggest putting statins in the water supply. Why, then, the insistence on half-joking? Half jokes seem to be an example of a rare kind of joke, what Sigmund Freud, in *Jokes and Their Relation to the Unconscious*, called a skeptical joke. Most jokes have a tendentious, cynical nature, conveying what cannot be said directly. Skeptical jokes, however, call into question the very ability to tell the truth. Freud provides an example: "Two Jews met in a railway station. 'Where are you going?' asked one. 'To Cracow,' was the answer. 'What a liar you are!' broke out the other. 'If you say you're going to Cracow, you want me to believe you're going to Lemberg. But I know that, in fact, you're going to Cracow. So why are you lying to me?'"[66]

What is being attacked in this joke, Freud suggests, "is not a person or an institution, but the certainty of our knowledge itself."[67] Instead of statins in the water supply as a truth that cannot be masked by humor—take this now, you don't need choice—it is the seriousness that must be reversed. What cardiologists perhaps wish to say but cannot even joke about is that statins are not such clear-cut solutions, despite their shiny-perfect clinical trials.

Overmarking it as a joke in a situation in which the expertise should be enough is a marker of the tragic trap of the facts, of the objective-persuasive force of clinical trials. Despite the facts, there is reason to be wary of the clinical trials, which is reason to be wary of your doctor, too.

We citizen-consumer-patients are often assaulted by facts and have trouble sorting out what to do and whom to believe. After the guideline changes in 2001, a recall of the statin Baycol by the FDA in December 2002 did not help matters:

> Amid reports that one of the nation's top-selling cholesterol-lowering drugs has been pulled from the market, heart doctors are worried that thousands of patients may be abandoning their regimens out of fear.
>
> The dilemma now, doctors say, is calming understandably confused patients. And that means education, on an individual basis, about what signs to look for and about the benefit-to-risk ratio of taking the drugs.[68]

Here is some postmodern irony: in an era of biological psychiatry, primary care doctors are in the position of talk therapists with regard to the fear and panic of their patients.[69] Facts are supposed to clear up confusion and calm the mind, but all too often they do the opposite and are mistakenly taken to be alarming.

The article on the recall repeats again the insistent mantra:

> The drugs are so effective, in fact, that cardiologists often joke—*and only half in jest*—"why don't we just put them in the water supply?" until the recall.
>
> The Food and Drug Administration immediately urged the millions of Americans who take any of the other statins not to panic. But panic they did. "And who can blame them? We have a sensational story out there that they kill people," Brown said. . . . Compounding the problem, experts say, is that many cardiologists are as stunned as their patients. . . . About 5 percent of patients on statins eventually develop muscle aches.[70]

How to make sure people are worried enough to see their doctor but not too worried about the drugs they'll be given? Ironically, the panic, anxiety, and depression generated by these facts are treated and managed psychologically by the same industry that makes drugs to treat the very same phenomenon as biological illnesses.

Side effects are not unnoticed in that many articles note that statins have them, especially at higher doses. This is the "one balancing thing that doctors have to remember"[71] when they use the drugs more aggressively.

The water supply joke resurfaced again in January 2012 when a new analysis of the large-scale Women's Health Initiative (WHI) study found that women who had taken statins were 45% more likely to be diagnosed with diabetes.[72] The WHI had originally been designed to test the efficacy of hormone replacement therapy (HRT) and had to be halted early because women on HRTs were found to be at increased risk of coronary heart disease and breast cancer among other problems.[73] The size of the study, over 160,000 women, enabled later researchers to detect many other population effects, including those of statins. A reporter at USA Today described the balancing act,

> Study authors advise patients not to stop taking their medications without talking to a doctor, because statins' proven power to prevent heart

attacks and strokes outweighs any potential increase in type 2 diabetes risk. But the results—a nearly 50% increase in diabetes among long-time statin users—should throw cold water on the idea of prescribing these drugs to healthy people, which some have recommended as a way to prevent disease, says co-author JoAnn Manson, a professor of medicine at Harvard Medical School. In recent years, statins' success in preventing heart attacks—even among people without high choles-terol—has led some doctors to joke about "putting them in the water supply."[74]

What is at stake here is the limit of the ethic of preventive medicine: the pharmaceuticalization of prevention. On one hand, prevention is so obviously the right idea that we cannot dismiss it. If a treatment reduces future disease and is tolerable, how can we not take it? On the other hand, by definition it depends on a slippery slope: is more prevention always better? What criteria and procedures are available socially and culturally to determine how much bad cholesterol is too much and in need of treat-ment?

In practice a small threshold change shifts large groups of people into or out of official diagnostic categories, with big market consequences for medications, and this is the explicit goal of conducting the trials; it is talked about in marketing brochures and business press coverage of the pharmaceutical industry. Thresholds are key operators in an emergent era of surplus health. Where to set a threshold should be a collective de-cision made on diverse grounds of health, ethics, economics, and politics. But we do not have a method to decide how to decide on a threshold.[75] Where is the right forum in which to discuss the limit of health risks?

Debates over how sensitive and how pervasive public screening for dis-eases should be enact a rarely public discussion of something the philoso-pher Michel Foucault called for in "The Risks of Security." Thresholds are the sort of decisions that have to be worked out empirically, experi-mentally, he argued, since they are necessary forms of rationing. He ex-plained that "a growth in the demand for health . . has demonstrated the fact that the need for health (as experienced) has no internal principle of limitation."[76] If we do not make rationing decisions explicit in new ways so that we are part of them, then they will continue to be made anyway, anonymously and systemically.

Where is the forum to figure out which health research can continue to be run for profit? As we have seen, in the hands of blockbuster, market-oriented clinical trials and PR, our situation has been naturalized. Can we say no to saving lives, even if those lives are future populations determined by clinical trials? And especially if those clinical trials are organized by pharmaceutical companies who first construct the future populations as contemporary market segments?[77]

Truth and falsity, health and risk chase after each other and become indiscernable, and as a result, choices become undecidable.[78] Reporters struggle to make sense of the medical announcements: "ANOTHER DAY, another medical breakthrough. . . . But with so much hype around so many medical discoveries, how do we know which ones we really need to pay attention to? Weeding through the clutter can be tough."[79] "Others see the same facts and come to different conclusions."[80] You cannot have a choice because there is no basis for deciding; therefore why not put it in the water supply and make the impossible nonchoice real?

As an aside, the half joke has another sinister side to it. Statins are already in the water supply, along with antidepressants, estrogens and other hormone replacements, and many other blockbuster drugs. The sheer tonnage of prescriptions ingested and excreted or thrown away is detectable in wells, in the ocean, and in fishes. This is a growing, if under-reported, concern.[81]

The drugs-in-the-water-supply half joke reveals a very real epistemo-logical deadlock. We know treatment cannot be infinite, yet risk reduc-tion seems like it has to be. Step by step it works and is rational, but there are choices in how to define health that still have to be made, choices that at one point seemed to have a built-in limit. In 1977, the physician, medical administrator, and essayist Lewis Thomas elegantly described the problem of coming to see ourselves as "fundamentally fragile, always on the verge of mortal disease, perpetually in need of healthcare pro-fessionals at every side, always dependent on an imagined discipline of 'preventive' medicine, [so that] there can be no limit to the numbers of doctors' offices, clinics, and hospitals required to meet the demand."[82] In 1991, the medical historian Robert Castel saw the growing system of mass treatment and concluded that it couldn't be sustained, "if only for the reason that the economic cost would be colossal and out of all propor-tion to the risks prevented."[83] Although all of these critical analysts, from Thomas to Castel to Hahn to Canguilhem, see absurd unsustainability in mass health, they fail to understand a perspective from which it makes sense to seek maximization, and they fail to imagine a rationality or logic in which more illness could be treated without quickly bankrupting the state or disabling the population.

In conclusion, despite its apparent economic unsustainability, mass health is a revolution in healthcare, a foundational reinterpretation of health: health as not the property of individuals but a way of helping individuals at a level below their conscious perception, before their bodies tell them they need help. Formalizing a notion of statistical causation, the concept of mass health allowed smoking to be understood and institutionalized as a true harm to all smokers and later to proximate nonsmokers. Mass health allowed the government, researchers, doctors, and patients to determine treatment effectiveness even when it happened at scales not able to be experienced by individuals. For these reasons, in the form of public health clinical studies and clinical trials it was enshrined as the gold standard for treatment evaluation. As a gold standard, however, it has certain weaknesses and flaws. Mass health does not tell us where to draw the line, only whether that line might make a difference. Mass health does not tell us what to do with risks discovered, whether they deserve to be treated as a disease or whether they are worth treating—those decisions require social discussion about costs, benefits, lifestyles, fairness, and justice. Nor does mass health as a concept and set of practices tell us what illnesses and risks to study. When these questions are left up to companies to decide, they do so on the basis of very specific criteria with which we as public citizens might not agree: market size and overall profit. Under those conditions, the open-ended possibilities of mass health have quite stunning results.

FIVE

Moving the Lines
Deciding on Thresholds

Using financial, contractual and legal means, drug manufacturers retain
a degree of control over clinical research that is far greater than most
members of the public (and, we suspect, many members of the research
community) realize.
—MORGAN, BARER, AND EVANS, "HEALTH ECONOMISTS MEET
THE FOURTH TEMPTER," 61

Mass health today is both fundamental and incomplete. Clinical
studies and clinical trials are wonderful tools, but they yield only partial answers to what we should do about our health. Their deployment
changes the very sense of what we understand by health and illness,
risk and treatment. I want to focus here on the point of view of pharmaceutical companies and how they decide which lines to research
and how they would like the lines to be drawn. They are in charge
of making these decisions because, as we saw in chapter 4, they are
paying for the large-scale studies that have become too expensive for
government to fund. Under these conditions, the image of illness via
mass health that we have come to take for granted has been turned
into a means of real and constant expansion of treatment markets.
As we will see, companies' choosing to study the most profitable illnesses with the biggest markets is only the starting point. They also
determine how those markets can be stretched wider by designing

clinical trials that will indicate that more of the population needs treatments.

The active promotion of threshold-defined diagnoses reinforces the new mass health image of illness and treatment. By image, I mean a basic, commonsense notion of what illnesses are, how they happen, and how they are to be treated. The image is one of persons being always on the way to illness through risk factors and other forms of measurement. In some cases, the threshold is rendered literally, as in this magazine advertisement for Paxil (fig. 17).

A better illustration of the new paradigm of illness is provided by the Kupfer curve, as illustrated on a number of antidepressant websites. A diagram from the Prozac.com website (now defunct) tells a story about depression, its course, and treatment (fig. 18). But it also assumes and reinforces a more basic story about disease and health, one that has far-reaching consequences for how we, as doctors, scientists, and laypeople, imagine drugs and normality.[1]

This curve is fascinating because it perfectly illustrates the redefinition of illness toward mass health. First of all, it represents a person as "normal," in quotation marks, to indicate that *normal* is a relative term now, not a reference in itself but defined in opposition to having a syndrome. The line between normal and syndrome is just that, a line drawn in a continuum of symptoms. The normal person has symptoms, just not enough to cross the line into syndrome. The line is also a dotted line, indicating its permeability and flexibility. If the curve is life, then one is always on the way to a syndrome, always at risk for crossing down into illness.

Depression checklists and score charts for risk of heart disease are operationalized into tools on websites, in news accounts, and in brochures in doctors' offices (fig. 19). The implication is that one should check often and that even if one is above the threshold, one is not safe. This image of symptoms adding up to a syndrome is standardized in both the *Diagnostic and Statistical Manual of Mental Disorders* and the ubiquitous checklists. The surveys are usually based on self-assessment of one's everyday symptoms—everyday in the sense that each symptom is quite common, and the only question is how often such a symptom occurs.

For instance, the Zung assessment tool for depression includes statements like "I feel downhearted, blue and sad" and "Morning is when

FIGURE 17 "Overpowered by Anxiety, Empowered by Paxil," magazine advertisement by GlaxoSmithKline.

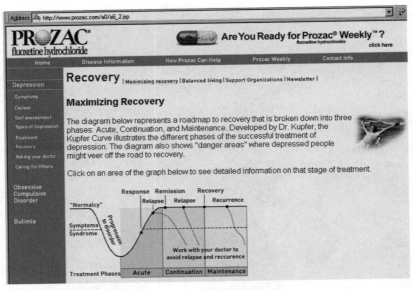

FIGURE 18 The Kupfer curve on the Prozac.com website by Lilly.

I feel best," both of which one answers by selecting from among "Not often," "Sometimes," "More often," and "All the time." A weighted algorithm or simple adding up of symptoms is then performed to realize a score that can be enough to suggest that one has passed from having symptoms into having a syndrome. In most of these surveys, no person is symptom-free. Learning to make sense of the diagram is therefore learning that one is always progressing toward the disorder. The consequences are apparent in terms of a concept or logic of health: the normal state is one of vulnerability and precariousness, requiring constant vigilance for further warning signs.

In figure 18 the dashed line between symptoms and syndrome, in other words, is arbitrary. The curve makes it obvious that a shift in the line upward, toward a diagnosis with less symptoms, is possible, and if one sees the curve as also representing treatment markets, then moving the line up would greatly increase the market size. The curve can thus be read as a strategic diagram for market growth as well as an image of illness. The line is dashed in part because the decision of where to draw it is based on judgments not about individuals, but about the existing set of clinical trials concerning the syndrome or illness. New curves with new dashed lines can be imagined if new biomarkers for the syndrome

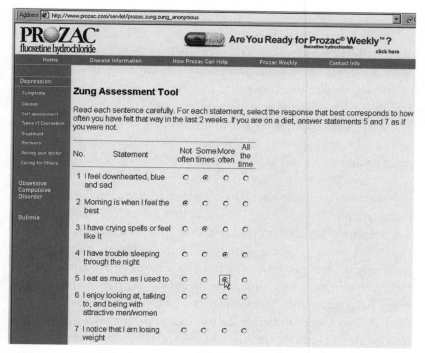

FIGURE 19 The Zung assessment tool on the Prozac.com website by Lilly.

are discovered or alternate modes of diagnosing the illness are deployed. Also, the area just above the line becomes questionable: if one were so close to the line, maybe treatment would help there as well. These so-called shadow syndromes or prediseases can themselves be imagined as syndromes.

The diagram itself should be upside down. Scores usually *add up* to an increased risk. Instead, the diagram looks like a roller coaster in which one is heading toward a plunge that could inevitably happen. But un-like a roller coaster, in which the first plunge generates enough momen-tum to get back up to the top, here it is only treatment that can rescue us from the valley of illness. Counter to the paradigm of an inherently healthy body, this diagram pushes us to accept that our bodies are inher-ently ill. Georges Canguilhem described the inherently healthy body as follows: "To be in good health means being able to fall sick and recover, it is a biological luxury."[2] In this diagram we are already at risk, on the way to illness, and we do not naturally recover but constantly need medical assistance.

The curve represents the course of illness as a fall, into a syndrome, from which one escapes only through treatment. This diagram thus dramatizes the preventive health pioneer Geoffrey Rose's insight that diagnosis has come to equal treatment, that the meaning of a diagnosis is to indicate medication rather than to identify a self-existent pathology. Taking one's medication appears to bring one back up the symptom list to normal again, and trailing dotted lines falling back into the syndrome indicate the risks of going off treatment. But the implication that treatment could be required indefinitely complicates this warning to comply with medication.

Another page on the same site directly warns against the notion that being "normal" equals cure. Titled "Feeling Better Is Not Enough," the page explains the need for continued treatment. At first the treatment appears curative, reducing symptoms. But continued or maintenance treatment is then indicated as prophylaxis because one is now at risk for future events. In this manner every illness can be imagined as chronic: drugs functioning simultaneously to treat symptoms and to reduce risk. Market size is more than just the number of people taking a drug; the bulk of market growth today is actually in the length of time a patient stays on a drug because that is a significant multiplier of the absolute number of pills sold.

By providing this diagram, the manufacturers of Prozac give us an image that is logically expandable, with transformations that make sense. The diagram is also not wrong, as it may have heuristic value in its initial design but it leans toward becoming the paradigm, the key example, or even the ground of future arguments.

THE DOTTED LINE

Clinical trials create lines. As the following quotation from an article in *Health Economics* indicates, the design of a clinical trial must assume and build in a number of threshold definitions:

> Drug companies commonly control the research question (with what products and what doses, and for what patients and conditions, is the new drug compared?), they control the selection of patients for the trials, they control how drop-outs and side-effects are reported and treated in the analysis, and they control what information makes its

way into scientific presentations and peer-reviewed publications. Drug companies often use surrogate endpoints to establish a product's efficacy (and to establish a market for the product), despite absence of evidence that the surrogate outcome and health status are in fact correlated, and sometimes, in the face of evidence that they are not.[3]

If verified, the threshold definitions come to define how the drug and therefore the illness are defined. These criteria include the following:

1. inclusion criteria, some kind of score or measurement of who can participate;
2. criteria of illness severity;
3. criteria of health, or how much less ill a person should be in order to be counted as improved or cured;
4. dose—often determined in earlier trials, the phase III or later trials use a standardized dose which often becomes the de facto standard dose;
5. criteria of side effects: what kinds of bodily reactions and complaints will be investigated and measured—how nauseated do you have to be to count?;
6. criteria of a successful trial result: how many people have to get how much better in order for the treatment to be considered good?;
7. generalizability—given the population, illness, health, and success criteria, how much can the results be generalized to other populations, other grades of illness, and other health outcomes?

Each of these seven criteria for designing and running trials are thresholds and can become, after the trial, naturalized working definitions in the world.[4]

The first assumption concerns whom to include as the study population. Most illnesses come in many degrees and many forms. In addition, there are often populations, even very young and very old ones, that suffer from multiple illnesses, and so on. Clinical trials must therefore define, as precisely as possible, criteria for inclusion. Typically, for example, a study will exclude anyone who suffers from other illnesses at the same time. This makes scientific sense, since the question concerns the effect of one drug on one illness. And it is probably unknown what the effect of that drug on other illnesses might be. However, it may be that many people who will eventually be prescribed the drug have other illnesses. For them, the clinical trials will have a different sort of relevance. Similarly, patients in clinical trials should be free of most other drugs since drugs can have bad interactive effects. A series of problems over the past ten years have highlighted this problem.[5]

Because humans are quite individual and variable in their bodies and illnesses, the designers of clinical trials prefer to have their populations as homogeneous as possible while still trying to represent the drug's target population. This kind of homogeneity includes trying to define the illness precisely and adapt or create a quantitative instrument for measuring how severe the illness is as well as a way to measure how much improvement the patient makes. A key point is that illnesses in the United States are redefined via continuous scales of measurement. Doctors' judgments, which may and do vary, are restricted and standardized. In this way, patients' illnesses are made comparable, allowing increasingly precise measures of average improvement.[6]

The inclusion criteria for a clinical trial can become a generalized threshold of risk. That is, if you fit the profile of those studied, then you would benefit from the drug. In the case of a breast cancer study, the inclusion threshold actually transubstantiated into a definition of high risk. The Breast Cancer Prevention Trial has been extensively investigated by social scientists because a prospective epidemiological study resulted in an inadvertent definition of high risk being produced and then appropriated and promoted. This trial was designed to assess whether Tamoxifen would help to prevent breast cancer. Because it was the first trial of this nature, it needed to set a standard for inclusion: women who were at enough risk for cancer within five years to enable the study to reliably produce statistically significant data. The eligibility criteria were set at the average risk that a sixty-year-old woman had of getting invasive breast cancer within five years, which was 1.66 percent. The sociologist Jennifer Fosket studied the development of this trial. She quotes the statistical coordinator, Joseph Costantino, as saying that the number 1.7 percent (rounded up from 1.66) represents "the average risk, if you took all the 60-year-old women in the United States and you took their average breast cancer risk, that's what it would be . . . that's where the number came from. . . . there's nothing really magic about it."[7]

What is magic is that the number 1.7 was then taken up in the mass marketing of chemoprevention for drugs like Tamoxifen and Nolvadex,

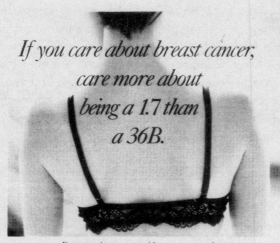

Know your breast cancer risk assessment number.
Know that NOLVADEX® (tamoxifen citrate) could reduce your chances of getting breast cancer if you are at high risk.

This new risk assessment test is a simple set of questions your doctor will ask you. The results will give you a number that estimates your chances of developing breast cancer over the next 5 years. A score of 1.7 or above is considered high risk. Most likely you won't be at high risk, but you owe it to yourself to find out.

Knowing your number gives you power, and knowing about Nolvadex should give you hope. Because even if you are at high risk, Nolvadex has now been proven to significantly reduce the incidence of breast cancer in women at high risk.

The proof: In a landmark study of women 35 years or older and at high risk of breast cancer, women who took Nolvadex had fewer breast cancers than women taking sugar pills. Nolvadex decreases but does not eliminate the risk of breast cancer, and did not show an increase in survival.

Nolvadex is not for every woman at high risk. In the study, women taking Nolvadex were 2 to 3 times more likely to develop uterine cancer or blood clots in the lung and legs, although each of these occurred in less than 1% of women. Women with a history of blood clots should not take Nolvadex. Stroke, cataracts, and cataract surgery were more common with Nolvadex. Most women experienced some level of hot flashes and vaginal discharge. Pregnant women or women planning to become pregnant should not take Nolvadex. You and your doctor must carefully discuss whether the potential benefit of Nolvadex will outweigh these potential side effects.

Call your doctor and ask for your Breast Cancer Risk Assessment test. For a free video, call 1 800 898-8423 to learn more about Nolvadex and the Breast Cancer Risk Assessment test.

Nolvadex® TABLETS
TAMOXIFEN CITRATE

There is something you can do

Please see important information on adjacent page.   NL1252 599

FIGURE 20 "If you care about breast cancer, care more about being a 1.7 than a 36B," Nolvadex advertisement.

appropriating the moral valence of high risk in order to promote the need for pharmaceutical intervention in all women at risk (fig. 20). In these advertisements the historical choice of 1.7 to meet the specific requirements of a five-year trial now becomes individual thresholds, internalized as meaningful (and scary) by women who encounter only the number and the words "high risk."[8]

Normal and healthy, average sixty-year-olds are de facto medicalized through this communication of facts.[9] Advertising campaigns focused almost exclusively on making the number into a fearful prospect of imperceptible but immediate risk: "Know your number if you care about breast cancer"; "Are you aware or do you want to prevent it?" As we saw in chapter 3, direct-to-consumer advertising designed these messages to bring viewers one stage at a time from awareness to personalizing their risk to taking action on it. These numbers also present and reinforce a threshold definition of disease by treating risk itself as the disease to be treated.

The rhetorical naming of the Breast Cancer Prevention Trial in the first place and of the class of drugs as "chemoprevention" show that the assumptions and language built into the design of a clinical trial can take on a life of their own after the trial.[10] Risk factors or biomarkers set into motion in order to run clinical trials, in turn, become diagnoses after the trial. In the case of breast cancer risk scores and cholesterol, one is literally diagnosed with being at risk, in the specific sense that on that basis a doctor prescribes for you a prescription-only pharmaceutical. In order to travel from clinical trials or guidelines into everyday awareness and self-fashioning, however, facts and thresholds must be carried to us by the media, which have their own logics and grammars.

What clinical trials authorize is more than a drug for a condition; they also define or redefine who counts as being ill enough to treat. In this way the National Cholesterol Education Program (NCEP) was able to claim in its guidelines that clinical trials showed that people with cholesterol over 200 or 100 should be treated with statins in addition to paying attention to diet and exercise. How these exact numbers were chosen as the cutoffs, especially why they are so even and neat, is somewhat of a mystery in each case. Often they are defined during the design phase of the clinical trial.

The tight coupling of clinical trials with the redefining of illness is not a bug but a feature. The very idea of comparing the improvement of a thousand patients over months or years drives designers to make the initial measure of illness precise enough to distinguish improvement between two treatments. That precise measure of illness may be different from previous diagnostic definitions of illness, but, given a successful trial, it now defines exactly the type of illness that the drug works on. The previous definition now looks less precise and has fewer facts behind it, and, perhaps most important, the new definition is easy to apply because it was designed that way, that is, to be a standard intake mechanism for the clinical trial across multiple sites and even countries.

MANY POSSIBLE LINES—WHICH TO CHOOSE?

> The challenge for the project team is to design the most efficient development plan, within the regulatory and ethical constraints, that will provide the largest market, and the best return on investment. The trials should be no larger, nor run longer, than required to provide evidence for efficacy and safety.
> —SCHACHTER, *THE NEW MEDICINES*, 117

The ability of a clinical trial to play a role in redefining how an illness is diagnosed means an opportunity for companies to choose measures of illness and improvement in order to maximize subsequent market size. With most illnesses there are often competing diagnostic measures described in the medical literature and used in practice. In some cases, for example, depression, there can be hundreds of possible scales to use in a clinical trial. The one that is used for a trial reinforces that definition and reifies that scale as the proper one. Co-produced as part of a clinical trial, the definition of an illness used is often marketed along with the drug as a package, further consolidating and reifying the drug via the clinical trial and via the diagnostic and therapeutic instrument as interdependent facts and protocols.[11]

How did the notion of mass health come into being? Here is an example: the Kupfer curve described above as a paradigmatic image of mass health was the topic of discussion at a conference in 1988 entitled "Depression in Primary Care: Screening and Detection." Kupfer presented on the use of the curve: in the late 1980s depression was not regularly looked for in primary care settings. Despite having a significant prevalence of between 3 percent and 8 percent in the population, most health plans and the U.S. surgeon general's report did not recommend screening for it during regular checkups.[12] But in light of the increasing attention to the disorder driven by surveys suggesting that 20 percent of patients in primary care have a depressive disorder, and of medical economic studies claiming that depression was the most costly mental illness to treat, a large debate was launched by the National Institute of Mental Health to explore how to screen for depression.[13]

One of the first challenges in evaluating a possible screen for depression is that there were, and still are, many depression screening instruments. Most of them are questionnaires or checklists that a doctor fills out while evaluating a patient. At the time, there were at least six survey tools and screens in use, each emphasizing varying aspects of depression, and each could be set to different cutoff points.[14] In other words, doctors and hospitals decided both what instrument to use to screen and what threshold score would indicate more action was needed. The result was an array of choices regarding sensitivity and specificity. A supersensitive test, like a supersensitive individual, detects anyone with even a hint of pathology. A superspecific test, like an auditor, makes sure that you are really in trouble.[15]

A central consideration of these debates was the political economy of the healthcare system. If a robust tertiary care system with capacity was in place, then a sensitive test would be appropriate. The cutoff would be set low, and the primary care doctor would send everyone who might be depressed on to mental health services. However, if tertiary care was full, then a highly specific screen with a high cutoff should be used, ensuring that only truly, clinically depressed people were sent on.[16] Other considerations brought to bear in this debate concerned the cost, the time efficiency of the screen—if it took a doctor too long, he or she would not use it—and the inadequacy of most screening instruments for special populations, which referred to diverse cultures, ethnicities, languages, and ages.[17]

A further crucial concern of almost every researcher was the uncertain purpose of screening. Was it to indicate referral to a psychiatrist? Did the screen itself constitute diagnosis of depression? Was there any evidence that screening improved patient outcomes? At the time, having no substantial clinical trial evidence, a family physician, Douglas Kamerow, concluded that "the current answer to the question 'Is screening for depression worthwhile?' is only a less than resounding 'probably.'"[18] Choosing to screen and setting a threshold involved a careful assessment of the entire healthcare system and the effect that the screen would have on each part of it. In the language of science studies, screening was understood to be part of a large-scale sociotechnical system.[19]

In sum, screening was seen to introduce a necessary but arbitrary threshold into a particular setting that would result in a large number of people testing positive for depression. Many of these people would not have depression, others who did have it would be missed, and many who were successfully screened would not be helped by treatment. Screening also raised the sociomedical problem of confusing the screen with the diagnosis and with proof of illness. Would a screen given to primary doctors to pass along possible depressives to psychiatrists so that they could be properly evaluated come to be taken by the primary care doctor and patient as a diagnosis of depression and indication for treatment? These problems were not condemnations; they were being raised by the researchers who were conducting the surveys, studies, and clinical trials and designing new and better screening tools.

Two preoccupations that, to a twenty-first-century reader, fairly jump out were absent from the papers. The first is that no one considered designing and promulgating the most sensitive instrument possible, a screen that would maximize the number of people diagnosed as depressed. Second, no one wondered whether primary care doctors might become the largest diagnosers of depression and prescribers of antidepressants, as indeed they were in 2004.[20] Peter Kramer's *Listening to Prozac* was three years from being published, and depression was still seen as a stigmatized disorder needing all the help it could get.

Statistics and data sets were and are the rule in the United States, reinforcing the idea that the truth was invisible to individual users and that quantification was its own justification. The question in 1988 by one of the original depression screen designers, Max Hamilton, was, What is an effective scale to help primary care doctors and other health professionals to diagnose mental illness? Today, when there are multiple scales that can be used and marketers help design clinical trials, the question becomes which one can capture the most profitable market? A survey of 2,000 trials of adults with schizophrenia in the 1990s found that 640 rating scales had been used! Such a profusion of scales not only makes it all but impossible to compare trials, but it also creates confusion among doctors and patients in evaluating diagnoses and treatments.

Another example illustrates the choices among thresholds that clinical trials present and the varying values and criteria that can be used to make those choices. An article by Douglas Manuel and colleagues in the *British Medical Journal* comparing cholesterol treatment guidelines in different countries made this dynamic visible. The researchers designed a graph that mapped the population indicated by each guideline and the lives that would be saved, assuming that the clinical trial evidence was correct and the guidelines were scrupulously followed (fig. 21).

The first thing to note about the graph is that the guideline commit-

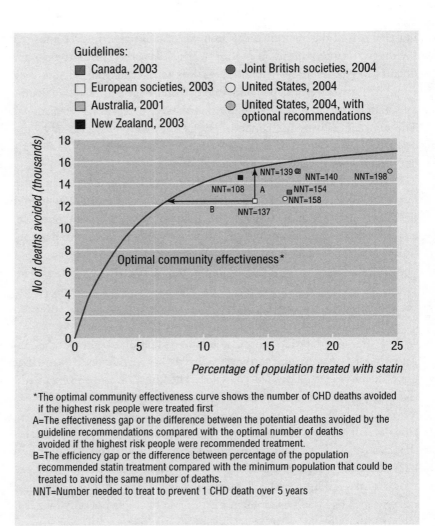

FIGURE 21 "Number of deaths from coronary heart disease (CHD) prevented over five years by percentage of Canadian population aged 20–74 years treated with statins for different guidelines for the management of dyslipidaemia." *Source*: Manuel et al. 2006.

tees in the various countries made very different choices at distinct times about how to implement the facts at their disposal. They came up with vastly different percentages of the population indicated for treatment and smaller differences in the numbers of lives potentially saved. The curve on the graph is the researchers' extrapolation of the ideal treatment-to-saving rate. The fact that it is a curve and not a point shows something very important about the graph as a whole. Any point under the curve is a potential guideline, and any point would save lives. The graph thus illustrates that thousands of potential clinical trials could be run, with consequent treatment indications.

In order to compare the guidelines, the authors describe the horizontal distance (arrow B) from the curve for each guideline as the efficiency gap. The efficiency gap implies that the same number of lives could be saved while treating fewer patients. The vertical distance (arrow A) to the line they call the effectiveness gap demonstrates how many more lives could be saved with a different guideline targeting the same percentage of the population. The authors imply thereby that prudent committees should design clinical trials and guidelines to move the points up and to the left. These would be trials that would suggest shrinking the population on medication. The researchers fail to consider the countervailing pressure of companies for whom the value of a clinical trial and consequent guidelines would be based on how far to the right the points would be placed, which translates into vastly more treatments.

When a pharma researcher such as Schachter states, "The challenge for the project team is to design the most efficient development plan, within the regulatory and ethical constraints, that will provide the largest market, and the best return on investment,"[21] she flips the considerations of effectiveness and efficiency on their heads. Saving lives becomes not the goal but the constraints within which the clinical trials are designed. As long as one can fit these constraints, then the company can concentrate all of the rest of its resources on designing for the maximum number of patients to be indicated for the drug. She continues, "The trials should be no larger, nor run longer, than required to provide evidence for efficacy and safety."

Not surprisingly, the guidelines used in the United States are the farthest to the right and getting more so with each guideline revision. This is a direct result of the guidelines themselves being the target of clinical trial design by pharma companies. As the medical historian Jeremy Greene discovered, Merck started conducting clinical trials for its drug Mevacor in order to reinforce the then-controversial cholesterol guidelines. Subsequent trials by many companies "came to exert a formative influence on the guidelines themselves."[22]

In terms of mass health there is nothing inherently illogical or illegal with any of these guidelines. According to the graph, the revised U.S.

guidelines are projected to save approximately 300 more lives per five years than New Zealand's (15,000 vs. 14,700). The fact that this comes at the cost of putting 12 percent more of the population on statins (24 percent vs. 12 percent) should be a concern, I think, but this is a social question about both how we think of risks and the extent to which we think we have enough data to make the call. A decision as to which guidelines we should follow is not something mass health, prevention, and clinical trials can determine. The fact that these countries have come to distinct decisions illustrates, again, the open-endedness of mass health.

Rose struggled with this decision gap in his proposal for preventive health and hinted at the inability of the logic of prevention to stop the biomedical appropriation of clinical trials. Ironically, he noted the folly of health service managers and policymakers who get so caught up in mistaking people treated for improved health that they say things like, "This has been a good year for the National Health Service. . . . We have treated more patients than ever before." He realizes that the number of treatments can, almost unconsciously, become an index for health itself. This would mean that more medicine comes to be a goal and is seen as inherently better than fewer treatments! Rose's assessment is that the National Health Service was managing health services "according to the principles of the market."[23] Precisely. Because he was probably writing within a world oriented toward government policy, Rose nowhere seems to recognize that what he calls this "blinkered attitude" is the very goal of pharmaceutical marketing.

Ironically, Rose's argument about the arbitrariness of illness and clinical trial definitions is cited by pharmaceutical companies in their understanding of how to grow markets. A passage in *A Guide to the Global Pharmaceutical Industry* by Mark Greener led me to Rose in the first place:

> Defining illness is somewhat arbitrary. Blood pressure and lipid levels, for example, have a normal "bell-shaped" or "n-shaped" distribution. In such cases, the abnormality is quantitative rather than qualitative. As a result, the point at which clinicians decide that something is abnormal and therefore warrants treatment, is an arbitrary decision usually based on population risk (Rose 1993, 6–8). This means that different clinicians can—and sometimes do—draw different conclusions about the point at which they will intervene. Clearly such factors can influence the success of a particular medication.[24]

Despite his attempt to say that this view of the success of a particular medication indicates a blinkered attitude, Rose is here fully enrolled to justify the use of that attitude to increase market size. Rose actually began his book with a meditation on the uneconomic consequences of preventive health, noting that it never really saves the state money since it usually only postpones but doesn't prevent health problems. He pointed out that the longer one lives, the more treatments one tends to require in addition to the screening and preventive treatments; therefore, mass health only gets more expensive. In the end, he argued for preventive medicine solely on humanitarian grounds, namely, that more life with less illness is better. Rose thus assumed that the point of designing a clinical trial was to maximize healthiness in society and that this required careful discussion of the tradeoffs between the size of population indicated by the clinical trial and the costs of treating that population. Greener turns this point on its head by making the arbitrary cutoff nature of clinical trials into a capitalist resource. As we have seen, marketing must insist that the clinical trial be designed so that if it is successful it will generate a bigger, more profitable market in prescriptions. It is Rose who unfortunately has the blinkers on. His lack of understanding of the political and economic context of clinical trials makes him miss the true function of the trials in biomedical capitalism.

MOVING THE LINE HAS BIG MARKET CONSEQUENCES

> By now you've seen the barrage of commercials starring good-looking people tripping over themselves or doing belly flops into pools because they have high cholesterol. Why all the commotion? In May 2001, the [National Cholesterol Education Program of the NIH] changed its guidelines for the first time in ten years regarding detection, evaluation and treatment of heart disease. For those of you with products to sell, these guidelines essentially tripled the market for the number of people who should be on drugs or some kind of lifestyle therapy by lowering the risk range of cholesterol.
> —WELLCHECK MARKETING BROCHURE (2002)

WellCheck, a pharmaceutical company interested in promoting a cholesterol-lowering drug, sells a portable cholesterol monitoring device, Cholestech, that can be installed in local pharmacies as part of a screening campaign. On one hand, moving the dotted line, that is, changing the threshold of illness diagnosis, vastly increases the market for treatments.

On the other hand, such a shift has profound personal and social consequences. On a personal level, it shifts a large number of people into or out of really being ill. Socially, it shifts these people into or out of official diagnostic categories, with big market consequences for medications. As we saw with the NCEP guidelines, millions of people transubstantiated into being unhealthy, at risk, and in need of treatment. Thinking with the Kupfer curve, through the raising of the bar, they were translated from being on the downward slope to being in the valley.

It is possible to move lines so profoundly because clinical trials were not designed to be used to move lines. They were designed to compare treatments for existing diagnoses, those that had known outcomes such as cures. When clinical trials are used to define a diagnosis along a continuum, they turn out to be remarkably flexible. In *Strategies for Prevention*, Rose detailed the social difficulty of deciding how to design a trial to help people. He uses the example of potential benefits from serum cholesterol reduction on coronary heart disease deaths. I have reproduced his table since it makes clear just how open clinical trials can be. He breaks down risk by age and sex (table 2).

On the basis of this table Rose discusses various screening programs that might be designed. Each could be verified by clinical trials as saving lives, but the cost of saving those lives varies greatly. On one hand, he points out how a screening program for men fifty-five to sixty-four years of age would require that 230 be screened and 100 of those be treated for five years in order to prevent one death on average. And this, he says, "relative to other preventive or therapeutic measures . . . would be reckoned a good value."[25] On the other hand, screening women twenty-five to thirty-four years of age would require screening 137,300 women and placing 20,600 of those on treatment for five years to prevent one death. The reason the number needed to treat (NNT) for women is so high is that the female demographic has so few coronary deaths to begin with (only 0.2 per 1,000, or 1 in 5,000 over five years).

Rose's disapproving response illuminates a crisis intrinsic to health prevention. Despite appearing to be objective, one must engage in a relative and arbitrary valuing of lives. "Unless one takes the extreme and wholly unrealistic view that the saving of a life is worth any price at all, then it is hard to justify."[26] Rose's need to increase the hyperbole, saying "extreme and wholly unrealistic," reveals the dilemma, since he is nonetheless talking about a program that would save lives. Like Canguilhem

TABLE 2 **Rose's Strategy of Preventive Medicine**

	AGE (YEARS)			
	25–34	35–44	45–54	55–64
Percentage with raised level				
Men	20	35	40	45
Women	15	20	50	70
Five-year deaths per one thousand in this group				
Men	1.2	5.8	21.3	48.1
Women	0.2	1.1	4.5	15.9
*Number screened to prevent one death in five years**				
Men	21,100	2,500	600	230
Women	137,300	23,200	2,200	450
Number treated for five years to prevent one death				
Men	4,200	860	230	100
Women	20,600	4,560	1,100	320

*Assuming a 20 percent reduction in deaths among all eligibles.

Source: This table was originally titled "Estimates of potential reduction in coronary heart disease deaths from screening for raised serum cholesterol (>6.5 mmol/l) in different age and sex groups," from Rose 2008.

and Robert Hahn, who could laugh at the absurdity of treating everyone for the smallest risks, Rose finds the crisis to be precisely that nothing in the logic of clinical trials prevents the result of an NNT of 20,600.

Empirically, a clinical trial could be designed to show a population goal of everyone over twenty-five being put on cholesterol-lowering drugs, despite the incredibly huge NNT. A pharmaceutical company would jump at such a market—everyone over twenty-five! For Rose, which clinical trial to run and where to draw the line are thus social and political dilemmas, questions for society to decide openly.

In the United States this dilemma has become a full-blown contradiction because of the following structural economic constraints. First, only a few of the many possible population and cholesterol groups can be studied, and, second, owing to their large size and expense it is pharmaceutical companies that are allowed to choose the groups. Make no mistake, the clinical trial will generate legitimate and true facts about health.

The clinical trial that is run will indicate treatment for whatever population subset it successfully studies. The tragedy for us is that this may be the only clinical trial that is run regarding this condition or risk, and therefore this trial may provide the only facts about this kind of health that we have access to.[27] If the other questions weren't asked, we could not know, and no one might know, whether some of us would receive almost all of the benefit of the drugs and the rest of us almost nothing. We would have no choice but to act on the basis of those facts of life that were generated by those whom we asked to generate them.

Now ask yourself: If you were running a pharmaceutical company and had to choose between a study that could show a high treatment benefit for men over fifty-five or one that would show a low benefit for everyone over twenty-five but still save lives, which would you fund?

There was a fascinating and frightening role-playing experiment run back in the 1970s and repeated hundreds of times since in various cities internationally. Based on a real-life scenario, it asked whether a pharmaceutical company should suppress findings about a deadly side effect for a drug "Panalba" for six months if it would result in an increased profit. While individuals responding were horrified at this prospect, when those same individuals were given role-playing tasks, including the chief executive officer (CEO) and other positions on the company board, they quite often decided to delay. What this Panalba study showed time and time again is that Americans, as well as global citizens, know how to be good businessmen and to see what "should" be done to keep companies alive and growing.[28] Even if we have other points of view, we maintain that perspective, and I think it is one of the reasons the current view of health and knowledge production makes sense to us.

Because the problem for pharmaceutical companies is how to keep growing under the constant pressure of stockholders, competitors, and the time bombs of their patents running out, clinical trials must be designed to maximize their markets in order to maximize their investment return. Schacter explained it this way to future pharmaceutical researchers: "If the team elects to seek approval for a narrow subset of patients with a certain condition, then the market for the drug may be too small to make financial sense for the company. If they seek the widest use, for example, for everybody with arthritis, they are at a greater risk of failing to demonstrate safety and efficacy and therefore failing to get approval. This is based on biology."[29]

The point is that there is an awareness in companies of the variety of clinical trials that could be run, and a conscious choice to pick those that address the desired profile for a large population with long-term needs. Schacter is demonstrating why clinical trials cannot be designed with general wellness as a priority: companies must see health as a *means* to profit through increasing treatments. In this way, clinical trials that result in larger NNTs (that is, less efficient drugs) come to be more valued than smaller ones. The dynamic of surplus health is at work in the fact that the larger NNT means that more people will be taking the drug without benefiting from it, but since there aren't any other facts about who will benefit, it appears as if everyone taking the pill is benefiting a little by reducing their risk. The thorny issue here is that health itself is being instrumentalized and made to grow by redefining it as treatments. Any critique of the process therefore seems to be antihealth.[30]

VIRTUALLY INFINITE PHARMACEUTICAL GROWTH

Guidelines introduced in 2001 by the NCEP of the National Heart, Lung and Blood Institute had lowered the recommended level of bad cholesterol, tripling the number of people defined as being at high risk. James I. Cleeman, the coordinator of the group that issued the guidelines, told reporters, "We want to recommend more aggressive treatment to people who are at very high risk." "And," he added, paraphrasing Shakespeare, "there are more of them out there than are dreamt of in your philosophy."[31] Cleeman's suggestion is that the implications of clinical trials should exceed not only what we think, but also our very imagination. A failure of our imagination is a proposal to reframe the problem. These people-at-risk (patients-in-waiting)[32] are not visible, even to themselves. If Americans want to be healthy in the future, they have no choice but to trust the clinical trials and treat the numbers that they propose. Inherent in Cleeman's declaration is an order of reality in which epistemology, where clinical trials redefine high risk, determines that these people *are* now ontologically at high risk, and, being at high risk, they should, as in need to, both ethically and imperatively, be put on treatment.

Even as he pronounced these words though, new clinical trials were under way that three years later would take the undreamed of numbers of people he refers to here and triple *them*, to two hundred million. And then the thresholds were further lowered.[33] Looking at the real and the projected rates of growth, I am confused. How does our pill taking continue to grow? I keep having conversations with colleagues, doctors, and economists in which the interim conclusion is that it makes no sense. I am now actively looking for projections that prescription rates will taper off in the future and can't find them. Instead, they are predicted to grow by 8 to 15 percent per year. It seems they have to stop growing, logically, but apparently there are other logics at work.

Roberto Goizueta, the former CEO of Coca-Cola, transformed the company in the early eighties with a different logic of growth. He had an insight, a simple but stunningly powerful one that he shared with his senior executives. What, he asked almost casually, was the average per capita daily consumption of fluids by the world's 4.4 billion people? The answer was sixty-four ounces. And what, he asked, is the daily per capita consumption of Coca-Cola? Answer: Less than two ounces.[34] As he stated in Coca-Cola's annual report in 1996, "We remain resolutely focused on going after the other 62."

However absurd Goizueta's redefinition of the Coca-Cola Company's market might seem,[35] it has been taken as a transformative insight throughout the business world, demonstrating the truth of the title of a book by Ram Charan and Noel Tichy: *Every Business Is a Growth Business*. Those who follow this vision claim "virtually infinite growth" is a matter of finding the right formulation for the virtual and then actualizing it. One pharmaceutical parallel to global liquid consumption by humans is illness risk and the capacity to take drugs to ward it off.

According to this logic, the solution to the growth demanded of pharmaceutical companies is clinical trials. They alone can increase the productivity of prescriptions, creating more drugs for more people for longer periods of time. The question is then how to see human health in terms of its potential treatment and create studies that can support that potential.

In biomedicine the current market for a drug is the limited viewpoint, and to reframe it we need to think about everyone who might possibly be able to take the drug. In this worldview the first step is not to look at who is already going to see their doctor, but to take a potential threshold diagnosis and then calculate how many people would fall within that threshold and therefore should be consumers of that drug. Interviewed in the industry journal *Pharmaceutical Executive*, Thierry Soursac, an executive with Aventis, describes this process: "'Up until now,' he says, 'when we were looking at the size of the market, we tended to open this market data bible called IMS and say, "Okay, the market of proton pump inhibitors is that much, and the market of hypertension is that much, and this is the size of the market we have to tap into.'" The problem, Soursac explains, is that IMS data represent a 'rearmirror view' of markets, a view of the past, not the potential."[36]

Soursac's reference to the problem with a "rearmirror view" of markets is almost an exact quote from another chapter in *Every Business Is a Growth Business*, this time by the CEO of General Electric Power Systems, Robert Nardelli, who said, "We were looking at the industry through a rear-view mirror," that is, using the historical basis of the market, not the prospective basis. Pharmaceutical executives, in other words, are already translating capital into biomedicine, substituting health for value and illness for labor.

One starts with the question, How big is the market for statins or other drugs? The traditional approach, used by most drug companies, has been to measure the amount of existing diagnoses for the indication and use this as a benchmark for market size. One company, IMS (now IMS Health), is the acknowledged leader in this type of information gathering. IMS tracks almost every prescription written by every doctor and then sells this information to marketers and drug companies so they can track exactly how well their campaigns are going. The interview with Soursac continues, "His entire marketing strategy hinges on his belief that pharma companies need to 'look at how many human beings on the planet have specific diseases that can be addressed by our drugs; this is the market. Whether this market has translated into any sales of drugs in the past is irrelevant.' Soursac cites the possibility that a market with low sales may be suffering from under-diagnosis of a condition or poor documentation of disease epidemiology in certain geographic areas."[37]

When Soursac suggests looking at "how many human beings on the planet have specific diseases," he means to estimate the number of people who could be determined to be within a specified threshold. Arguing from this potential, he outlines a strategy for achieving it, beginning with changing how the disease is diagnosed and how it is documented. This way of growing a megamarket begins with emphasizing an under-diagnosis by identifying a hidden epidemic. In the following account of producing a market in Japan, newly targeted epidemiological studies are designed to show undetected, even unimaginable levels of disease that could literally create a market: "'People in the company said there are too few patients in Japan,' he says. 'But I looked at the U.S. and Europe . . . [a]nd thought this is sure to be a big market.'"[38]

Again, this approach is a textbook business growth tactic, emulating Goizueta's admonition to base the projected consumption of Coke in Southern California not on its average soft drink consumption but on the largest consumption in the world. Southern California's potential could be tripled because Hungary's consumption was three times greater per month. Goizueta premised growth on the notion that ideals, not averages, were appropriate target norms. So Soursac commissioned a third-party epidemiology study that found rates in Japan to be identical to those in the United States. "'Suddenly, [Soursac says,] by having that data in your hand and being able to share it with the health authorities and medical institutions, you certainly create the market for diagnosis and treatment of DVT [deep vein thrombosis] which didn't exist before.'"[39]

The slippage between growing a product market and growing a diagnosis seems to go without saying. National populations and potential markets are made equivalent through epidemiology and bodies that set international standards. Factual humanitarian claims of disease prevalence are mobilized to invoke nation-state ethical responses, thereby opening up markets.

Soursac views health facts as highly contestable things. If epidemiological data suggest one conclusion, another study might counter it. The result would seem to be a contradiction or even a controversy: the ability to commission a new, latest study to promote greater disease prevalence. But, when properly shared, emphasized, and amplified, a new patient-population-in-waiting can be created out of whole cloth, where one didn't exist before.

We can now see how the unimaginable numbers of people at high risk and in need of treatment, "more than are dreamt of in your philosophy," can be so easily talked about. One reason we cannot imagine the number of people is that the population does not exist until the questions are posed, the epidemiology conducted, and the treatments indicated.

MULTIPLYING LINES THROUGH NEW BIOMARKERS

Another strategy for creating megamarkets is to make more curves that indicate more risk and treatments. Producing new biomarkers or checklists that define diseases in new ways can do this. These serve as proxies or surrogates for the diseases and are in many cases risk factors. Greener describes why biomarkers save time and money in research: "Ideally [a] study would look at the drug's effects on the so-called 'hard' endpoints — death or a heart attack, for example. However, such studies tend to be large, expensive, and lengthy. So many studies rely on 'surrogate' endpoints. These predict the risk of suffering a hard endpoint either for each patient or from a population perspective. . . . Taken across the whole population these are associated with, for example, a risk of stroke, asthma or heart attack. However that does not show that any particular patient will develop the disease."[40] In this manner, biomarkers undergo a transformation from additional signs of an illness into the means of defining a new risk or illness for treatment. Symptoms become the only way to decide on illness. The person is dependent on the evidence from the clinical trial for knowing whether or not he is at risk or ill and needs treatment. And the patient has no way of knowing whether or not the test finds a real thing or whether the treatment works. The switch to preventive, population-based medicine makes this happen.

In *Forecasting for the Pharmaceutical Industry*, the pharmaceutical management consultant Arthur Cook gives an example of how a condition that many men die with, but not from, can be transformed into a market by developing a diagnostic technology:

> For the patient-based forecaster success-stories revolve around diseases such as benign prostatic hypertrophy and HIV. Benign prostatic hypertrophy (BPH) is a disease that affects men, usually in older age. Cadaveric epidemiological studies suggested that the prevalence of BPH was as high as 95 per cent in men over the age of 65. However, the number of men treated for BPH was significantly lower. With the advent of new diagnostic technologies, physicians were able to monitor for an enzyme associated with BPH and were able to diagnose patients earlier in their disease. This led to market growth through an increase in diagnostic rates.[41]

In this case BPH is found in as high as 95 percent of men over the age of sixty-five, meaning that the potential market not only for diagnostics but also for treatment is basically every man over sixty-five. Realizing that potential market is the goal of developing the diagnostics. For market purposes it is not necessary to know whether the diagnoses saved lives.

Given that the pharmaceutical companies, as Cook shows, have run the clinical trials that define the facts about illnesses and risks, the patients have no choice but to rely on those facts and to submit their healthiness to screening and diagnosis. One way of increasing the market size is by studying younger pools of risk patients. Tamas Bartfai and Graham Lees explain how biomarkers enable this extension: "Drug companies do not have the time to wait for the actual therapeutic effect to manifest itself. . . . That is why the designers of clinical trials are always looking for 'surrogate endpoints'; that is you look for something which indicates the therapeutic effect indirectly."[42]

They use the example of chronic, slowly progressing diseases like osteoporosis, rheumatoid arthritis, and Alzheimer's:

> If you want to look at the disease progression of say a neurological disease such as Alzheimers (AD), the length of the study becomes a major financial and marketing issue. Since the disease can be detected much earlier, one can elect to perform the trial on patients with mild to moderate symptoms, as defined neuropsychologically, and try to show efficacy against a slow decline, but that can take 24 to 36 months. The market size will of course be much bigger; they are younger and there are more of these patients who are less likely to die from other causes during the trial.[43]

Bartfai and Lees demonstrate how, by choosing to study the mild, earlier forms of a disease, one can vastly increase the number of people in the market as well as the NNT and the length of time each of those people is on the drug. The pressure on corporate and corporately funded trial designers is enormous to redefine diseases in this way, that is, by studying them with the purpose of identifying a market that is as large as possible. But what of the excess or surplus? The switch to studying patients with mild versus major symptoms changes the perceived efficacy of the drug: say it now has an NNT of 500 (versus 100 for the major symptom study), then for every person who is diagnosed and benefits from the drug, 499 do not need the treatment, versus 99 before. Not only are millions more now indicated for the drug, but its efficacy has decreased. Choosing which trial to run thus increases the illness that is apparently treated; it appears as if more health is possible. Designing the trial is a way to generate surplus health.

This is the public secret of capital-driven health research. Clinical trials can and are used to maximize the size of treatment populations, not the efficacy of the drug. By designing trials with this end in mind, companies explicitly generate the largest surplus population of people taking the drug without being helped by it. Since the trials are the major evidence for the treatment indication, which effectively becomes the definition of the illness or risk, there is rarely any outside place from which to critique or even notice this bias.

Trials can be used to find new biomarkers, ones that respond better to one's own drugs. This is often done through phase IV or V trials in which an approved drug's markets can be broadened.[44] Some statins work better on LDL, others on HDL. A month after the NCEP guidelines came out in 2001, a set of studies indicating a new biomarker, C-reactive protein (CRP), was publicized. CRP was offered as yet another "acronym to add to your storehouse of medical knowledge."[45] The studies were covered with the same breathless, fearful hype as the new cholesterol guidelines, leading to a conflict of measures: "Cholesterol under Threat" read one headline, while two others read "Study Says a Protein May Be Better Than Cholesterol in Predicting Heart Disease Risk" and "New Test for Risk of Heart Disease; Study Shifts Focus from Cholesterol."[46] The new tests were incorporated as a possible answer to the problem that more than half of the population who suffered heart attacks has normal cholesterol.

But the implication that every new study should change guidelines was premature: "Sidney Smith, the chief science officer at the American Heart Association and a former president of the organization, said it was too early to change the guidelines to treat people with high C-reactive protein levels. 'The guidelines came out a month ago—they are not going to be changed within a month,' said Antonio Gotto of Cornell University in New York, one of the new paper's authors. 'Eventually this will be incorporated into guidelines.'"[47] This quote is revealing because it illustrates that health does not drive guidelines directly. Guidelines have their own timetable, in this case a slow, step-by-step progression.

When possible, though, all the pieces of co-producing a market, brand, biomarker, and trial come together. An example is Aventis's work on HbA1c levels in diabetics. At the time the following statement was made, Aventis had products for diabetics but needed a new biomarker to become common sense in order for the market to grow. *Pharmaceutical Executive* enthusiastically reported on the attempt to change the way we think:

In November 2002, Aventis launched its "Aim. Believe. Achieve. Diabetes A1c" initiative, part of an ongoing effort to increase professional and consumer awareness and testing of HbA1c. The company works with organizations such as the American Diabetes Association [ADA], the American Association of Diabetes Educators, the International Diabetes Centers, and Take Control of Your Diabetes. With those efforts, the company's objective is nothing short of revolutionizing the way the average person thinks about his or her illness and its management. Part of that is general public education, but the other part is more specific to the role Aventis' products will play in the reshaping of diabetes into a long-term lifestyle management issue rather than a chronic illness.[48]

This is an explicit lifestyle management approach. Campaigns like "Aim. Believe. Achieve." work to substantiate the general sense of threshold-defined illnesses for chronic management, everyday risk factor management, and continual surveillance of biomarkers while also targeting specific thresholds, illnesses, risks, and tests. In other words, campaigns like this reinforce the image of preventive health while growing the market for a specific treatment.

The challenge, as perceived by Aventis's chief operating officer, Richard Markham, is one of capturing attention and changing belief at the individual, commonsense level, building on the results of previous campaigns. He sees marketing, education, and research as part of a seamless whole:

> Markham likens the challenge of educating consumers and primary care practitioners about the significance of HbA1c to the challenge of convincing people of the significance of high cholesterol decades ago. "Having an HbA1c level of 7 percent now, and with future guidelines, 6 percent, has not risen to the same level of importance in people's minds as having a diastolic blood pressure above 100 or having LDL cholesterol above a certain level," he says. "Until there were tools available to prove that statins worked, that you could take someone with high cholesterol and give them medication, that it would make them look like someone who doesn't have high cholesterol," he explains, "the case hadn't really been made in a bulletproof and persuasive way that you could control cholesterol's effects on heart disease." Similarly, he argues, "There's still room around the edges, people think, to argue

about whether the level of diabetes control has an effect on cardiovascular events."[49]

Cholesterol is cited as the sort of cultural change that can be achieved through co-produced PR, facts, and measures. Markham understands the production of consumer awareness as a template that can be emulated. To this end, a clinical trial is being created precisely to draw attention to and ideally prove the marketing claims. "That's why Aventis is launching the ORIGIN (Outcome Reduction with Initial Glargine Intervention) Trial, a four-year, 10,000-patient study that [Markham] says seeks to 'further demonstrate with hard data that there is a big difference in the longer-term health consequences of good versus suboptimal HbA1c control.'"[50]

The aim of this study is to contribute to the gap in evidence-based marketing that Markham has identified. Ideally, it will enter into the logic of diabetes, as "bulletproof and persuasive," especially when it has been marketed in press releases. The clinical trial will also seed the drug to hundreds of doctors, who will be likely to use the drug in the future and who can become potential spokespersons for its effectiveness. Combined with the anticipated lowering of the HbA1c threshold, this form of coordinated campaign will substantially grow the market for the drug. In this manner we can see how each new biomarker functions as a surrogate for a new disease, multiplying the number of risk factors and therefore the reasons for treatment.

NEW "PREDISEASES" CREATE NEW MARKETS: METABOLIC SYNDROME

> What makes a blockbuster has been evolving into not just branding the class [of drugs] or the science [of a condition,] but branding the patient. . . . We're creating patient populations just as we're creating medicines, to make sure that products become blockbusters.
>
> —VINCE PARRY, PRESIDENT OF Y BRANDING (QUOTED IN KOBERSTEIN,
> "WHEN WORLDS COLLIDE," 56)

Even as a threshold line creates categories of sick and not sick on either side, nearness to the line creates its own categories: almost sick, borderline, or at risk. Because the curve is continuous, one is always either closer or farther from crossing the threshold. The area just above the syndrome line becomes itself liminal as a kind of risk territory as well as worth defining as a penumbra of the disorder, a kind of protodisorder.

TABLE 3 **Selected Prediseases**

PREDISEASE	NUMBER AFFECTED	YEAR GUIDELINE CHANGED
Prediabetes	40 million	2004
Prehypertension	45 million	2003
Borderline high cholesterol	104 million	2001

The historian Charles Rosenberg has noted the irony with which proto-diseases are the artifacts of laboratory-oriented medicine, yet "each such problematic physiological status presents a potential site for moral action."[51] Despite, or rather because of, the mushiness of the category, prediseases have become explicit objects of attention in government and pharmaceutical companies.

As I noted in chapter 3, prediabetes had for two decades been a site of incredulity and struggle by researchers and doctors, yet it is now an operationalized form of rhetorical authority, as a predisease is defined as being somewhere between wellness and full-blown disease. In 2004, a *Washington Post* headline was "Making Us (Nearly) Sick: A Majority of Americans Are Now Considered to Have at Least One 'Pre-Disease' or 'Borderline' Condition." The conditions included "pre-diabetes, 40 mill, 2004; pre-hypertensive, 45 mill, 2003; borderline high cholesterol, 104 mill, 2001" (see table 3). The story explained that the terms to describe these conditions were chosen to psychologically manage people: "The [National Blood Pressure] committee felt that the term 'pre-hypertensive' would be more of a motivating tool to get people—physicians, clinicians, and patients—to do things."[52] Focus groups and other research techniques are conducted on words and phrases, testing them for how much tension and fear they create.[53] As opposed to borderline hypertensive and other notions suggesting nearness to the line, the concatenated condition "You *are* prehypertensive" apparently works more effectively. Behavioral science and marketing research are thus employed to manage the objective self-fashioning of all those involved by getting them to redescribe the state of patients in the charged form of a disorder that requires immediate response. In this formulation, clinicians and physicians are seen as being in need of as much motivation as patients. By establishing a new disorder, the committee hopes to overcome most people's reluctance to take risk seriously as a condition requiring treatment.

The psychiatrist and popular commentator Peter Kramer calls the process by which shadow disorders become newly named diseases "diagnostic creep." But where Rosenberg, Kramer, and others sense a slippery definitional slope, committees and companies see a challenge that is to be solved by using a combination of test scores, grammar, and marketing. A market can thereby be produced by inventing a new syndrome, especially since the syndrome itself is a compilation of risk factors. The ATP [Adult Treatment Panel] III guideline changes in 2001 did just this by legitimating and making real and public something called metabolic syndrome." Newspapers called attention to the new nature of it:

> Another new aspect of the guidelines is the emphasis on the dangers of something called the "metabolic syndrome," which has emerged as being "as strong a contributor to early heart disease as smoking . . . and is important to recognize and treat," said Scott Grundy, chairman of the National Cholesterol Education Program panel that wrote the guidelines.
>
> The metabolic syndrome consists of a constellation of risk factors, including being overweight or obese (as measured by a waist circumference of 40 inches or larger in men; 35 inches or larger in women); elevated triglyceride levels (200 mg or higher); low HDL; high blood pressure; high blood sugar levels; and a tendency to form blood clots. It is estimated to afflict one in every four Americans.[54]

Literally, a disease-sounding syndrome is produced by correlating risk factors and naming it in such a way that it becomes common sense to think about treating "it" as a disease in and of itself. Just a few months before, Forbes covered metabolic syndrome under the name Syndrome X, emphasizing both its constructed nature and its lucrative market potential. In a typically Forbes manner, the reporter revealed both skepticism of the illness as a marketing tool and admiration for the marketing ploy of constructing an illness that had such great profit potential.[55]

For companies, an event like death, a heart attack, or even heart disease is always a risk, and their question is, How far in advance can they market that risk? The challenge for companies is explained as one of changing how doctors and therefore patients think of that risk. The goal is to get them to treat it as early as possible, as an article in *Pharmaceutical Executive* on "Metabolic Syndrome: The Making of a New Disease," explains:

> In the short run, the key to unlocking the potential of the metabolic syndrome market may lie in the establishment of a "pre-diabetic" state. The diagnostic criteria are already in place. In fact, [Richard] Nesto says that the ATP III diagnostic criteria make it easier to diagnose metabolic syndrome than using the Framingham risk score for coronary disease. However, in a society in which even hypertension is undertreated, companies face a formidable challenge in moving physicians to think about treating patients 10 or 15 years before they get sick.[56]

Prediabetes is used as a precursor diagnosis; it opens the door to constructing a new diagnostic, the metabolic syndrome. A careful look at this marketing view of metabolic syndrome will illustrate both how a threshold disease is explicitly "socially and scientifically constructed" and how this construction should be more properly thought of as a corporate construction.[57] The *PE* article about metabolic syndrome, written by Joanna Breitstein, an editor, celebrates the process:

> Science is beginning to understand the role of insulin resistance. Now it's industry's turn to draw the blueprints for the biggest market yet.
>   Unlike a new pathogen bursting from the jungle like Ebola or mutating from something familiar like each year's "new" strain of influenza, metabolic syndrome must be both socially and scientifically constructed. Well-known medical facts have been reorganized into a new understanding. And with that knowledge comes the need and opportunity for new research, new modalities of treatment, and, on the pharma side, new market risks, demands, and opportunities.[58]

Moving step by step through this article will help us understand the careful work with which companies are able to exploit the cutting edge of medical knowledge and uncertainty in order to maximize treatment market size. As with the development of strategic ubiquity discussed in chapter 1, marketers draw on the insights of social scientists in figuring out how to change our common sense. Breitstein quotes a medical anthropologist who worked at Integrated Marketing Associates and admired how much effort and innovation disease creation takes: "Cholesterol wasn't something people talked about 20 years ago. Merck spent years getting physicians to think about it as a big problem. Now they do."[59] Critical analyses of social constructivism and medical anthropology can be used to show the entanglement of social and scientific processes in order to offer critical alternatives, and they can be used to accelerate them.

With regard to cholesterol, the anthropologist as marketer sees in social construction solutions the ability to respond to corporate problems by creating a market. Getting a topic like a new syndrome into public discussion is called agenda setting, and even controversy over a biomarker or disease serves to draw attention to it and place the burden of disproof on those who wish to argue that the disease being talked about is not real. The article continues, "The emergence of cholesterol reduction as a market was a major event for pharma. Metabolic syndrome promises to be as big or bigger. Like any new disease, this one offers significant challenges to pharma. But for companies that meet them—especially the challenge of finding an appropriate role for medication in treating a disease with a large lifestyle component—metabolic syndrome will be a force reshaping products, companies, and markets for decades to come."[60]

Emergence as a disease is tracked as an institutional achievement, one of coordinated science, publicity, and an "infrastructure of journal articles, meetings and associations."[61] The article implicitly struggles with a chicken-and-egg problem, that is, whether scientific research discovers a new risk that calls forth an effort at market creation or whether the market potential itself pulls together a constellation of correlations, organizing them into an exploitable object. On one hand, the NCEP guidelines of May 2001 defined metabolic syndrome as a disease that was also a high-risk factor requiring pharmaceutical treatment, and the International Classification of Diseases (ICD) gave metabolic syndrome a code. As narrated by Breitstein, these apparently objective decisions by neutral scientific expert bodies, gatekeepers, could truly be said to have produced metabolic syndrome as social and intuitive fact, "To [Yehuda] Handelsman, who can methodically recount the syndrome's genesis, as a parent recounts the maturation of a child, that was the tipping point. 'Nothing helped metabolic syndrome more than the establishment of the ICD9 code.'"[62] Breitstein concludes, "In a world in which a condition isn't really a disease until it becomes part of physicians' paperwork, metabolic syndrome had crossed an important threshold."[63]

From a patient's or clinician's point of view, before a code exists syndromes may be thought of as, at best, claims. The tragic corollary of the code as "tipping point" is that persons suffering from conditions that have no codes may easily be dismissed as not suffering at all. Hilary Johnson, in tracing struggles with chronic fatigue syndrome, discusses a patient being told by insurance companies, "We don't even have a code for this disease, so we're not going to pay you."[64] The lack of a code is an explicit reason for a denial of insurance benefits, and its absence may lead the friends and family of the sufferer to not believe in the illness. In a world in which a "condition isn't really a disease until it becomes part of physicians' paperwork," those who are not yet classified fall through institutional cracks.[65]

As these comments make clear, bureaucratic codes and institutional definitions are obligatory passage points for facts to become real and effective. Science studies scholars have traced the social, cultural, international, and highly political nature of these classification systems.[66] What they have not done sufficiently is to connect those battles with the people seeking to use the classification systems to grow markets.[67] As the story in *PE* unfolds, the fights between factions within the medical community and the wider public come to blows over definitions.

> Already, some critics complain that the syndrome is simply the industry's effort to medicalize obesity. "Pharma companies understand the potential market, so they are trying to bring some light to it and push their products towards it," says Nikolaos Karachalias, Datamonitor senior endocrinology specialist.
>
> "It is being medicalized—but not just by the pharma companies," says [John] Buse. "The American Diabetes Association is also doing so by giving it a name and calling it a risk marker. Although there are some overweight people who don't have the syndrome, obesity is, in essence, the problem."[68]

The interests of pharma companies here coincide with those of patients' groups like the ADA. Those who look for conflicts of interest here will find them, as pharma companies fund most of the researchers in this arena, and they also contribute to patients' groups.[69] The *PE* article, however, takes the pharma company point of view, looking at how hard it is to grow a market even with the help of patients' groups because the treatments are for asymptomatic conditions. Getting patients to be aware of obesity and worried enough about it to do something requires redefining it as a risk factor, metabolic syndrome. "'Pharma companies are running for this market,' says Ajit Baid, manager of Frost & Sullivan's pharmaceuticals group. . . . But most patients are asymptomatic. And many would respond well to lifestyle changes. Finding pharma's niche in a massive, prevention-oriented campaign against metabolic syndrome won't necessarily be easy."[70]

Physicians and the public must be made aware of the risk as being objective, sanctioned fact, and then they must be convinced there is something to be done about it. We have seen that this process of critical persuasion can be dissected into discrete microsteps of conversion (see chapter 2). Breitstein's article covers the institutional aspect of persuasion: publicly funded market development initiatives by pharmaceutical companies to raise physician awareness, including the following:

> The American College of Cardiology and the ADA recently launched "Make the Link," a campaign that informs physicians and consumers that type 2 diabetics run an increased risk of heart disease and stroke.
>
> MSAToday.com, an alliance with a corresponding website funded by unrestricted grants from GlaxoSmithKline (GSK), offers physicians information about metabolic syndrome and continuing medical education credit.
>
> November 2003 saw the launch of the first annual scientific meeting devoted to insulin resistance, which most scientists believe is the cause of metabolic syndrome.
>
> In early 2004 a new society devoted to metabolic syndrome called the International Society of Diabetes and Vascular Research is expected to launch and begin publishing its own journal [now publishing *Diabetes & Vascular Disease Research* since May 2004].[71]

These and other initiatives have achieved "critical mass," according to Richard Nesto, a physician and researcher, "and if you look at the websites that have anything to do with high blood pressure, diabetes, cholesterol—many of them supported by drug companies—you'll see there is enough out there that the average mindful physician should have heard about it."[72]

With awareness covered, the challenge of convincing physicians that treatments are available requires that pharma companies "harness clinical evidence to show physicians the benefits of using pharmacologic therapy to prevent patients from developing CVD [cardiovascular disease] and type 2 diabetes." One solution, in addition to producing more clinical trials, is actually the production of yet another intermediate disease, another protodisease: "In the short run, the key to unlocking the potential of the metabolic syndrome market may lie in the establishment of a 'prediabetic' state."[73] In this sentence, the active agent is the market potential, which drives the establishment of a disease state. As epidemiological estimates range from 20 percent to a future 40 percent of the population, the potential for metabolic syndrome is obviously planetary.

By establishing new disease categories or states, the shift of treatment to a point earlier in time is redefined as proper treatment of an existing illness. With the production of prediabetes, prehypertension, and metabolic syndrome, risk is personally and socially reified into new discrete and singular disorders.

CHRONIC TREATMENT, DEPENDENT NORMALITY

Maximizing markets by choosing the most profitable diseases and maximizing the number of people indicated by clinical trials are only the first steps. The next, according to marketers, is to maximize the length of time people stay on a treatment through increasing the number of prescriptions per diagnosis. In an article titled "Moving beyond Market Share," James Vermilyea and colleagues write,

> Health care has changed dramatically in the past 35 years, as treatment has increasingly migrated from the doctor who directed care in the hospital to patients who now prevent illness through medication use in an unsupervised community setting. . . . medications [now] treat illnesses early in their natural history, long before painful or disabling symptoms are apparent. . . . With [these] asymptomatic conditions, patients are often unable to determine if they need treatment at all and/or whether the product is working. . . . This difficulty is only likely to grow. As researchers unravel the molecular basis of an illness, *manufacturers increasingly turn incurable diseases into merely chronic ones.*[74]

Constructing diseases as chronic moves beyond fighting for a share of the market because it grows the whole market by leaps and bounds into drugs for life. In the Kupfer curve diagram (see fig. 18), the length of time one stays on a drug is represented by the extension of the "treatment" line into the future. In the best case, one returns to "normalcy" by using the medication.

The new normalcy is thus not a return to the previous set of symptoms but a virtual or dependent normalcy, one that depends on the medication. But normalcy is now truly in quotation marks because it is now threatened with a series of dotted lines that indicate the dangers of going off the medication at any time. Initially, one must stay on it in order to stabilize the curing of the depressive episode. But at this point there is a danger of relapse. The illness is here reconstructed as risk: because one has had a depressive episode, one is now more at risk of having another. Hence the quotation marks; one is now normally at risk, and the pharmaceuticals are needed to maintain one's normalcy. One is now dependently normal.

If we were to construct an image of treatment to match this Kupfer curve, it would look like a mountain in which we were a marble balanced precariously on the peak. With tremendous genetic and environmental luck, some of us might stay up there for a long time, but most of us would do better to continually monitor our position in order to recognize when we start to roll off in one direction or another toward illness. In the image of health as a mountaintop, once one has slipped off in a particular direction, one has to be forever wary of slipping off again. Medication not only pushes one back toward the top but it is also needed to keep one propped up indefinitely.

The idea that removing the symptoms of depression can cure it is explicitly attacked by the argument inherent in a headline that appeared on the Prozac.com website, "Feeling Better Is Not Enough," and is reinforced by the invisible accumulation of symptoms and risk factors that cross thresholds (fig. 22).

The website and the doctor agree here with statistical medicine that your intuition and sense of wellness are deceptive and even dangerous in their ability to suggest that you discontinue treatment. Even though there are suggestions in the text of medication inserts that some people are able to discontinue their medication after six to twelve months, the implication of the final phase, "Maintenance," is that depression is not like a bacterial infection, cured by a week of antibiotics (see fig. 18). The ubiquity of this image comes from patient speech as well. The co-construction of this discourse floats between patients and marketing.

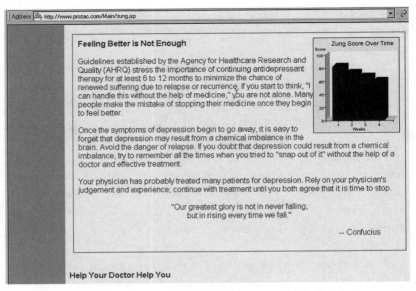

Feeling Better is Not Enough

Guidelines established by the Agency for Healthcare Research and Quality (AHRQ) stress the importance of continuing antidepressant therapy for at least 6 to 12 months to minimize the chance of renewed suffering due to relapse or recurrence. If you start to think, "I can handle this without the help of medicine," you are not alone. Many people make the mistake of stopping their medicine once they begin to feel better.

Once the symptoms of depression begin to go away, it is easy to forget that depression may result from a chemical imbalance in the brain. Avoid the danger of relapse. If you doubt that depression could result from a chemical imbalance, try to remember all the times when you tried to "snap out of it" without the help of a doctor and effective treatment.

Your physician has probably treated many patients for depression. Rely on your physician's judgement and experience; continue with treatment until you both agree that it is time to stop.

"Our greatest glory is not in never falling,
but in rising every time we fall."

-- Confucius

Zung Score Over Time

Help Your Doctor Help You

FIGURE 22 "Feeling Better Is Not Enough" on the Prozac.com website by Lilly.

One patient blogged his personal understanding: "If you happen to have a serotonin imbalance in your brain . . . ssri's [SSRIS, selective serotonin reuptake inhibitors] can change that. . . . [T]hat I have to take some pills every day to maintain my life is no different from my friend who takes sulfa drugs daily to stave off a recurrence of colitis, or another who injects herself with insulin."[75]

The sociomedical logic of the threshold here is objectively compelling. If your cholesterol is high, you must get on a statin. If subsequently it falls, then the statin is working, and you should stay on it. If your cholesterol doesn't fall, then you should increase the dosage or change statins. Save for intolerable side effects no part of the algorithm enables you to get off the statin. And this is taken for granted in reporting on statins: "Some patients are not told, or don't understand, that they have to use statins for the rest of their lives, not just until their cholesterol falls."[76]

Variability, one's score going up and down over time, will appear only as pathological, not natural, in this model. Once one has crossed the threshold and been diagnosed and treated, any improvement will be interpreted as the drug working. A returning of symptoms will be seen as a need for a greater dose. In this diagram there is no way off the treatment once you get on it. The psychiatrist Joseph Glenmullen found an additional driver toward drugs for life: "Especially in managed care settings, little or no effort is made to periodically reassess whether a patient's dosage can be reduced or the drug stopped."[77]

This thresholding of variability is not unique to pharmaceuticals. A medical anthropologist, Elizabeth Cartwright, found that a similar situation emerged when electronic fetal monitors were introduced into hospital labor rooms. Once a woman was hooked up to such a machine, its interpretation of fetal heart rate became the shared definition of fetal health. If the rate dropped below a certain threshold, an alarm went off and a legally shaped set of responses had to be initiated by hospital staff, even though *normal* variability in fetal heart rates indicated that most babies would cross the threshold more than once during labor. Cartwright describes a self-reinforcing feedback loop that can happen when an alarm causes an intervention that itself requires more and more adjustment.[78] With pharmaceuticals and thresholds, this can result in a "spiraling medication regime."[79]

The risk model reinforces a fear of going off medications even when they might be causing side effects. Rather than investigating the causes of the effects and changing the therapies altogether, many doctors follow a protocol of adding another drug to suppress the side effects. Glenmullen explains how this prescription cascade can lead to problems:

> Instead of stopping Prozac, another medication (Cogentin) was added to suppress the side effects. The use of additional drugs . . . to treat muscle spasms is well known to doctors from their experience with the side effects in patients on major tranquilizers. Although many doctors suppress medication-induced movement disorders in this way, I worry that ongoing exposure to the offending drug will cause damage eventually leading to tics. My preference is always to take patients off the offending agent, whenever possible.[80]

The shape of the diagram from beginning to end implies a certain inevitability to the course of the illness. Once one starts going down toward the threshold, there is no going back. Neither is there a way back to normalcy except through treatment.

Dependent normality consequently has two related meanings. The first meaning preserves the biological definition of normal as what your body needs to be and stay healthy, in this case a drug. In the second meaning it becomes socially common and normal to be on drugs. David Healy has noted that there is often surprise, but not outrage, over the rapid shift in the past ten years so that 6 percent of children under the age of six are on long-term psychoactive drugs.[81] At the end of this diagram we can see the normal become normative, and parents of children who are noticeably active may be asked by other parents, "Have you thought about Ritalin?"[82]

CHRONIC PROFITS AND PATIENT RESISTANCE

> As the old pharma saying went, 'While it's good to have a pill that cures the disease, it's better to have a pill you have to take every day.'"
>
> —HAWTHORNE, *THE MERCK DRUGGERNAUT* (CITED IN SHAH, *THE BODY HUNTERS*, 44)

The engine of expansion through chronic treatment comes into existence in the eyes of marketers who see it as the most efficient way to increase prescriptions. They calculate treatment value based on total prescriptions sold. This was brought home to me when talking with a group of marketers about chronic illness. Poring over a large flowchart of patient decision points, I was directed to a loop in one corner where repeated prescriptions were encapsulated. "We would love to increase the number of prescriptions a patient takes" said the marketer, "because the profit is the same if one patient takes a drug for four months, as it is for four patients taking the drug for one month." This interchangeability of patient numbers and prescription consumption is reflected in the Express Scripts report under the combined figure of "utilization" which is prevalence, the number of people indicated for the drug, times intensity, the average length of prescription per patient.

The consequence of this form of calculating value is that if a drug is approved for an indication, its possible market becomes its expected market in the eyes of pharma. And every person who could be indicated but is not taking the pills is seen as a loss of revenue. Mickey Smith's *Pharmaceutical Marketing* includes a chart headed "Decomposition of the Market," which lists the math through which Patients with Chronic Condition X (1,000,000) end up with only 7,350,000 prescriptions whereas there was an estimated "Original Potential" of 12,000,000 prescriptions (1 million patients multiplied by twelve prescriptions each) (fig. 23). So the rest is termed "Prescriptions 'Lost'" with *Lost* in quotation marks, as if Smith knows he is treading on ethically suspect grounds. In the sum-

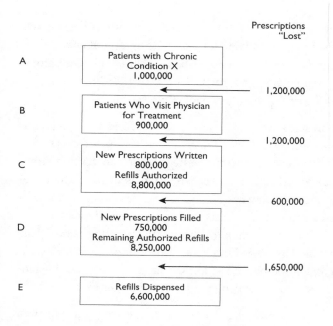

Prescriptions "Lost"

A — Patients with Chronic Condition X 1,000,000

← 1,200,000

B — Patients Who Visit Physician for Treatment 900,000

← 1,200,000

C — New Prescriptions Written 800,000 Refills Authorized 8,800,000

← 600,000

D — New Prescriptions Filled 750,000 Remaining Authorized Refills 8,250,000

← 1,650,000

E — Refills Dispensed 6,600,000

Original Potential (1 Million Patients x 12 Rx)	12,000,000 Rx
Total New and Refill Prescriptions Dispensed	7,350,000 Rx
Total Prescription Loss	4,650,000 Rx

FIGURE 23
"Decomposition of the Market." *Source*: Smith 1968.

mary chart, however, defined in terms of the Potential, it is simply listed as "Total Prescription Loss." Smith uses this chart to make the point that increasing compliance may be cheaper than increasing market share.

The effect of quantitatively extending risk in this way not only places more people in the category of "at risk" but also essentially changes the quality of the disease, rendering it chronic. This is an illustration of the fact that, as a pharmaceutical report from 2002 states, marketers consider that "the economic driver in health care has shifted from the physician to the patient. While physicians continue to control episodes of short-term, acute illness, such as hospitalizations, patients increasingly drive the financial and clinical outcomes for chronic diseases through the simple daily act of taking a pill, often over a long period of time. In financial terms, the shift from acute to chronic care medicine means that between 75–80% of a prescription's value is now concentrated in the patient's return to the pharmacy for refills."[83]

The point being made in this report is that if one were comparing two clinical trials, one for a cure and one for a chronic treatment approach to a disease, the latter has a four to five times better chance of being a block-buster. Similarly, the economists Michael Kremer and Christopher M. Snyder ask, "Why are drugs more profitable than vaccines?":

> In a simple representative consumer model, vaccines and drug treat-ments yield the same revenue for a pharmaceutical manufacturer, im-plying that the firm would have the same incentive to develop either ceteris paribus. We provide more realistic models in which the reve-nue equivalence breaks down. . . . The second reason for the break-down of revenue equivalence is that *vaccines are more likely to interfere with the spread of the disease than are drug treatments, thus reducing de-mand for the product.* By embedding an economic model within a stan-dard dynamic epidemiological model, we show that the steady-state flow of revenue is greater for drug treatments than for vaccines.[84]

As Kremer and Snyder make explicit, in too many drug studies, cures get in the way of repeat revenue. The corollary of seeing clinical trials as instruments or means for maximizing prescriptions, especially when used to lengthen treatment time, is that everything that gets in the way of those treatments becomes a loss. Because the expected return on in-vestment for a clinical trial is the total possible prescriptions, everything that impedes their realization is seen as a loss and a barrier to overcome.

A version of the flowchart the marketers showed me concerning the patients' return for prescriptions appears in almost every pharmaceutical textbook. The issue I didn't understand at the time (as I was at an early stage of my research) is that what the marketers call utilization (the num-ber of pills or prescriptions a person consumes in a set period of time[85]) is, from the user's point of view, bioavailability, the overall availability of their metabolisms for the maintenance of pharmaceutical flows.[86] The consequence of this formulation is that marketers envision patients as points of resistance rather than of consumption. Patients' physiological rejection of many drugs, their desire to stop taking different treatments, even their sense of their own wellness are all obstacles to be overcome. The authors of "Moving beyond Market Share" explain why this is the case: "What is needed are new measures of product performance that are consistent with the long-term use of chronic disease medications and that reflect how individuals use products in routine practice. Two such measures are persistence, or the percentage of patients who remain on medication, and the days of therapy obtained, which is a measure of the intensity of product use. Applying such metrics to a variety of chronic disease states reveals that a marketer's real enemy is less the share lost to competitors than the cumulative effects of patient attrition over time."[87]

This means that marketers are directly opposed to your decision not to continue taking a prescription even if you feel better or want to try an alternate form of medicine. The business magazine *Forbes* reinforced this battle image with a cover story entitled "Pharma's New Enemy: Clean Living" (fig. 24). Recalling Goizueta's redefinition of the Coke market as a war on coffee, tea, and tap water, the point here is that for good business reasons pharma has found a way to continually grow medicine by declaring war on living without drugs.[88]

What seems absurd here is that medical research could see healthiness as its enemy rather than a goal. It is only the notion of possession by the spirit of capitalism and growth that enables me to understand the following claim, made by Bartfai and Lees, which otherwise leaves me apoplectic:

> Looking at the business of mental disease objectively, but without cynicism, a common denominator of these indications is that they share the distinction of not being cured by these pharmacological treatments. This makes the market even more attractive. The patients have to take the drugs chronically. Not only are the diseases not cured, but there are few treatments that give 100% relief to those who have a syndrome. All usual response rates are 60 to 70% for a really good drug. . . . This gives a double opportunity: (1) one can enter a partially saturated market with a drug that works on patients unresponsive to existing treatments; and (2) one can improve on the side effect profile or the efficacy in terms of the time required for the onset.[89]

"Objectively, but without cynicism," it is as if some small part of them realizes how outrageous the rest of the paragraph will seem, and yet they cannot stop writing because it *is* objective. The world they live in, our world, is a world in which medical research *is* a financial investment demanding returns. In our world, it is objectively true that drugs that cure people or stop the spread of a disease, like vaccines are supposed to do, reduce revenue. It is true that research into chronic treatments will generate vastly more pill sales than research into cures. As we have also seen,

FIGURE 24 "Pharma's New Enemy: Clean Living," cover of *Forbes*, November 29, 2004.

it is true that drugs that work only on some people, that is, have a large NNT generating more prescriptions by indicating a larger market, are more valuable than those that help everyone they are indicated for, those that have an NNT of one. These are the realities of biomedical capitalism within which we and the pharmaceutical companies must operate and survive.

Bartfai and Lees say their view is expressed "without cynicism." That is, while it might appear they are speaking in a scornful, bitterly mocking tone, as if only selfish interests motivated them, they are not. They are saying they are consciously possessed and understand they have no choice but to "excessively lengthen treatment time . . . beyond all bounds set by human nature."[90] They are not cynical because that would imply they selfishly chose their analysis and believe it to be the product of human nature. But they know instead that it is precisely the product of the objective contradictions of today's healthcare.

Two researchers writing in the *British Medical Journal* (in 2003) proposed a related logic. On the basis of a meta-analysis of existing risk, biomarker, and threshold trial data on cardiovascular disease, the authors proposed a single "polypill" that will save lives to such an extent, they argue, that everyone over the age of fifty-five should be mandated to take it. Their logic is an extension of Rose's prevention analysis. In a nod to cost but not consent, they suggest that a low-cost version of this polypill, using generic components off patent, would work, even if 10 percent of the users were intolerant. Intolerance here is a formulation of the literal limit of the body's resistance to too many drugs. It vomits them up. Their proposal involves calibrating the drug to the maximum number of effects and side effects and to the highest cost society will bear before rebelling.[91]

The NNT of the polypill was estimated to be between six hundred and eight hundred. About half of the discussants online thought the article was an absurd joke. But the other half were genuinely excited by pushing preventive health to its limits. The polypill article concludes with a call for an end to thresholds altogether by taking them to their natural limit: "It is time to discard the view that risk factors need to be measured. . . . everyone is at risk."[92] This is a naturalized form of the suggestion to put statins in the water supply, no longer even a half joke but a policy proposal.

SIX

Knowing Your Numbers

Pharmaceutical Lifestyles

> Now, after the advent of statins, Christmas may be enjoyed—though not to
> absurd excess—by those with a history of cardiovascular disease or high
> cholesterol levels.
> —STUTTAFORD, "LONG-LIFE STATINS"

> Great brands not only become part of patients' health and perception of
> well-being, they become part of their lives.
> —BOLLING, "DTC: A STRATEGY FOR EVERY STAGE"

In so many ways pharmaceuticals have become integral to daily life
in America. They help those on diets to have Christmas dinner; they
help schools fill up with attentive kids; they are part of our identities
as well as our lives. According to surveys of Americans, we are becoming more attentive and more self-conscious about health while
taking more drugs than ever before. As the advertisement for the
ADHD drug Strattera suggests (see fig. 25), this is neither shocking
nor exciting, it has become ordinary.

As we have seen, however, the information we need to take in to
keep up with our health is overwhelming and partial. A majority of
health facts are produced as part of investment strategies whose primary aim is, first, to grow the amount of medicine in our lives and,
second, to keep coming up with more facts and more "health" for us to

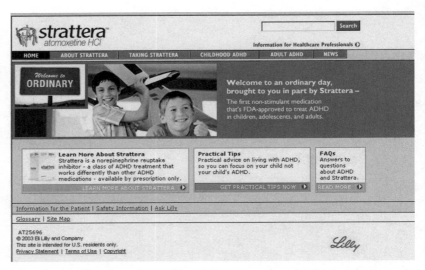

FIGURE 25 "Welcome to Ordinary" on the Strattera website by Lilly.

to take care of. Even doctors cannot keep up with the deluge of risk facts and health revisions. When a colleague asked her doctor about the necessity of a recommended colonoscopy screen, she was handed a fifteen-page document that outlined a number of contradictory positions: some groups, like gastroenterologists, recommended it; others did not. The extra information in the packet did not settle the issue at all but made it more complicated and at the same time seemed to make her responsible for any adverse outcomes because now she had been informed.

So how do we survive this flood of facts? I want to consider different modes of living with the notion of mass health described in this book, in which our environment is that of risk management, surplus health, maximum prescriptions, and we are doing everything possible within it. Most patients are not passive in the face of facts, advertising, and culture.

On the basis of my analysis of interviews with people about their pharmaceutical living, and accounts of practices online and off, I have identified three modes of biomedical living within a constant flow of health information: expert patienthood, fearful subject of duties, and better living through chemistry. Each of these modes exists within a "risk society" as described by Ulrich Beck, where risks are pervasive and catastrophic but also unseeable and barely controllable. All of the modes of biomedical living presume that we are responsible, self-managed individuals; each is suspicious of the clinical trials and marketed facts that permeate our informational environment; and each is actively inventing solutions to the contradictions of too many facts and too many competing risks. Within this shared discursive space, people have nonetheless adopted diverse pharmaceutical lifestyles.[1]

These modes are not types of people, but different ways that each of us has of relating to information, risks, facts, and newly discovered symptoms. We switch between them depending on the illness, the risk, the treatment, our knowledge, and our current situation. These modes are promoted to us in ads, in health pamphlets, and by our doctors; they are amplifications of our own inventive ways of making sense of the facts we are told about our world. They are logical forms that are worth separating because they reveal how effectively we have adapted to the notions of inherent illness, mass health studies, and drugs for life.

EXPERT PATIENTHOOD—HEALTHY LIVING

The first mode of biomedical living, expert patienthood, is embodied by Andy Grove in the extreme of obsession and paranoia. The expert patient is an expert at being a patient, at living the lifestyle of the good patient. The expert patient knows all of his or her numbers, watches them, and will help others do the same. Headlines like "Healthy Living a Numbers Game; Knowing Your Cholesterol Levels Crucial" reinforce the generalized anxiety that Grove lives with, that danger is ever-present but can be reduced and managed with enough research and effort.[2] Expert patients often volunteer advice guides and columns, especially online. Both Grove's and Alexander's articles (see chapter 1) are exemplary in this regard. Grove looks at the facts and seeks aggressive treatment while Alexander looks at the same facts and adopts a wait-and-see attitude, yet both have thoroughly researched what actions to take and chosen what is best for their health. They tell personal narratives by presenting facts, advice on how to keep current, and exhortations to be more involved with one's health.

To Grove, health is an ideal that can be achieved through the mists of facts. It exists, as an optimal, but also as something that future research might contradict. Therefore it is a mode of optimizing the available facts and correcting for the biases inherent in their production. It is a paranoid or skeptical mode, but also an optimistic one: an optimal choice can be made and even if it includes risk, this can be borne proudly. The truth is out there. With pessimism of intellect and optimism of will, one is guided by the facts and one's lifestyle becomes one's healthstyle. Health is the rational basis of actions.

The expert patient who lives to be healthy is the idealized product of the past fifty years of pharmaceutical marketing. As Jeremy Greene documented, the "Know your level" campaigns of the 1970s created alliances of public health, pharmaceutical companies, and doctors' associations to identify the 25 percent with undetected high cholesterol. These efforts led to ads and articles in women's magazines and to health lobby groups "brokering disease definitions and their promotion in late-twentieth-century health politics."[3] We can think of the expert patient as a consumer who adopts a public health attitude toward himself or herself and is always on the lookout for better information.

Contemporary ad campaigns add more risky numbers to one's concerns. Interviewing women about their reactions to breast cancer chemoprevention campaigns like "Know your number," Linda Hogle found that many women assumed the role of expert patients "who are in control of information and confident that they can sift through the good, the bad, and the commercial." "I think information is always good," said one woman, explaining the agenda-setting advantages of awareness. "Advertising gets women thinking about [these conditions]." Another expressed more skepticism and said she "would have researched it." Hogle notes that most of the women assumed that the ads were screened and therefore biased but not false. The ads, she argues, emphasize women's autonomy and informational empowerment through prevention and self-care. But she notes, "The women's health movement promoted preventive health as a way to be less dependent on the medical establishment, and to preserve women's autonomy in decision making. Co-opted by medicine, prevention has become a marketing technique to link women to specific health providers for their future health needs."

This notion is very explicit in ads: "Are you a helpless female? [. . .] Will you simply sit back and ignore a way to possibly reduce your chances of getting breast cancer? We think not."[4] This rhetoric has called the reader into the expert patient position and pictures the only variable as whether the patient might not know something. The experts that the patient might want to rely upon, like her doctor, are systematically disqualified, since obviously her doctor did not tell her about this (see chapter 3). Crises for the expert patient take the form of uncertainty and controversy. Critical information is often missing, and the field of facts is tragically filled with scandals and problems. Time is spent collecting and correlating information to counter these in an attempt to be healthy.

The power of the expert patient is reinforced by the growth in markets for home testing,[5] and the rise of direct-to-consumer lab services is one indication that numbers and risk monitoring are becoming common. David Healy suggests that without the home weighing scale, anorexia would not have been possible in its current form. Whatever the underlying pathology, the ability to constantly weigh oneself is integral to the identity of an anorexic. Similarly, João Biehl found that AIDS testing among the middle class in Brazil created the possibility for new forms of techno-neuroticism to develop.[6] Numbers take on a magical or fetish-like quality not only in marketing campaigns and news media, but also in the advice of patients to one another who have learned to negotiate a dysfunctional medical system. Expert patients understand that they have to take charge of their medical care from beginning to end, beginning with demanding the right tests and then literally keeping these results with oneself so one can chart one's progress. The journalist Mary Linton describes how to become an expert: "Don't wait until your number's up to get to know your numbers, my doctor told me. Heart disease is a numbers game and all the latest evidence indicates that we could all learn to play it better. . . . And that's as easy as one-two-three. One, demand your doctor give you a fasting blood cholesterol test every couple of years; two, discuss the results with your doctor; and three, ask for a copy of the lab report so you can have your own record and reminder that you need to work on those numbers."[7]

Grove underlined the idea that numbers motivate. Numbers as measures of risk give you time, he argued, and it is your job to make the most of this time. Newspaper articles often boil down trial results into a series of easy-to-follow steps. Discussions like the following are a common type of advice:

> If you're concerned about cholesterol, these are some of the things you should ask your doctor about, suggests Dr. Matthew Sorrentino, a cardiologist at the University of Chicago: "What are my specific cholesterol levels—both LDL, or 'bad,' and HDL, or 'good?'" If a person knows

what his LDL and HDL levels are, that can motivate a patient to work at lowering the bad and raising the good," he said.

What level of risk am I at? Someone at a 1 percent "risk per year" of developing heart disease will have a different treatment plan than someone at a much higher risk. "The higher the risk, the more aggressive the treatment," Sorrentino said.

What can I do in my daily life to improve my health? The American Heart Association recommends that you reduce fat to less than 30 percent of daily calories, and that you exercise 30 minutes to an hour three to four times a week.[8]

The expert patient aims at health by adopting a healthy lifestyle. Health is a state that may never be fully achieved but that organizes a part of one's attention, energy, and lifestyle. It appears on the to-do lists and on one's online bookmark lists. As I suggested in chapter 2, the expert patient can be seen in the image of outsourced health. The medical system should take care of us and tell us what to do, but it does not, and when it does tell us what to do we do not trust it. Health as a fact-finding mission is too crucial to leave to the experts. As Grove says, if you manage your money, you should manage your health.

One extreme form of expert patienthood is hiring your own health consultant. Some HMOs have even started offering *prospective medicine* that one-ups preventive medicine and includes a personal health coach, one's personal health mission statement, and a long-term plan.[9]

Another extreme form of expert patienthood is to adopt the polypill approach to every risk. As discussed in chapter 5, regarding the polypill article, Wald and Law suggested that measuring risk was a time waster since everyone was at risk and *being* at risk was the proper starting point. Confirming this regress of pursuing risk to the earliest possible point, an issue of *Newsweek* in 2005 included a special advertising section—an advertorial—on women's health containing a section called "Keeping your heart healthy is a risky business." It critiqued the classic Framingham Heart Study (which discovered the high cholesterol link and conceived the concept of risk factors) as not looking deeply enough into the nature of risk. The problem with existing risk scores, the authors argue, is that they only treat risks for heart attacks in the next ten years. They accuse these horizons of being too small and the imagination as being too limited.

In place of primary prevention for intermediate risk women, the advertorial introduced "Primordial Prevention . . . identifying women likely to develop a heart condition before any symptoms arise." The method for this ur-prevention is for women to ask their doctors to treat them as if they were already seventy years old. Risk-time is collapsed into the present and onto the bodies that now must bear their possible futures in the form of treatment. Similar to what the sociologist Silja Samerski encountered in her analysis of genetic counseling, women here are asked to "see themselves as risk profiles" and in this way to become "physically compatible" with pharmaceutical treatment.[10]

The advertorial is written as an objective account of research but nevertheless directly demands that all women respond to the inferior treatment they must be getting. It identifies you as the heroic expert patient who should demand that your doctor treat you as if you were already seventy. Literally, you are being encouraged to see that the purpose of your life, your health right now, is to care as much as possible about your future health. You are being told to use the current health that you do not immediately need to consume medications so that your future self will have improved health chances. It makes sense, and yet the surplus health logic has slipped in: if you *can* take drugs that may help you, then you should.

The expert patient oscillates at this edge of paranoia. You must learn (become sophisticated), determine (self-diagnose), and demand (emplot your doctor). It is really in your hands now, as it looks like you can't take one step beyond awareness without sliding down the slope toward acting on it. You have a Hobson's choice, really only one choice. Yet you can never be well enough informed, up to date, ideally medicated. Between Grove's calculated gamble on the best future and ur-prevention's extreme consumption of the future lies the healthstyle.

FEARFUL SUBJECTS: UNAVOIDABLY COMPROMISING HEALTH

> Fear factor got my life back in shape. . . . The doctor conducting the test stopped it after three minutes and said: "There's no doubt you've got coronary heart disease." I was terrified and decided to change my life there and then. When people say to me, "How did you change your eating habits and give up smoking both at the same time?" I say one word: "Fear."
>
> —CLEMENTS, "WHY IT'S BEST FOR YOUR BODY IF YOU ASSUME THE WORST"

The second way people may incorporate biomedical facts is through fear and pressure. These persons do not so much seek health as try to avoid illness and risk. They see themselves as threatened by, but ever avoiding, becoming patients. Whereas the expert patient changes his or her lifestyle in order to be healthy and to live healthily in a fairly systematic or unified manner, the fearful subject struggles with the pressures of avoiding harm from multiple directions. An article in the *Milwaukee Journal Sentinel* puts it this way: "As you sit there right now (and I apologize for assuming that if you're actually reading this on a treadmill), do you know where the debate stands on the health benefits and risks of drinking a glass of wine every night? How about an aspirin a day? One thing I know for sure: you could eat your weight in fruits and vegetables every day and it wouldn't be enough to satisfy the health police."[11]

Life is seen as being in competition with health. Health takes away enjoyment, constrains actions, cramps your lifestyle, and adds to worries. Jokes about the health police indicate an anxiety about how to respond when there is too much to know and too many facts to listen to. Health promotion throughout the twentieth century has argued that food and lifestyle are to be intensive objects of responsible self-action. Exercise, special diets, activities are promoted for their health-giving properties as part of positive lifestyles that looked and felt fit and healthy. Robert Crawford has argued that in the 1970s health promotion accelerated dramatically with risks, self-management, and health as a goal and state to be achieved. Risks as imperceptible dangers contributed to a sense that feeling one's own body and experience, could no longer guide action. Expert knowledge, epidemiological correlation, and possibilities had to be attended to.[12] Biomarkers like blood pressure and cholesterol and checklist diagnoses of depression contributed a need for constant objective surveillance through tests. One can follow rules, but one can never be sure one is safe.

Following the release of the 2001 guidelines, journalists tried to understand how to follow them: "[Dr.] Orchard acknowledged that meeting another set of goals could be hard for some patients. 'They do have a lot of pressure achieving their own blood sugar controls and now to add more stringent blood pressure and lipids is a further challenge to them,' he said. 'But I think it is one that the evidence suggests is well worth taking.'"[13] The patient is here assumed to be naturally resistant and noncompliant. Public health can respond to this patient only by upping the ante of pressure and fear. Fearful subjects are the product of many marketing campaigns starting from a public health perspective in which "even before the value of medication has been proved, a disturbing test result could provide added motivation to stop smoking or get moving on a heart-healthy diet and regular exercise. A nation where more than half of all adults are overweight or obese needs every tool it can get to head off cardiovascular problems."[14] In turn, some subjects identify their ability to change as a direct product of fear.

Whereas the expert patient adopts a healthy lifestyle, the fearful subject sees his or her lifestyle as being at odds with health yet dependent upon it, leading to a terrible double bind solved not by choice but by fear. Marketers recognize that pharmaceuticals integrated into lifestyles in this way require constant reinforcement that cannot always be negative images of death to be avoided.

Part of the growth of fearful health is owing to the medicalization of food. Food increasingly comes to be judged not just for its taste and nutritional value (meeting daily requirements) but as medicine, as treatment for risks on a par with that of pharmaceuticals. These are traditional foods, breakfast, lunch, and dinner fare, that have either been shown to have preventive benefits in clinical trials or actually have medicines embedded in them. Variously called functional foods, designer foods, nutraceuticals, and true health foods, they are one approach to maintaining an everyday awareness of the need to be vigilant about avoiding risk and illness. Cheerios, one of the leaders in this category, features commercials in which a man cannot stop telling everyone he meets that he lowered his cholesterol. Viewers are informed that he did this through his breakfast cereal.

In the commercial, one car pulls up next to another at a stoplight, and a man motions for the neighboring driver to roll down his window. The first man says, "Hi. I . . . uh . . . lowered my cholesterol." The other car driver looks confused; the commercial continues to show scenes of the happy man telling his office workers and someone on his cell phone that his cholesterol is down. At one point, a male voiceover announces, "In case you haven't already heard the news, Honey Nut Cheerios [the camera then zooms in on the "may lower cholesterol" label on the box] can help lower your cholesterol as part of a heart-healthy diet." The commercial concludes by asserting that Cheerios is "the only leading cold cereal clinically proven to help lower cholesterol in a low-fat diet." Health in this commercial is defined as *not* being ill or at risk. The ad implies that one's aim should be to minimize one's risk. Health is not a state to be achieved but a form of vigilance in which one is always behind, always at risk, involving a pessimism of will in that one is always failing to be as healthy as possible. It seems that one is always finding out that a previous food may have been riskier than one thought.

The fearful approach to health struggles above all with lose–lose dilemmas, impossible choices between two risks. One must decide whether the benefits of a treatment are worth the risks (side effects) of taking it. In either case, one takes on the responsibility for the results: one will either be responsible for side effects or for the risky event: lose–lose.

A paradigmatic example of this is a study in 2004 that found that farm-raised salmon contained high levels of cancer-causing PCBs.[15] The study was quickly picked up and publicized by newspapers and other mass media. In an article entitled "Salmon: Health Food or Pink Poison?" the fearful subject was directly addressed: "Like alcohol and chocolate before it, salmon is now the subject of contradictory science. So what is the bewildered, bemused consumer to do, pelted with so many admonitions about what to eat, what not to eat, and how to eat it?"

This article and many others treated the study as one more outcry in a cacophony of cost-benefit risk factors. Readers are urged to "gauge the size of the study" and "ask what standards were used." In the case of salmon, however, there is an additional level of difficulty in that salmon is supposed to have protective, medicine-like benefits. The dilemma is that not eating salmon, like not taking a statin, would appear to increase one's risk of heart disease, while eating it would increase one's risk of cancer. To help readers solve this impossible choice, two nutritionists from Tufts University were consulted. They offered a new iteration on the idea of personalized medicine, one in which one's imagined genetic makeup is used to tailor drug treatment:

> "We're all bombarded with so much information every day," [the nutritionist named] Lichtenstein said. "So we have to customize it and take our own individual situation into consideration." . . .
>
> "If you're worried about family histories of arrhythmia and Alzheimer's, I would say you probably want to err on that side and eat the fish," said Katherine Tucker, director of the Epidemiology and Dietary Assessment Program at Tufts. "But for other people, especially those

who have endured cancer or who have a family history of the disease, the equation might work out differently."[16]

Literally, it is one's fear that guides one's objective calculation of a generalized health plan and diet, a determination of whether one worries more about heart disease, Alzheimer's, or cancer. The result is a tension at the level of the fear itself.[17] With the forced choice of whether to eat or avoid salmon, of deciding which is the lesser of two potential evils, one finds oneself in a position where one must actively put oneself at risk and take responsibility for the outcome. Choice here becomes deeply regrettable: if one gets cancer or heart disease or Alzheimer's, one will have been responsible for it. While assuming responsibility for the outcomes of our health behaviors is a laudable goal, here it reaches an absurd and exploitable limit: one must do everything possible precisely because one can never do enough.

Along similar lines, two new margarines have been "manipulated to pack a medical punch."[18] So far, most of these functional foods are aimed at cholesterol and heart disease because cholesterol is easily measured and therefore trials are easier to conduct. These foods all market facts in the form of special labels and claims that clearly aim to increase consumer anxiety over eating the wrong food—at the same time, they reinforce the image of mass health that can be managed only scientifically through treatments. "The growth of functional foods represents a more positive message that 'plays very well,' said David B. Schmidt, senior vice president of food safety for the International Food Information Council. 'It tells people, "What you do eat may be more important than what you don't eat."'"[19] This is a form of consumptive doing: "'The advantage of having these margarines on the market is that they provide consumers with yet another food choice in an overall diet strategy to lower cholesterol,' Carr said. 'The disadvantage is if they give the false impression that using these margarines by themselves will prevent heart attacks.'"[20]

The same article goes on to add a worrisome point: "But could there be too much of a good thing? . . . Consumer advocates worry about possible side effects of functional foods."[21] Medicalization of food goes hand in hand with the generalization of biomedical living. Every choice of what to eat intersects with an anxious duty to be healthy.[22] This duty is in turn fraught with worries over not being informed enough.

Many people describe being healthy in this manner as an additional anxiety. Surveying health attitudes, Crawford found that people wanted what they felt were two contradictory things: to be healthy, which required denying pleasures, and to enjoy life, which required sacrificing health. They often settled into an oscillation between the two: ritualized ambivalence, acknowledging that both were important and hating that fact. Crawford writes, "The healthy self is likely to become more disciplined while continuing to assert her freedom to consume, relax and have fun. Anxiety and resentment are momentarily managed both by the assertion of control and by the continued 'resistance' to health norms in the name of pleasure."[23]

The opposition between what is pleasurable and what is healthy is characteristic of the fearful subject. This could be experienced as a constant tension between healthstyle and lifestyle.

BETTER LIVING THROUGH CHEMISTRY: LIFE AS PLAYFUL

> An obese diabetic who now exercises, "... continues to indulge his weakness of heart-stopping entrees, ... but he also knows he doesn't have to worry about cholesterol as long as he takes that little pill every day." It's better living through chemistry, he says.
> —NOONAN ET AL., "YOU WANT STATINS WITH THAT?"

Despite and because of the worries generated by overwhelming facts, many patients consume pharmaceuticals as a means of maintaining rather than changing a lifestyle. It is crucial to analyze the grammar of the obese diabetic's "better living through chemistry" comment. He is happy because he is still himself; part of his core identity, a "weakness for heart-stopping entrees," can still be indulged in. The subtle manner in which a weakness is not a flaw but a badge indicates that he sees his lifestyle as a biologically justified choice. His weakness is a physiological enjoyment that he chooses to indulge. Facts intervene twice in this enjoyment: first, they make him worry because they inform him of the risk he is at for heart disease; second, they allow him to counter this risk with a pill. Biomedical facts cancel each out in this pharmaceutical care of the self.

The pharmaceutical solution to the dilemma of health versus pleasure represents an innovation vis-à-vis Crawford's ritualization of ambivalence.[24] Pharmaceutical living offers a new choice through reconfiguring what is considered foundational and fixed and what is changeable

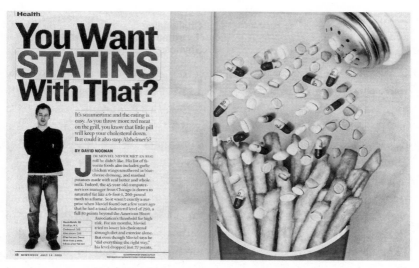

FIGURE 26 "You Want Statins with That?" *Newsweek* article, July 14, 2003.

and can be countered. The foundational message is one of risk. Given the many risks like high cholesterol for heart disease, you need to act. One *USA Today* article exhorted, "Lower your cholesterol by any means necessary: There's diet, exercise or medication."[25] The assumption is that the "you," in this address is always making choices. Pharmaceutical companies suggest that you are making a choice about your biology in any case: through exercising or not, getting a test or not, taking a drug or not. But also that if you choose any one of these you are at least doing something.

The *Newsweek* cover article that contains the diabetic's statement about better living through chemistry is entitled "You Want Statins with That?" (fig. 26). A following headnote reads, "It's summertime and the eating is easy. As you throw more red meat on the grill, you know that little pill will keep your cholesterol down. But could it also stop Alzheimer's?" The graphics, which include a mouth-watering steak on the cover and an image of statins spilling out of a saltshaker into a container of French fries, reinforce the sense that chemical living is a joke that needs to be taken seriously because biomedical facts are getting increasingly hard to swallow. Paul Braverman, a statin user and self-styled gourmand, states, "As a weak man without willpower or self-motivation, it's a lot easier for me to take the pill than to eat the damn veggie burger."

While the idea that one might balance one risk with another might seem nonsensical, the pharmacoepidemiologist John Urquhart provides a logic by which even proven-dangerous drugs like Vioxx should be ethically consumed. He argues that we should not panic over drugs like the Cox-2 inhibitors (Vioxx) that occasionally cause bad side effects or deaths. Borrowing the analogy of companies trading pollution credits, he points to "the possibility of 'risk-swapping,' in which a patient with a mix of risks and benefits has the option to omit or modify one or more life-style risk-factors in order to 'make room' for, for example, the use of a pain-reliever that seems to be providing the patient with uniquely strong analgesia."[26]

Urquhart decodes the underlying commodification of risk that the statins-for-steaks folks have independently invented. Treating risks as exchangeable is an eerie echo of pharmaceutical companies' treating of treatment numbers as exchangeable. There being no moral reason to distinguish between treatment profits, the lopsided research into Western, chronic disease treatments is fully justified. Similarly, the people who can best consume dangerous drugs like Vioxx are those who are full of other risks they can reduce, leading to a paradox, as Urquhart notices:

> Obviously, the tofu-eating, normotensive, non-diabetic, non-smoker who has an occasional drink (for its 10% reduction of coronary risk), and who daily exercises and consumes fruits and vegetables, leaves little, or no room for advantageous risk-swapping, but those with a probably more prevalent mix of risks and benefits might risk-swap advantageously.[27]

Urquhart's fuming disgust with healthy people and non-pill-takers assumes a norm in which most people have multiple known and measured biomedical risks. Epistemology again precedes ontology: what matters primarily is what you know, not what you have. One can swap risk only if one knows what those risks are, and therefore we need to grow our known risks in order to be able to take our medications. Being too healthy is the same as being ignorant!

Urquhart's language might strike us as being extreme, but in fact doctors and news media routinely normalize the kind of risk swapping he describes, allowing the transparent exchange of behavior, risks, and treatments. Sidney Smith, a former president of the American Heart Association, states, "The problem is that the changes needed are frequently very difficult. For some it is an inability to break habits, but for many, the reality is, it's just not palatable."[28] Often the logical claim is buried within a seeming opposite statement. After praising the discovery, need for, and value of statins, a doctor adds an apparent caveat: "Having said all of that, I most definitely do NOT believe that a medication (whether you take Zocor or another cholesterol-lowering drug) is the only thing that you should do."[29] His defensive qualification, "most definitely do NOT believe ... [it] is the only thing," actually asserts that medication does do quite a lot. Similarly, a doctor who is worried about overprescribing statins based on the new guidelines commented that doctors need to present their patients with all the options, "You've got to give the intelligent patient a [choice]. . . . I wouldn't want to be on the Ornish diet because I'm a carnivore. But if you follow his diet you will not have to take any pills."[30] Medication is here one option among many that can be matched to one's dietary style.

Medical defensiveness is often rendered as despair. One doctor wrote to the *Journal of the American Medical Association* to say, "While ATP [Adult Treatment Panel] III gives requisite lip service first to an attempt at instituting therapeutic lifestyle changes (with the quaint acronym TLC), one senses in the guidelines the hopelessness that those of us in clinical practice feel. I cannot persuade the vast majority of my patients to restrain their appetites and perform supplementary exercise. The ATP III recommends that we throw in the towel on TLC [and prescribe statins] after only 2 months."[31]

In all of these comments, the doctors no longer contemplate the causes of high cholesterol or heart disease. Pervasive existence is assumed as the starting point, and the crucial question is, What do we do about it? The prevalence of heart disease risk is fully naturalized as part of the condition of Americans, either currently or in their imminent future.

For the risk swapper, informed consent and consumer preference are fused so that intelligence is a means of rationally choosing one's lifestyle. Pushing Canguilhem into the era of direct-to-consumer marketing, life as "Lifestyle" here functions as normative, adapting to changing circumstances, circumstances that include both worries and knowledge. This is a newly adapted form of creative self-preservation.[32] People pose questions like the following to their doctors and to newspaper columns: "Q: If I take drugs to lower my cholesterol, can I chow down on cheeseburgers whenever I want?"[33]

The conclusion here is intriguing: one's DNA and biology can be managed now; they are what one makes choices about. Biology is man-made;

it is culture. Lifestyle, on the other hand, one's taste for meat, desire to be a gourmand, one's habits, are fixed. They are natural. Being self-styled is a natural right.

While it may seem a bit ludicrous to look at pill taking through the lens of lifestyle in this manner, it has some important consequences. First of all, side effects are actively attended to. Whereas the first two ways of living—expert patient and fearful subject—are predisposed to choose the best drug, statins-for-steak folks are oriented toward enjoying their lifestyle, and if a statin causes headaches or requires too many other drugs they will find another solution. Second, these patients are often actively noncompliant, inventing ways of getting the effects they want, as judged by their experience. Long-term risk-prevention drugs may be turned into "take as needed" drugs. Large NNTS are less persuasive.

CONCLUSION

Living in a World of Surplus Health

Frequently Asked Questions

The very concept of health has changed in ways that are both utterly familiar to us and unbelievably alien. In this new health we are dedicated to measuring our health by understanding our risks and taking practical steps to reduce them. This just makes sense to us. At the same time, as I've shown in chapters 3 and 4, this approach to health has the actual consequence of causing us to spend ever-increasing amounts of attention, energy, and money on health, vastly and continually increasing our pharmaceutical consumption. While this new health has strengths as well as weaknesses, it has been fitted into corporate research agendas and become something quite different, namely, surplus health, which looks like health but is valued only in terms of treatment growth because only that translates into corporate growth. As we have come to accept and live within this new notion of health, we have come to naturalize and desire this notion of health growth in ourselves. While there are many other concerns about the pharmaceutical industry, my book has attempted to isolate this specific aspect of the redefinition of health research.

The case I make on this transformation of research agendas is a strong one because I have taken it directly from the explicit goals of pharmaceutical marketing, and it is echoed by many other players in the pharmaceutical world. There is a growing recognition that marketing has taken over clinical trial design and therefore shapes the universe of known facts. Building on quotes from marketers' published literature, I have intended to make the logic of this treatment growth clear. In this conclusion, I've used the format here of an FAQ document to address a number of questions I am often asked when I talk about my work as well as questions about whether the FDA, the patent office, Congress, insurance companies, watchdog groups, alternative medicine, and pill resistance can help us. These institutions are each very important for other aspects of our health, but not for the growth of surplus health. Being an optimist, however (no matter how scary this book may seem), I end by looking at what might help.

FREQUENTLY ASKED QUESTIONS

1. If our actions are about health though, are things really so bad?
2. What is this new health as risk reduction?
3. How is health shaped by the questions we ask?
4. What is surplus health?
5. Should we regulate clinical trials better and get rid of the bad research practices of pharmaceutical companies?
6. Hasn't medicine always been driven by profit?
7. Are you against drugs? Many good doctors prescribe them. Aren't you generalizing too much in your statements?
8. What is the solution then? Aren't those ads on TV the real problem?
9. Are there other solutions? What about changing the patent system?
10. What about alternative medicine?
11. Are there doctor-suggested solutions?
12. Why can't we just do more studies?
13. Is comprehensive health surveillance the answer to our current health crisis?
14. What about the insurance industry?
15. Will any of the national health insurance plans change this?

1. IF OUR ACTIONS ARE ABOUT HEALTH, THOUGH,
ARE THINGS REALLY SO BAD?

This question launched my entire research project and continues to haunt me. I have two responses to it. The first is this book and my argument about mass pharmaceuticals: what we think of as health are facts based on clinical trials that have been designed to increase treatments, not decrease them. Our health is no longer indexed either to our felt sense of wellness or to our life outside of medicine. Rather, *being healthy* has come to mean spending more and more time, energy, attention, money, and side effects with medicine.

My second response is that there is overwhelming empirical evidence that every year Americans are getting more tests, more prescriptions, and prescriptions for longer periods of time, and they are worrying more about their health. At the same time, compared with people in other industrialized countries we are not living longer or suffering less. Researchers like Gilbert Welch have shown that the increased five-year survival rate for cancer, for instance, is an effect of earlier testing, not a decrease in annual cancer death rates. While there are amazing new drugs for some illnesses, caring doctors, and lives saved throughout the medical system, the topic of this book—health as risk reduction through mass-consumed screens and pills—is deeply contradictory.[1]

In other words, I am arguing not against health or even public health but against the hijacking of a logic of public health to claim that all population risk reductions are healthy. As I suggested in chapter 4, the statistical medical revolution that took place in the 1950s through the 1970s gave birth to clinical trials as we know them now, that is, trials based on the argument that some effects can't be seen individually in patients but require us to take a group of patients, treat them regularly, compare them to a control group, and measure the outcome. An important part of that practice is that it is done for a condition that is known and defined in advance. In those cases, it is great and effective and does what it is supposed to. What Geoffrey Rose showed in defining preventive health was that clinical trials could also be conducted on risk factors; trials discovered biomarkers (bodily measures) that were correlated with future adverse events like heart attacks. These measures are on a continuum, however, and cannot themselves tell us where to draw the line between treatable conditions and general variability. Rose worried about the risk that public health officials would come to measure health by the number of interventions rather than by the overall reduction in illnesses. Then there would be a drive to treat the smallest amount of risk because it would count as increasing health.

This logic of increasing treatments is precisely what pharmaceutical companies feel themselves driven to do in order to maintain the growth in revenue that shareholders like ourselves demand. Even though clinical trials cannot tell us where to draw the line on whom to treat, we nonetheless allow them to do so. Most large trials simultaneously test a treatment for reducing risk and define what counts as a treatable condition. And that reduction in a biomarker comes to count as being more healthy, and having that risk becomes a kind of illness. A lot of people, all of us, in fact, talk about having a risk as a disease. It is a sliding kind of measure, and where we draw the line in terms of health is a social decision.

2. WHAT IS THIS NEW HEALTH AS RISK REDUCTION?

In a lecture delivered in 2005 entitled "Health Care in the Twenty-First Century," then–Senate Majority Leader William H. Frist tells a utopian story of healthcare in 2015 in which a fictitious patient takes a single (eight-in-one) pill each day, is constantly monitored, and spends a great amount of time not only monitoring his health but also checking in with his team:

> The patient, Rodney Rogers, is a 44-year-old man from the small town of Woodbury, Tennessee. He has several chronic illnesses, including diabetes, hypercholesterolemia, and hypertension. He is overweight. He quit smoking about eight years ago. His father died in his early 50s from a massive myocardial infarction. In 2005, Rodney chose a health savings account in combination with a high-deductible insurance policy for health coverage.
>
> Rodney selected his primary medical team from a variety of providers by comparing on-line their credentials, performance rankings, and pricing. Because of the widespread availability and use of reliable information, which has generated increased provider-level competition, the cost of health care has stabilized and in some cases has actually fallen, whereas quality and efficiency have risen. Rodney periodically accesses his multidisciplinary primary medical team using e-mail, video conferencing, and home blood monitoring. He owns his privacy-protected, electronic medical record. He also chose to have a tiny, radio-frequency computer chip implanted in his abdomen that monitors his blood chemistries and blood pressure.
>
> Rodney does an excellent job with his self-care. He takes a single pill each day that is a combination of a low dose of aspirin, an angiotensin-

converting-enzyme (ACE) inhibitor, a cholesterol-lowering medication, and a medication to manage his blood sugar. That's one pill daily,
not eight. He gets his routine care at his local clinic. He can usually
make a same-day appointment by e-mail.[2]

The new form of health I have been outlining in this book is built of
a number of components. The primary one is that health is defined in
large part by risk. Being at risk seems to be something we can easily talk
about, and it is a basic way in which we make sense of the world: which
foods to eat, drugs to take, car to drive, mutual funds to invest in—all
these are matters of risk that we assess and make decisions about. If I am
at risk for a heart attack, then I am to some extent unhealthy and should
take steps to reduce that risk. It appears to be a no-brainer that to reduce
one's risk is to increase one's health. As savvy new-health consumers
(see chapter 2), we seek out the latest information on risks and attempt
to reduce them. This makes perfect sense, but it has an uncanny consequence. As this risk-reduction notion of health becomes more prominent
in our lives, we begin to see our current wellness as a resource to spend
to reduce those future risks. And because each risk, however small, is
about one's health or even life, almost any exchange that reduces it can
seem worth it. These exchangeable resources include our free time, our
expendable income, our attention and worries, and our bodies. Among
the other things, we take pills now, with all of their attendant costs, including to our bodies through side effects, because we understand that
they are preventing future illnesses. We essentially start treating our current wellness as surplus health that can be used to increase our future
health through reducing risks. If each case of risk reduction seems worth
it, however, the aggregate may not: at some point you might be spending
all of your surplus health for your future health, putting up with a life of
side effects for the sake of living longer.[3]

One of the greatest triumphs of the twentieth century, public health is
founded on the principle of early risk reduction. Mass change in certain
behaviors, diets, and drug taking improves general health. The idea that
statistics can be used to discover low-level health changes in a population
is an important part of public health. As historians like Jeremy Greene
have pointed out, pharma companies have extended and invested risk reduction numbers with expertise. By reducing health to a series of numbers that require expert interpretation, they have "black-boxed" the status

of our health. Our health data are seen as value-neutral and now the subject of expert knowledge.

This is a relatively new way of thinking of health, one that we, as a culture, inhabit. Such thinking is not the sole fault of pharma companies or the healthcare industry; they are part of this health, but they are reframing it in ways that are not easily analyzable. One way they extend this notion of health involves drawing lines in order to create categories like high cholesterol as being at high risk for a heart attack. If a line is moved slightly it often indicates millions more people for treatment. Clinical trials are not capable of telling us where to draw the lines, but they are nonetheless being used this way.

Risk is a highly fungible concept when it comes to health. It depends on large-scale trials in order to be discovered at all. And the flipside of risk as discovered by trials is that it is no longer connected to how you feel or to something a doctor can see, though it can be transformed into biomarkers like cholesterol. Another problem is that many risks are incredibly small, far in the future, and possibly not in fact present at all. It is part of our basic understanding of health today that if you are measured and found to have high cholesterol, then regardless of how you feel you are at risk, and you should do something or take something to reduce that risk.

The problem with this way of understanding health is, again, that it takes a part of risk and treats it as one-size-fits-all. How much at risk for heart disease does your cholesterol score indicate? The line you cross for high cholesterol keeps getting lowered, four times in the past two decades, each time transferring millions of people from a not-at-risk category into an at-risk one. Whether they are truly at risk or not is not the right question; in fact, it is a nonsensical question. On an absolute level there is a risk, and on a very obvious level we are all at risk of dying within ten years, five years, one year. What has changed is that health is no longer keyed to either an experiential sense of wellness or an absence of disease and imminent danger. Rather, our nonhealth, or risk, is defined by the fact that we can reduce it by taking a drug (see chapter 4). To put this more starkly, if a trial shows that a population may have fewer adverse events in the future by taking a medicine now, their current status shifts from being healthy to being at risk, and they are indicated to take the drug. The trials define our nonhealth.

Yet it may not in fact be our risk. Imagine a clinical trial conducted on men and women over thirty that found that taking a drug every day for a year reduced the overall heart attack rate by one in five hundred. In aggregate, the drug helped the population. Depending on how you think of that number, it may seem obvious that the drug may help you as a member of that population. But individually it may be helpful to only a small subsection of that population that may not include you at all. Another trial of the same drug could show that almost all of the effectiveness is in men over fifty-five. If you knew only about the first trial or if that had been the only trial conducted, then it seems you have no choice but to act as if the risk reduction applies equally to everyone over thirty. You have no choice because the kind of fact you and your doctor and all of us are confronted with is a statistical fact, and one so difficult and expensive to produce that it is almost impossible to question it.

One crucial insight of this book is that if clinical trials define our non-health, then the questions they ask or don't ask determine the extent to which we understand ourselves as being ill or at risk, and they determine our obligation to treat and reduce that risk. If that risk is a deadly one, then, no matter how small, it is hard not to be caught up in morally doing everything one can to reduce it, including accepting short- and long-term side effects and high costs both individually and as a nation. The issue becomes one of understanding how those clinical trials are designed.

3. HOW IS HEALTH SHAPED BY THE QUESTIONS WE ASK?

Before we can ask how questions about which clinical trials to run are chosen, we need to ask who chooses them. So far in this conclusion, I've discussed clinical trials in terms of medical risks and health values. But clinical trials are big business. It seems another no-brainer that if clinical trials are incredibly expensive to run, then the nation should outsource their running to pharmaceutical companies, who, after all, use them to show that their patented medicines work. Yet everything changes when that outsourcing happens.

First of all, companies run clinical trials as investments. Even as this makes sense, it means a shift takes place in the notion of health value. When we consumer-patients think of the value of a clinical trial, we measure it in terms of how it reduces our illnesses and contributes to our well-being. A company, however, measures the value of a clinical trial in terms of the potential sales of medicine it promises. The larger the market for the drug, the more valuable the trial is for them. And when it comes to deciding which clinical trials to run, one that has the potential to indicate treatment for tens of millions (even if the drug needs to be given to five hundred to help one) is clearly more valuable to a company than a drug indicated for only fifty thousand (even if that drug would help most of those treated). We can see in this that because health has come to depend on the clinical trials posed, health becomes manipulable.

One paradox, therefore, is that if trials determine what counts as risk, health, and nonhealth, then these all can be grown. One way to think of this is that health can be grown because risk can be grown. According to marketing textbooks (see chapter 5), risks can always be grown because no matter how much risk you have reduced through healthy living and treatments, you still have 100 percent risk of dying left to reduce. Each new trial potentially defines or creates a new risk and the treatment for it.

Health can also be grown precisely because it has been defined in terms of treatments. This is a second paradox. A traditional view of health sees medicine as being needed when one is ill, and as *not* being needed or taken when one is healthy. But if you are reducing your risk by taking a cholesterol pill every day, are you healthy or sick? If, in the United States, 5 percent more people are taking cholesterol-lowering pills this year compared with last year, are we sicker or healthier as a nation? Once we, in our everyday parlance, come to understand our health through the treatments we take, we actively participate in growing health.

Together these two paradoxes create a lived contradiction for us consumer-patients such that we are indicated to take more pills every year. Pharmaceutical companies have an incentive to design clinical trials that grow treatments rather than reduce illness because as companies they are under pressure from their shareholders to maintain revenue growth, which means treatment growth. They literally value ineffective drugs that reduce risk the smallest amount (but still something) over those that might be much more effective (and therefore have a smaller market). As consumer-patients, however, often the only facts we have about these drugs and these risks concern the questions posed in the trials. In this manner we can see how each year the number of pills we consume "naturally" increases.

In terms of knowledge, another way to put this is that to the extent pharma companies design clinical trials and therefore the facts we have about risk and health, then almost all the facts we have about treatments are about increasing their numbers. Health itself becomes what the anthropologist Michael M. J. Fischer has described as an "ethical plateau" where multiple technologies interact to challenge the very form of our decision making.[4]

To give an example of one ethical plateau, an article in the *New York Times* in March 2010 stated that the FDA was going to recommend a statin drug for *healthy* people. Doctors cited in the article were opposed to it. This article represents one of the limit cases I have been examining. A clinical trial of almost eighteen thousand people was sponsored by Astra-Zeneca to test healthy people and was widely reported as finding a 55 percent reduction in heart attacks in a year for those taking Crestor, among other claims. This sounds phenomenal, but because the risk of a heart attack in the population studied is so small, less than a half percent, the absolute reduction in heart attacks was 0.2 percent, or one-fifth of 1 percent. This means that five hundred people would have to take Crestor every day for a year to prevent one heart attack. According one cardiologist interviewed, "That [reduction is] statistically significant, but not clinically significant. . . . The benefit is vanishingly small. It just turns a lot of healthy people into patients and commits them to a lifetime of medication."[5]

Digging deeper into the approval process, the FDA voted twelve to four that the drug was valuable enough to be recommended for healthy people (the article is concerned with the possibility that market forces were acting both on the trial and within the FDA). Surprisingly, because the study had relatively quick success, it was halted after only 1.9 years instead of the planned 5. This means we will not know whether the effect holds up year after year, or whether there are longer-term side effects. In a meta-analysis of the trial data published in the *Archives of Internal Medicine* in June 2010, other researchers suggested that the data did not show such a success story and criticized the early halt. In other words, the design of the trial (whether or not it was directly influenced by AstraZeneca) was oriented toward producing only enough data to justify approval of mass treatment, not to confirm that mass treatment was effective in the long term.[6]

Two issues are at play here. First, as a consumer or as a doctor, one wants to know whether the approval of the drug means that everyone over fifty basically should be taking Crestor. Perhaps a subset in the study received more benefit from the drug than others. This may be impossible to tell from the study because the benefit came down to thirty-seven patients (out of the eighteen thousand). The tragic problem, from the point of view of my research, is that there is no incentive to do the research to figure out who would really benefit from the drug. That would involve an even more expensive study with the most probable result being that it would destroy AstraZeneca's market. The second issue is a very real worry regarding the circulation of knowledge about this study, as if Crestor were a miracle drug cutting heart attack risks in half (Crestor being a me-too drug, not the first but the sixth statin). This way of putting it encourages patients and doctors to overvalue the pill's benefits relative to its side effects and costs. But my analysis does not mean that the FDA is wrong in its decision. Rather, the FDA and all of us (doctors and patients) have been put into a position in which our capacities for decision making are exceeded by the material economy of fact production.

4. WHAT IS SURPLUS HEALTH?

Beyond letting pharma companies essentially decide what facts are available about treatments, there are even more troubling aspects to their control of the questions. When deciding what diseases or risks to research, and within that what populations to study, they have every incentive to maximize the number of future treatments they will sell. This means they aim to maximize both the number of people indicated for treatment and the length of that treatment, that is, the number of pills each of those people is indicated to take.

On one hand, that approach means that the most valuable illnesses are those that are treated as chronic: five-year risks are more valuable than one-year risks, and any long-term treatment is orders of magnitude more valuable to companies than cures (see chapter 5). That this is not a scandal is testimony to the fact that we have naturalized the notion that medical research can be seen in terms of an investment.

On the other hand, there is an incentive to study a risk in the widest possible population that will still show an effect. Companies will design the trial so that it picks out a very large population, for example, everyone over fifty in the Crestor study, even though groups of people in that study will have either no risk reduction or very little. Including these groups, though, vastly increases the size of the market. In technical terms, the companies aim for the largest NNT (in the case of Crestor, five hundred treated to save one) that will get approved. This means, counterintuitively, that they aim for the most minimally effective, the most ineffective effective drug.

In both cases, the purpose of treatment is no longer to reduce the need for future treatments but to increase that need. One way to understand the extension of the NNT is as surplus illness. If a study could be designed to find a population in which 1 out of every 20 people treated with Crestor for a year had one less heart attack, Crestor would be an amazing drug, but it would have a relatively small market. By studying a much larger population, the study effectively made everyone over fifty seem equally at risk and in need of the drug—technically it spread the risk out more thinly across a larger population, while keeping the dose steady. As a result, 480 more people are indicated for Crestor than my ideal 20. Because they are treated as being equally at risk and indicated for the same amount of medicine, we might consider understanding this process as surplus illness. As a result of the way the clinical trials were designed, 480 more people than necessary are labeled as ill and potentially will be treated.

I have made up the ideal number of 20 to illustrate the process of surplus risk expansion. The fact of medical research today is that there are many drugs whose NNTs are in the hundreds and for which there are clinical trials that could be done to cut that NNT in half or by much more. The result of such a trial would be taking millions of people off of drugs they are not being helped by, but another result would be cutting large markets in half or more. A drug company has no incentive to conduct such a study. Sadly, such studies are extremely expensive, involving even more variables than the clinical trials, so the incentive for the government to conduct them is very small as well.

The research that creates surplus illness fits quite comfortably with our commonsense idea of surplus health. The more we find out about new risks, especially remote ones for which there are pills, the more we can do about our future health and seemingly the more healthy we can become. Campaigns that imply that feeling well is a bit dangerous because it might lull us into not getting screened enough are both strategies for market expansion and the lived experience of new health.

Ironically, the more traditional view of health, in which being healthy was connected with not having to take medicines, not going to the doctor, not worrying about one's body, quite literally becomes one enemy. In chapter 4 I showed how the commercials we see on TV, namely, direct-to-consumer advertising, imply precisely this idea: there are many everyday experiences that are actually symptoms, we should be more concerned about this, we should go to the doctor to make sure, we should probably be taking even more drugs in order to be healthy. The transformation will be complete when, rather than trying to avoid healthcare or to live so that we do not need it, we more and more live to accumulate healthcare.

5. SHOULD WE REGULATE CLINICAL TRIALS BETTER
AND GET RID OF THE BAD RESEARCH PRACTICES
OF PHARMACEUTICAL COMPANIES?

Yes, we should regulate clinical trials better, but that is not what I am talking about in this book. One of the hardest parts of trying to present my research has been the polarization around pharmaceutical companies as either life-saving or evil and corrupt capitalists. Yes, there are terrifying abuses of clinical research going on at every level of the clinical trial, reporting of research, marketing of drugs, and concealment of emergent side effects. This is a crucial issue to study, and I have tried to point to the many excellent works that do this. It is a never-ending struggle in part because the scale of the pharmaceutical industry is so vast and the money involved so overwhelming compared to what is available to regulators that the incentives to cheat and deceive are truly frightening (and, as I discuss in chapter 5, when everyday citizens were asked to role-play what pharma company board members would do when faced with an emergent scandal, they all too easily knew how to play the uncaring capitalist).

I am talking about a different issue: what happens when companies do play by the rules and therefore use clinical trials to grow treatments. I have shown that if companies are allowed to design clinical trials, they end up shaping the very meaning of health, a health known only through those trials. Their valuing of clinical research in terms of how many pill prescriptions will result means that basically the only facts of health we have these days are about the value of more medicine. Other facts could be produced, those that would tell many people to take less medicine and that they are less at risk than previously thought, but they are few and far between because facts are expensive to research.

In the case of cheating on clinical trials, the FDA has a difficult mission partly because it has relatively few resources compared with the companies it is in charge of regulating and partly because regulating companies is a politically charged issue, and the FDA has had periods of greater and lesser government support. Despite this, the FDA continues to set the global tone for pharmaceutical regulation. When it comes to asking questions about the growth of treatment rather than about reducing illness, however, the FDA has no teeth and may not even have jurisdiction. By and large the FDA's mission is to evaluate the trials that have been conducted, not to insist that companies ask other questions.[7]

Even more tragically, what seem to be the most important issues in health today, namely, those illnesses that continue to devastate the developing world, are explicitly rejected by pharmaceutical companies as unworthy objects of research. Worth is quite literally turned on its head once clinical trials are seen as investments because if the potential patients cannot pay for the treatments, then the treatments are not valuable. Moreover, I have shown that the pharmaceutical industry is quite aware of this paradox: they explicitly discuss it in their textbooks, and they blame us for their predicament. We are addressed as citizens and shareholders who have created the monster they have to be, unable to produce unprofitable treatments. While it may seem disingenuous for companies not to take responsibility for the choices they make in research, I do think their refusal to do so is a direct consequence of the generally accepted notion that health can be turned into a growth industry. As shareholders, especially as holders of retirement accounts, pension funds, and mutual funds demanding good returns, we require companies to maximize their profits in the short term, and we punish them for not growing.

6. HASN'T MEDICINE ALWAYS BEEN DRIVEN BY PROFIT?

Historians would locate the shift from traditional health to the new health in the postwar period of the 1950s. As I outline in chapter 4, my claim is that there is a narrative within the pharmaceutical industry that a shift happened during the 1980s. Financial mergers and acquisitions led to corporate consolidation, and companies had to take on a lot of debt to survive, which meant they needed steady, short-term growth (versus long-term bets with short-term variability). This put great top-down pressure on the industry to look at research in terms of its relatively immediate payout.

At the scale I'm talking about, that is, blockbuster drugs, how much freedom do the pharma companies have? They would experience it as none. In clinical trials, which are by nature long-term, such constrictions meant showing that a trial, if successful, would have a huge payout: hence the pressure on the companies to bet only on large-market chronic drugs. They experienced this as losing the freedom to set their clinicians loose to do research on whatever is interesting. The large companies' current tactic for making long bets is to let small, so-called boutique companies do the research and then acquire the companies when they have a promising molecule. But only those new molecules that promise a huge market.

There are accounts in textbooks, for instance, about Lilly saying,"We used to be a medical company, now we are a financial one." I try to show how companies themselves started lamenting the loss of their souls: "No one cares about patients any more, just market share." I think there is a transition here when the debate has reached the point where the tensions have to be said out loud, and companies start asking us (society and shareholders) to save ourselves from their need for growth. The contradictions within the system about health have reached a crisis point: what used to be a question of how to make a profit out of health has now become a question of health *or* profit. I was surprised that this critique appeared first within the industry, but this is a crisis of expansion that the industry cannot help but become conscious of: however much they would like to make better drugs, they must research bigger ones. From within the system of corporate growth the very people making the decisions cannot decide otherwise. The question of ethics today thus becomes not what decision to make, but how to make a decision within financialized medicine.

7. ARE YOU AGAINST DRUGS? MANY GOOD DOCTORS PRESCRIBE THEM. AREN'T YOU GENERALIZING TOO MUCH IN YOUR STATEMENTS?

I am trying to get at a phenomenon that is not easily pointed out. I've been calling it mass pharmaceuticals or blockbusters. In addition to the large number of people who need to take these drugs in order for them to be effective in one person, there are two other crucial things about these drugs that are aimed at the largest possible markets.

One, they are not directed at specialists like psychiatrists or cardiologists or oncologists. Pharma ads on TV always say "ask your doctor," not "ask your specialist," even when they are talking about an antipsychotic or an anticancer drug. As I discussed in chapter 2, one of the aims of the industry is to have the blockbuster drugs prescribed by primary care physicians and nurse practitioners, precisely those who have the heaviest throughput of patients and are most dependent on pharmaceutical representatives for their information. The aim is to get the primary care provider to prescribe the drug on the basis of a short list of indications, and then you just keep repeating your prescription with them: you never go to see your specialist.

Two, in talking to specialists I have learned that the questions asked by the clinical trials are not the ones doctors would like to ask: When can I take a patient off of a drug? How do these three or four drugs interact? What are the long-term effects? These are critically important questions, but they would all result in shrinking the number of pills people take. Many drugs are supposed to be monitored post-marketing, in so-called phase IV trials. But by and large these have not been conducted by pharma even when required. And for simple reasons: they are expensive, there is no enforcement, and therefore there is no incentive for a pharma company to look for what could only be data that endangers their product.

8. WHAT IS THE SOLUTION THEN? AREN'T THOSE ADS ON TV THE REAL PROBLEM?

Certainly the vast panoply of pharmaceutical direct-to-consumer (DTC) ads on TV play a role in strengthening a commonsense attitude that health depends on continual risk reduction through drugs and that there are a seemingly endless number of risks to stay on top of. The companies expect us to be savvy consumers in search of information on symptoms and risks, information that we will then act on. The research conducted on DTC shows that they are effective in reframing people's expectations regarding treatment and risk prevention. These ads and their accompanying campaigns in print and online also teach people how to lobby their doctors (see chapter 3). Research into the effect of these ads on doctors has shown they are even more effective: patients who request treatments they have seen advertised on TV do in fact get more prescriptions than those who don't make the request, even though both groups present the same symptoms.

The key arenas for growth in mass treatment are at the trial-design stage, the establishing of mass risk levels, and our cultural attitude that risk reduction is always healthy. I began my research thinking that DTC ads were driving pharmaceutical consumption, but they turn out to be only mildly successful, and they are only a small part of the growth in posttrial health. The larger drivers of mass treatments are guideline committees and public relations (see chapters 2 and 3). The sheer scale of resources available to pharmaceutical marketers that allows them to shape human interest stories, newspaper articles, daily news videos, and internet facts enables them to shape our everyday knowledge through strategic ubiquity.

9. ARE THERE OTHER SOLUTIONS?
WHAT ABOUT CHANGING THE PATENT SYSTEM?

Many people in the industry claim we would have a less absurd system if we lengthened patents; they say patents are too short. While the notion may seem counterintuitive, consider the following argument: in the current regime, most drugs that come to market have a maximum period of about seven to ten years before their patent expires and generics can be made. At that point, the drug goes immediately from being a profit center for the company to the company's worst enemy. Worst enemy because the company's next generation of drugs needs to overcome all of the marketing for the original drug. The company needs to prove to doctors and the public that the drug it touted last year is now relatively ineffective next to its new one. This means more research, more marketing, and more expense to destroy the reputation of a drug that in many cases works perfectly well: its own drug. This adds greatly to the cost of the new drug. Extended patent life might actually enable the best drugs to be fairly tested and discovered, and it might cut down on the number of me-too drugs.

Getting rid of the patent system for drugs altogether is another proposal. That certainly seems like a good thing for health. I don't see why health should be patentable. Life shouldn't be either (as I'm writing this, decades of patents on genes are in the process of being overturned, thanks to the efforts of the American Civil Liberties Union). The argument for patenting has been the need for innovation, but one of the few things people regularly dedicate their life to with no financial incentive is saving lives. So thinking that financial incentives are necessary for health research seems absurd. But that is not what the industry says.

10. WHAT ABOUT ALTERNATIVE MEDICINE?

When I hear the question "What about alternative medicine?" I hear the following: if the medical industry values health in terms of treatment rather than a more holistic form of wellness, why don't we turn to alternative systems of taking care of ourselves? I thought so, too. But to my surprise, when I have conducted preliminary interviews with people about their alternative health practices, I found the same logic of health as risk reduction creating issues similar to those I have been discussing.[8] Many people take herbs and supplements because they stay on top of the latest clinical literature about these medicines and calculate their reported benefits in a manner similar to Grove (see chapters 1 and 6). To the extent that these clinical trials also study drugs for their improved risk outcomes, the result is that more and more people take more and more herbs and supplements. Like pharmaceutical trials, these trials are usually designed with the idea that the diagnosis of risk coincides with the indication of treatment. Partly this notion stems from the same problem with expensive clinical trials that come to be seen as investments. And it results in the same type of runaway logic, namely, that any evidence of risk reduction is good and should be followed. As in the case of pharmaceuticals, the improved risk may be approaching a vanishingly small number, and the possibility of side effects owing to interactions among the various substances being taken increases.

11. ARE THERE DOCTOR-SUGGESTED SOLUTIONS?

Given the current system in which the facts that have been produced are not sufficient to enable either patients or doctors to make good decisions about health and treatments, one suggestion echoed in a number of books by psychiatrists, cardiologists, and other specialists is to allow most chronic medicines to be sold over the counter. Why? Because the marginal risk benefit will be weighed more directly against side effects and costs. This is a mass democratic response to mass health.

A clue toward understanding the side effects of mass treatment might be seen in the work of Gilbert Welch, the author of *Should I Be Tested for Cancer? Maybe Not and Here's Why.* Among other fascinating and scary examples, he discusses the seeming paradox that being screened for colon cancer (through a fecal matter test) can increase one's risk of death. How can this be? In a study that compared fifteen thousand people (aged fifty to eighty) who were screened yearly for thirteen years to fifteen thousand who were not screened, 82 people died from colon cancer in the first group versus 121 in the no-testing group—screening saved 39 people from colon cancer. However, the overall number of deaths in both groups was the same: in the screened group, more died from other causes, especially heart disease. The study couldn't say why, but the mechanism Welch contemplates is that there are so few people who will get colon cancer in the first place that even with a good test the false-positive rate is high: about five thousand people were indicated for further exploration, including a hospital visit and sometimes minor surgery. Those five thousand have the fear of cancer; go into a hospital, which increases your death rate; have anesthesia; drive home afterward, and so forth. Together, these cause at least as many deaths as the few cancers that screening saved. But you do save some people from that cancer, and therefore it can be reported as saving lives.

Here is the tragic rub of risk prevention: clinical trials that study risks are limited to the populations they study, and shorter studies especially are not designed to check the limits of the risk reduction; neither are they able to say anything about real-world patients who often have multiple illnesses and are on multiple other drugs.

12. WHY CAN'T WE JUST DO MORE STUDIES?

One seemingly obvious solution to Pharma's designing and conducting the trials would be to have the government run more long-term mass trials like the Nurses' Health Study. Trials like this have resulted in the knowledge that hormone replacement therapy, long thought to provide great health benefits, was in fact quite detrimental to health. But such trials are too expensive to run continuously. And it is not easy to imagine how to take the design of clinical trials, the questions they ask, out of the hands of companies, who see them as investments.

The key ingredient missing in the circulation of knowledge today is the most surprising: data on the actual outcomes of long-term mass pharmaceutical usage. It is surprising because the data exist in all of our health records if we could find a way to study it in aggregate. Some steps in this direction are being taken, for example, in movements among doctors and the government to conduct much more "comparative effectiveness research."[9]

We have the best opportunity now to change that: more and more records are electronic. Healthcare is a spiraling cost that everyone agrees needs to be reined in, even if we disagree on how. If we had a way to analyze the mass facts that exist in our records, we could answer the most pressing questions that patients need answers to (and that HMOs want answers to) and that pharmaceutical companies say they want answers to. The questions include the following:

- What are the long-term effects of drugs?
- How long do chronic treatments stay effective? When can we stop treatment?
- What are the effects of multidrug interactions?
- What are actual long-term risk reductions versus overall mortality costs?
- What important population-specific issues are there?
- What potential effects do drugs have on diet, environment, hospital stays, treatments, and longevity?

Despite promising starts in this direction like the Sentinel Network at the FDA, outcome monitoring has been resisted for various reasons, HMO privacy and fear of lawsuits among them. HMOs won't share data because they are proprietary and a competitive secret and because of liability. Drug companies won't even collect the data because the results could potentially shrink their market and because of liability. Current privacy regulations like the Health Insurance Portability and Accountability Act of 1996 actively impede our ability to do research on outcomes.[10]

Maybe the whole country should be treated as an ongoing trial, a mass-observation study drawing on actual patient outcomes, rather than as a set of large-scale improper clinical experiments, its current state. I have talked with a number of people about taking this seriously. It would involve the open-ended collection of health records from as many people as possible stored in a public-key database, to which information could be added over time about an individual without allowing anyone to retrieve private data about that individual. Instead, only aggregate slices of data could be retrieved and analyzed. Ideally this could preserve privacy while allowing actual long-term outcomes data to be investigated.

13. IS COMPREHENSIVE HEALTH SURVEILLANCE THE ANSWER TO OUR CURRENT HEALTH CRISIS?

No. At best it is a stop-gap measure. It is an idea that takes the new understanding of health as risk reduction and evidence-based medicine to their ultimate extreme, challenging the limits of clinical trial value with an actual commitment to evidence. It definitely would help us understand the wellness value of current drugs and get many people off of them.

But this sort of solution would not solve the deeper issues of health research based on a model of capital growth. Neither would it alter the ongoing access issues of healthcare for the poor. These require a serious rethinking of the very meaning of health we have come to depend upon and of the value of healthcare in aggregate. And that means rethinking the relationship between health and the economy. Our nation's economic health seems dependent on the growth of the health sector. The Merck joke—it's good to have a pill that cures the disease, but it's better to have a pill you have to take every day—may be true for all of us in a most ironic way.

This book makes clear that the usual critique, namely, that profit motives work against our health, is both right and beside the point. The point is that corporate marketing logics are redefining health and our relationship to it in such a way that they are actually completely compatible and therefore very hard to criticize. Health facts are no longer neutral arbiters between different treatments but often the means to drive treatment growth. Faced with such interesting facts and strategic ubiquity, we as patients and consumers are placed in a position of deep critical uncertainty. Furthermore, outsourcing health research to companies grants them the choice in how to value which diseases to research and what sorts of treatments to design. To repeat, analysts inside the industry are calling for changes in incentives to save us from their structural violence. Taking on the reform of healthcare thus requires challenging the current infrastructure of health research.

14. WHAT ABOUT THE INSURANCE INDUSTRY?

When I started this research I thought HMOs and insurance companies were big enough to stand up to pharma companies, to criticize trial design and do research on reducing treatments. They were doing some of the best critical readings of clinical trials; some insurance companies have a whole group of analysts trying to figure out whether a drug really does something. They were highly critical of clinical trials for reasons very similar to mine. Then I presented this perspective on a panel that included a vice president of a large insurance company. After the panel he came up to me, put his hand on my shoulder, and said, "Well, in the short run you are right: we are against the pharma companies doing this massive expansion. But in the long run we have to grow too!"

So in the long run, to the extent that we all accept the new health model, with its ever-expanding health cost, the insurance industry can grow. It can grow because it can demand higher payments and premiums for good health reasons. The following quotation from the literature makes the point: "While analysts say drug firms and the companies that manage prescription benefits will gain from the increased sales, the costs will ultimately be borne by consumers. 'Managed care is no longer trying to control costs,' says Todd Richter of Bank of America Securities. 'Insurers will simply take whatever they have to pay for these drugs and pass that cost along directly to employers, who will raise co-payments and deductibles for their workers.'"[11]

Such views tell the story. When you see the growth, it is phenomenal. Every government projection for national expenditure on health shows a constant increase in treatments, insurance, time, money, and attention toward health (see chapter 1). It is taking an ever-greater percentage of our gross domestic product. And the insurance industry fights this only competitively because health growth is congruent with its growth model.

15. WILL ANY OF THE NATIONAL HEALTH INSURANCE PLANS CHANGE THIS?

In short, no. As they are structured, the national health insurance plans all start with the assumption that research is too expensive for the government to do and is instead the proper pursuit of for-profit companies. My sense is that pharma companies and insurance would grow either way. I wrote this book to help clarify the notion that until we recognize that health can be grown and that trials are being designed to maximize "health as treatment" rather than "health as freedom from treatment," there is no way not to grow it. We'd have to be against health!

If we define being healthy as not needing treatment, then the goal of medicine becomes reducing the amount of money and time we spend on it. But health is not only a significant proportion of our economy, it is also one of the major growth sectors, and we are regularly reminded by our political leaders that "the economy has to grow."[12] Or as Stephen Colbert might say, in order to save our companies and make the economy healthier we should all take more medicine.

We all say we want to cut healthcare costs and make medication more effective, but do we really mean it?

NOTES

Introduction

1. IMS 2011.
2. Akinbami et al. 2011; Express Scripts 2007; NCHS 2007; Pratt, Brody, and Gu 2011.
3. Pollock 2012.
4. Marks 1997.
5. Greene 2007.
6. The stories of these drugs and conditions are the subject of Greene 2007.
7. Ernst & Young LLP 2006.
8. Kremer and Snyder 2003, 2.
9. Bartfai and Lees 2006, 221.
10. See the Centers for Disease Control (http://www.cdc.gov/chronicdisease/over view).
11. Kleinman 1988a, 1988b; Strauss 1984.
12. Beck-Gernsheim 1995, 82. Risk and pharmaceuticals, especially psychopharmaceuticals, are the object of a growing body of social science scholarship. A number of these scholars have used a discursive analysis of the self in the late twentieth century to develop important critiques of the geneticization, somaticization, molecularization, and psychiatrization of society. These analyses focus on how the promise of therapy and the threat of risk form the kinds of persons we take ourselves to be: beings influenced by biology and amenable to social control through what we take to be self-chosen or managed freedom. They attend to the uses by hegemonic institutions like schools, the workplace, healthcare, and the military of pharmacological and genetic discourse for what Foucault called governmentality, acting on our actions so that we act in accordance with their objectives. On governmentality used in this way, see N. S. Rose 1999. On risk, genes, and pharmaceutical discourse, see Lakoff 2004; Nelkin and Lindee 1995; Nelkin and Tancredi 1989; Rabinow 1996; Rapp 1999; N. Rose 2003.
13. Centers for Medicare and Medicaid Services 2011.

14. Express Scripts 2007; Gu, Dillon, and Burt 2010.

15. "The health share of GDP is projected to reach 16.3 percent in 2007 and 19.5 percent by 2017" (Centers for Medicare and Medicaid Services 2008).

16. Light 2009. See also Angell 2004; Avorn 2004; Healy 2004; Kelleher and Wilson 2005; Moynihan and Cassels 2005.

17. At the same time, as I discuss in the conclusion, the doctor's pronouncement resonates with the practices of people who follow medical and alternative literature diligently and take handfuls of vitamins and supplements daily. My surprise in this case involved the apparent negation of side effects, long-term effects, and generalization of clinical trials to a general population that had not been studied.

18. Robert Aronowitz, 2004, talk presented at Harvard History of Science.

19. Wilkes, Bell, and Kravitz 2000; Wilkes and Shuchman 1989, 88, 90, 126, 128–29.

20. Kommers and Rainie 2003.

21. Greene 2007.

22. Zola 1972.

23. Trials are now oriented toward defining health according to the lowest possible threshold. Trials and epidemiological surveys are designed to maximize as much as possible the number of people eligible for treatment. Then, given a particular trial and a treatment, the imperative for the pharmaceutical company is to induce as many people as possible to take the drug or get the treatment. This outcome is a banal tautology repeated in every pharmaceutical marketing article. But it has profound consequences for traditional definitions of health, medicine, facts, and risk. These concepts become the instrumental means for realizing the goal of maximizing treatments.

24. Winslow 2004.

25. Bartfai and Lees 2006, 73.

26. Klein et al. 2002.

27. For these and more up-to-date figures, see Center for Information and Study on Clinical Research Participation (ciscrp.org), the Clinical Trial Registry (clinicaltrials.gov), IMS Health (imshealth.com), and M. Martino, "The Most (and Least) Efficient Big Pharma Companies," FiercePharma.com, September 28, 2010.

28. Cost data are at "Kaiser Fast Facts" (http://facts.kff.org/); clinical trial data are available at "Clinical Trials.Gov" (http://clinicaltrials.gov); Ernst & Young LLP 2006.

29. Ernst & Young LLP 2006.

30. Ecks 2005, 2008; Epstein 2007; Greene 2007; Hayden 2003; Hayden et al. 2007; Lakoff 2006; Peterson 2001, 2004; Pollock 2012.

31. Petryna 2009, 82; Fisher 2009.

32. Sunder Rajan 2008, 179.

33. She continues, "All the artefacts we make and the relationships we enter into have in that sense 'cultural' consequences, for they give form and shape to the way we think about other artefacts, other relationships" (Strathern 1992b, 33).

34. Extended interviews were conducted with twelve persons about their pharmaceutical use. This was done as part of the Working Group on Pharmaceuticals and
Identity that I started at MIT. Six participants and I conducted these interviews
and then collectively discussed their transcripts. Half-hour interviews were conducted over the phone or in person with thirty doctors by myself and a gradu-
ate research assistant and transcribed. Approximately two thousand messages
were collected from online discussions (GoogleGroups) about pharmaceuticals
and analyzed as "very large-scale conversations" using ConversationMap software
designed by Warren Sack. One hundred forty television pharmaceutical ads were
collected and transcribed. Eight thousand newspaper and magazine articles
were collected from LexisNexis by using keywords, and seven hundred articles
were selected for coding. All messages, interviews, transcripts, and articles were
entered into the program Atlas.ti for indexing and preliminary coding (Thomas
Muhr, Atlas/ti. Scientific Software Development, Berlin, 2005). They were then
printed out, hand coded, and analyzed through a method of grounded theory
adapted from Glaser and Strauss 1967. This method is described in more detail
in Dumit 2006. See also Clarke 2005.
35. The two main archives I used were twelve years of *Pharmaceutical Executive* and
two years of *MedAd News*. Business press coverage was obtained through Lexis-
Nexis and Factiva database services. Key articles (approximately 120) were selected
from these and added to Atlas.ti.
36. Talks were given to eight groups of doctors, including the Massachusetts General Hospital Psychiatry Department, Cambridge Hospital Residents, MIT Mental
Health Services, Grand Rounds at Alta Bates Medical Center in Berkeley). I also
spent six days consulting with marketing companies, arranged through the MIT
Industrial Liaison Program; these involved signed nondisclosure agreements and
the participation of ten marketers. The presentations were followed by question-
and-answer sessions that, with one exception, I taped and reviewed as well as
by extended discussions afterward and often by later e-mails. I call these activities constant ethnographic engagement because my ongoing formulations of the
structural problems of fact production and information navigation were actively
shared and critiqued by these groups, including many people who were actively
writing about similar problems. I also taught over six hundred students for seven
years in an undergraduate course, "Drugs, Politics and Culture," in which discussion, response papers, and term papers contributed another kind of focus group
setting for informed commentary and feedback.
37. Strathern 1992b, 33. She writes, "By 'ourselves' I do not claim to speak on behalf
of contemporary British society, but simply to identify myself with those who are
exposed—whether they wish for it or not—to a range of ideas and images now in
cultural currency. One does not have to be governed or preoccupied by such ideas
in order to be aware of their significance; it is sufficient that they have been conceived, expressed and thus made available as vehicles for further ideas. The issue,
then, is not whether these technologies are good or bad, but with how we should
think them and how they will think us." This "we" and "ourselves" are grammatical

subjects as opposed to what linguists call enunciatory subjects. It is also a grammatical collective as opposed to a plural first-person pronoun. These slippages or splittings are part of the performatives of rhetoric and of persuasion. On the historical and critical development of these forms in anthropology, linguistics, and philosophy, see Fisher 2009, chap. 1; see also Biehl, Good, and Kleinman 2007.

38. Bartfai and Lees 2006, 14.
39. Greener 2001, 122.

One. Responding to Facts

1. Grove 1996b. All quotations attributed to Grove in this chapter are from this article.
2. Grove's highly reflexive, self-aware account allows me to present a thick and dynamic description of the expert patient in a manner similar to Max Weber's use of Benjamin Franklin's writing in *The Protestant Ethic and Spirit of Capitalism*. See also Whyte, Van der Geest, and Hardon 2003.
3. Appadurai 1986; Kopytoff 1986.
4. Dumit 2004.
5. The work of the medical anthropologist Mary-Jo Delvecchio Good on the nature of physician competence in the United States, on narratives of hope, and on what she calls the "biotechnical embrace" is crucial in making sense of encounters like this. She describes the ethical difficulties of embracing and being embraced by biotechnology's promises, statistics, and failures. See M.-J. D. Good 1994, 2001.
6. Austin 1962 discusses the success and failure of statements seen as performatives. To the extent that we can attribute a performative goal to the doctor in this case, wanting Grove to talk to an oncologist, the doctor was unsuccessful.
7. On troubles with winking, see Geertz 1973.
8. "An exercitive is the giving of a decision in favour of or against a certain course of action, or advocacy of it. It is a decision that something is to be so, as distinct from a judgement that it is so; it is advocacy that it should be so, as opposed to an estimate that it is so; it is an award as opposed to an assessment; it is a sentence as opposed to a verdict. . . . Its consequences may be that others are 'compelled' or 'allowed' or 'not allowed' to do certain acts" (Austin 1962, 155).
9. Interview with a doctor by phone, 2003.
10. Del Vecchio Good et al., 1994; Fisher 2009; Gordon and Paci 1997; Mattingly 1994.
11. Many patient narratives have this serendipitous structure, both for illnesses treated by pharmaceuticals, in which they tend to be felicitous, and for illnesses that are undiagnosed or untreated, in which they tend to be tragic. On the latter, see Dumit 2006.
12. Grove 1996b.
13. For a review of PSA tests, problems, and ongoing controversies, see Hadler 2004. Also see http://www.mayoclinic.com/health/prostate-cancer/HQ01273 and http://tinyurl.com/HealthCrossroadsPSA.

14. This wider sense of medical emplotment is described in Mattingly 1998 and White 1973.
15. Mol and Law 2004.
16. Nelkin 1979. Modes of controversy studies are reviewed in B. Martin and Richards 1995.
17. Grove 1996a.
18. Monopolies in the pharmaceutical industry are explicit targets of critique in Angell 2004 and Abramson 2004.
19. In real life cases, then, we are dealing with a specific circumstance, a specific purpose, and a specific audience. With the idea of a description, just the facts, or what Austin calls the "constative," "we use an over-simplified notion of correspondence with the facts—over-simplified because essentially it brings in the illocutionary aspect. This is the ideal of what would be right to say in all circumstances, for any purpose, to any audience, &c. Perhaps it is sometimes realized" (Austin 1962, 146). He provides two examples: "France is hexagonal" and "Lord Raglan won the battle of Alma," in the latter case remembering that the battle was a soldier's one and that Raglan's order never made it to the battlefield. In both cases we respond with something along the lines of "it is true for certain intents and purposes," good enough for this but not for that. Austin suggests that there is no final true or false: "It is just [a] rough [description], and that is the final answer of the question of the relation of 'France is hexagonal' to France. . . . [It is] exaggerated and suitable to some contexts and not to others" (143–44).
20. These aspects of facts have a long history. See, for example, Chandler, Davidson, and Harootunian 1994; Poovey 1998; Shapin 1994; Shapin and Schaffer 1985.
21. See Epstein 1996; Klawiter 2002; J. S. Kroll-Smith, Brown, and Gunter 2000.
22. Wittgenstein 1991, 94.
23. For exhaustive reviews of these problems, see Avorn 2004 and Angell 1996.
24. Dr. Renata Albrecht, acting director, Division of Special Pathogen and Immunologic Drug Products, FDA, said, "And no one yet knows how to choose a population sample size or design that would alter that state and everybody would like to, because failed trials are a burden for everyone" (Anti-Infective Drugs Advisory Committee [AIDAC] 2002).
25. Attributed to Tom Laughren three years earlier, in U.S. Department of Health and Human Services, Food and Drug Administration, Center for Drug Evaluation and Research, Committee for Advanced Scientific Education Seminar Series, "The Use of Placebos in Clinical Trials and the Ethics of the Use of Placebos." Wednesday, April 21, 1999 (retrieved March 15, 2012, from http://www.fda.gov/downloads/Drugs/GuidanceComplianceRegulatoryInformation/UCM117671.txt).
26. Ibid.
27. The source of this controversy appears to be that the FDA and pharmaceutical companies actively prevented analyses of the data from taking place. Only after Attorney General Eliot Spitzer of New York launched a lawsuit against the SSRI manu-

facturers was it learned that GSK had suppressed the data. See also Healy 2003, 2012.

28. Fox and Jones 2009; Kommers and Rainie 2003.
29. Walker 2000, 4. In the early 1990s pharmaceutical companies were initially shy about going online, especially for legal liability reasons. But since direct-to-consumer advertising was allowed in 1999, they have developed named and sponsored websites in force.
30. Holliday and Grant 2003.
31. The key finding of Henwood and colleagues (2003) was that the women they interviewed about HRT relief for menopausal symptoms had developed a wide variety of information practices, ranging from outright skepticism to credulity to denial.
32. See Bloor 1983.
33. Holliday and Grant 2003.
34. Ibid.
35. Turett 2002.
36. Cox 2002.
37. For a history of this activism in AIDS and breast cancer, see Epstein 1996; Klawiter 2002.
38. Cox 2002.
39. Ibid.
40. Ibid.
41. See Angell 2004, 152.
42. Grefe and Linsky 1995.
43. Dumit and Sensiper 1998; see also Bell 2009.
44. Dumit and Sensiper 1998.
45. Good 2001; see also Good et al. 1990.
46. Healy 2002, 186–87.
47. Ibid., 160.
48. For a review of these studies, see Abramson 2004, chap. 7.
49. Rapp 1999.
50. Alexander 1996.
51. Ibid.
52. Rebonato 2007.
53. Crawford 2000.
54. Rapp 1998.
55. Alexander 1996.
56. Ibid.

Two. Pharmaceutical Witnessing

1. For histories of DTC advertising rules and regulations, see Hartgraves 2002; Hilts 2003.
2. Bolling 2003.
3. Express Scripts 2007.

4. Kaericher 2007.
5. Kravitz et al. 2005.
6. Aikin 2002.
7. Shalo and Breitstein 2002, 84.
8. The drug approval process has many variations. A patent on a treatment molecule is granted for twenty years and it often takes eight to twelve years of that time for the FDA approval process to be completed. The remaining years of the twenty are then for the owner of the patent to exclusively sell the drug. When the patent runs out, competitors may make generic versions. The FDA also grants its own market exclusivity that may or may not overlap the patent time as an additional incentive to gain approval. Patent terms may also be extended. See http://www.fda.gov/Drugs/DevelopmentApprovalProcess/ucm079031.htm.
9. Chomsky and Barsamian 2001; Herman and Chomsky 2002; Tye 1998.
10. Nelkin and Tancredi 1989.
11. Austin 1962; Kahn 1978.
12. Halliday 1985.
13. Sacks and Jefferson 1992.
14. Franklin 1997; Nelkin and Tancredi 1989.
15. Bordo 1993; Marchand 1986.
16. Althusser 1984 (1970); Pêcheux 1982.
17. Dixon-Woods 2001, cited in Henwood et al. 2003, 591.
18. Hone and Benson 2004, 98.
19. Prounis 2004, 152.
20. Ibid., 152.
21. Shalo and Breitstein 2002, 84.
22. Kelly 2003, S6.
23. Ibid.
24. Hone and Benson 2004.
25. Bolling 2003, 112.
26. Prounis 2004.
27. Bolling 2003, 114.
28. See, especially, Clarke et al. 2003; Conrad 1992, 2007; Illich 1975; Klawiter 2002; Lock 2002; Zola 1972.
29. Dumit 2006.
30. Frankenberg 1993.
31. Garfinkel 1967.
32. Harding 2000, 58–59.
33. Ibid., 57.
34. This is consonant with Turner's distinction between liminal (pertaining to traditional societies, in which rituals involved the whole social group) and liminoid (pertaining to industrial societies, in which individualization both flattened rituals into ceremonies and invented the social categories of leisure and the arts). The process Harding describes is individualized and, more important, antagonistic. It borders on manipulation and is, not unsurprisingly, called brainwashing by those

who are outside of evangelical culture and see only the external effects of conversion. Conversion as a practice and coming under conviction as an experience require an extension of liminality in the direction pointed to by the felicitous term *subliminal*, a word that connotes a form of liminality at a subconscious, subsocial, or social unconscious level.

35. According to his byline, "Vern Realto is a virtual contributing editor to DTC Times, a composite of regular staffers and other advisors" (1998, 14). As a composite, Realto thus speaks the collective wisdom of the pharmaceutical marketing industry, precisely the level of enunciation I am interested in analyzing.

36. Dumit 2004.

37. D. Smith 1998.

38. Ibid.

39. Cf. J. S. Kroll-Smith et al. 2000.

40. Realto 1998, 14.

41. Bolling 2003, 114.

42. Sunder Rajan 2007.

43. V. Turner 1982.

44. Burke 1984.

45. Harding 1987, 140.

46. S. Kroll-Smith 2003, 641.

47. Ibid., 640.

48. Edlen-Nezin 2003, S18.

49. Dumit 2006; E. Martin 2007.

50. Melucci 1996; Strathern 1992a.

51. Breitstein 2004a, 95.

52. Pêcheux 1982.

53. Bolling 2003, 114.

54. Healy 2002, 350.

55. Castel 1991.

56. Express Scripts 2012. See also Abboud 2004.

57. Lee 2006, 94; Mark, Levit, and Buck 2009, 1167.

58. Lee 2004, 53.

59. Dumit 2006.

60. Melucci 1996.

61. Beck 1992.

62. Kravitz et al. 2005.

63. Realto 1998, 14.

64. http://www.effexorxr.com/p/p10.jhtml, retrieved May 4, 2002.

65. Bell, Wilkes, and Kravitz 1999; Kravitz et al. 2005; Wilkes et al. 2000; Wilkes and Shuchman 1989.

66. Hone and Benson 2004, 104.

67. Bolling 2003, 117.

68. Ibid., 116.

69. Ibid., 117.

70. V. W. Turner and Turner 1992, 137.

71. Dumit 2006.

72. On "prescribing cascades," see Rochon and Gurwitz 1997. For a review of the problems, see Rochon, "Drug Prescribing for Older Adults," http://www.uptodate.com/contents/drug-prescribing-for-older-adults?view=print, retrieved March 15, 2012.

Three. Having to Grow Medicine

1. Petryna and Kleinman 2006. The large-scale efforts by the Gates Foundation and the World Health Organization are examples of direct responses to this critique of neglected diseases, but these methods of funding research are still driven by a growth model of health. See Broadbent 2011; Kadetz 2011; Kelly and Beisel 2011.

2. Bartfai and Lees 2006, 14.

3. Greener 2001, 122.

4. Schacter 2006, 116.

5. Tone and Watkins 2007.

6. Perkins 2002, 148.

7. Greener 2001, 25, 36.

8. Spilker 1989, 427–28.

9. The sole focus on blockbusters that the researchers here discuss has been mutating as more and more drugs come off patent. See Pollock 2012.

10. Perkins 2002, 122.

11. Bartfai and Lees 2006, 71.

12. Schacter 2006, 219.

13. Luce et al. 2009.

14. Kassirer 2005.

15. Weber 2006, 13, citing a Peter Jennings interview of Drummond in 2002 on *Bitter Medicine*.

16. Greener 2001, 1.

17. Morgan, Barer, and Evans 2000, 660.

18. Califf 2004.

19. Ramspacher 2004.

20. See chapter 5 for Geoffrey Rose's discussion of how treatments come to be seen as the meaning of health.

21. From the perspective of health as prescriptions, biopolitics in terms of care of the population is only meaningful when such care involves an expanding and constant domain of prevention. Normalization in a Foucauldian sense is meaningless in this regard—the only state of normality that generates value is one that expresses an increasing potentiality of future illness.

22. On statistical medicine, see chapter 5.

23. Bartfai and Lees 2006, 73 (emphasis added).

24. M. C. Smith 2002, 32.

25. And then there will be an opening in the market to produce drugs that are targeted to offset the side effects of your primary drugs.

26. Cutting Edge Information 2004.
27. Daly and Kolassa 2003, 11.
28. Ibid., 11.
29. Cutting Edge Information 2004.
30. Daly and Kolassa 2003, 12.
31. Jasanoff 2004.
32. The way in which marketers have deconstructed clinical trial research into component parts is not unlike what happens in science studies. But whereas science studies scholars have shown that science, because it happens as part of a social world, needs to be socially and rhetorically savvy in order to be science, marketers see this situation as an opportunity to produce designer science, that is, desired messages that function and persuade through science. When science studies scholars examine how facts are made, their aim is not to discredit the facts produced but to show how much work goes into achieving a fact. The classic text *Laboratory Life* by Bruno Latour and Steve Woolgar (1979) focused on how experiments had to be designed so that they would produce the right sorts of texts, that is, journal articles that would convince others, especially scientists' peers, of a fact. Scientists did this in the name of truth but knowing that truth counted only if it looked like truth and was packaged in the right manner. Some critics of science studies have charged that this account of how science is socially constructed demeans scientists and reduces the truth value of their work. But what Latour, Woolgar, and others actually show is that good science is much harder than anyone thought. In addition to designing and carrying out the right experiments in the right ways, scientists must be experts at gathering allies by fitting their work into that of their peers, at managing institutions by translating their proposals and results into terms that the funders and the public will accept, and at crafting the facticity of their claims. The word "claims," as related to objectivity, refers to the rhetorical and literary crafting necessary to help us believe in facts, in statements about the world that rise above their history so that they are truths we can depend on. One reads science studies and understands how much work is required to get results and to make the world safe for them. In this case, we can read the analysts as science studies scholars who are teaching us how to produce the right kinds of facts.
33. Srinivasan 2004. At the time, Srinivasan was a senior research biostatistician.
34. Bartfai and Lees 2006, 44.
35. See, for example, Abbasi 2004; De Angelis et al. 2005; Dickersin and Rennie 2003; Laine et al. 2007.
36. Fauber 2001.
37. Aoki 2001.
38. Ibid.
39. Sunder Rajan 2006.
40. Califf 2004, 272.
41. Ibid.
42. Allen and Smith 2004, C1. "Bristol-Myers Squibb had funded the Harvard Medical

School research in hopes of proving that its cholesterol-lowering drug was just as good as a more-potent rival. Some cardiologists even scoffed at the boldly named PROVE-IT study, suggesting it was rigged to favor Bristol-Myers' product."

43. Califf 2004, 272 (emphasis added).

44. Bartfai and Lees 2006, 14.

45. They say earlier, "A more profound 'revelation' [than that drug companies deceive us] is that members especially of the US society are prepared to take too many drugs with little provocation" (xv). This is similar to Mickey Smith on society as the problem. And it is insightful, in that it goes to the heart of why we expect drug companies or any other company to look out for us. Even that they would tell the truth (as Althusser says, the bourgeoisie tell lies easily because the lies go on all by themselves). "The risks of production have to be compensated, if no gain, profit, then waste of money. Mania for wealth = productivity. Infinite urge to wealth" (Marx 1973).

46. This call echoes an industrial practice that Marx notes in a chilling footnote, when even raids to kidnap children to work twelve-plus hours per day in factories was unstoppable as long as competition with other capitalists existed. One group of factories actually submitted a petition to the British government in 1863 pleading, "Much as we deplore the evils before mentioned [kidnappings], it would not be possible to prevent them by any scheme of agreement between the manufacturers. . . . Taking all these points into consideration, we have come to the conviction that some legislative enactment is wanted" (1976, 381–82, fn 82).

Four. Mass Health

1. Laino 2002.

2. See http://www.fluoridealert.org.

3. Henig 1997, 85.

4. Brandt 2006, 211–17.

5. Berridge 2007, 15.

6. Cf. Brown and Williamson Tobacco strategy document from 1969: "Doubt is our product, since it is the best means of competing with the 'body of fact' that exists in the mind of the general public. It is also the means of establishing a controversy. . . . Spread doubt over strong scientific evidence and the public won't know what to believe." See also Oreskes and Conway 2010.

7. Brandt 2006, 137–51.

8. Ibid., 218.

9. Ibid., 239.

10. Sturdy 1998, 283. He is citing Cantor 1992 and Marks 1992.

11. Marks 1997. A major problem for clinical medicine was that it was seen as secondary to laboratory and theoretical research, where the bulk of funding was directed.

12. Ibid., 126.

13. To many clinicians the basic procedures of the randomized controlled trial were unfamiliar. Allowing a roll of the dice to determine a patient's treatment, withholding innovative therapies from one group of patients, keeping treating physi-

cians in the dark about what medications their patients were receiving—these were all innovative and somewhat disturbing practices. Ibid.

14. Ibid., 156.

15. Ibid., 161.

16. According to the historian J. Rosser Matthews (1995), what enabled randomized and double-blind trials to finally get established as regulatory was another scandal, that of the use of thalidomide in the 1960s, which caused many babies in Europe to be born with birth defects: "It became apparent to Congress that the medical profession needed the kind of quantitative oversight for experimental drugs that clinical trials could provide. In this manner, statistical health based on mass experimental medicine was defined and institutionalized" (564). Arthur Daemmrich's comparative analysis of the regulatory "therapeutic cultures" of the United States and Germany highlights the FDA's insistence on clinical trials over experience after the 1960s. Even five years of use of a drug in Europe did not "equal well-controlled quantitative" studies, so the FDA would not consider it tested. In discussions following Ayerst's failed application for the drug propranolol, FDA officials in essence helped them design the protocol for an acceptable clinical trial. A key difference, according to Daemmrich, between the United States and Germany is that support in the United States for quantitative clinical trials "sought to replace clinical judgment." "By discrediting Ayerst's application, FDA officers and members of the advisory committee were striving to standardize practices in clinical trials. . . . They wanted companies to submit data of a more formal statistical nature, instead of relying on case reports . . . [they] sought to use the company to change how doctors carried out clinical trials. The agency's detailed critique therefore eventually served as a template for designing clinical trials of propranolol" (Daemmrich 2004, 76).

17. G. A. Rose, Khaw, and Marmot 2008, 47. Rose uses "precautions" because treatments, for him, mean lifestyle, diet, and behavioral changes first, and he reserves extreme caution regarding prescriptions, since he points out that the large NNTs would greatly amplify long-term side effects, many of which would be all but impossible to detect without other massive, long-term, and prohibitively expensive clinical trials.

18. Healy 2002, 350.

19. Greene 2007, 83–84, 92.

20. Ibid., 106.

21. Ibid., 112.

22. Diller 1998, 2002.

23. Greene 2007, 43–55, 84.

24. Ibid., 53.

25. Ibid., 59–65. Greene discusses how the queries over exact and round numbers happened at the inception of this type of medicine.

26. Pickering 1968, in Greene 2007.

27. Pickering 1968, in G. A. Rose, Khaw, and Marmot 2008, 42.

28. Brayne and Calloway 1988, quoted in G. A. Rose, Khaw, and Marmot 2008, 42.

29. G. A. Rose, Khaw, and Marmot 2008, 45.

30. Greene 2007, 84.

31. Hahn 1995, 31.

32. Welch 2004.

33. Canguilhem 1989, 198–200.

34. Cf. Snyderman and Williams 2003.

35. Fauber 2001; Ferraro 2001; Rubin 2001.

36. Deleuze and Guattari 1987, 90.

37. Fackelmann 2001.

38. Gilbert 2001.

39. Deleuze and Guattari 1987, chapter 4.

40. Gilbert 2001.

41. Fauber 2001.

42. Prounis 2004.

43. Fauber 2001.

44. Fackelmann 2001.

45. Aoki 2001.

46. Deleuze and Guattari 1987, 89–96. This transformation contrasts with the "torque" that follows when personal biographies do not match the classificatory systems that have been created to contain or narrate them, described in Bowker and Star 1999.

47. Canguilhem 1989, 134.

48. Best 2001.

49. Jeremy Greene has traced the transformation of cholesterol from this contested marker into a generalized risk factor. Calling cholesterol a biomarker for risk means that serum cholesterol levels offer an insurance agent a population-prediction about heart disease.

50. Hall 2001.

51. Khan 2000.

52. Ferraro 2001.

53. Fauber 2001.

54. Rubin 2001.

55. Kolata 2001.

56. Ibid.

57. Staff reporter, "MD Prefers Lifestyle Change to Cholesterol Drugs," *Ottawa Citizen*, July 8, 2002, A11.

58. Nagourney 2001.

59. Squires 2001.

60. Fiely 2001.

61. Dr. Cynthia 2003a.

62. Doyle 2002.

63. Squires 2001.

64. "Enter tibolone, a synthetic steroid available in Europe for a number of years. Tibolone seems to tickle all the right receptors and block all the wrong ones. As

efficient as estrogen on hot flashes, mood problems, and dry vaginas, it works even better than estrogen on improving libido. It prevents osteoporosis, doesn't stimulate the uterine lining or fibroid growth, and decreases cholesterol levels. So why is tibolone not yet in the water supply?" (Paley 2007).

65. Haney 1999a. He explained, "Behind the obvious is a complex web of problems and uncertainties, and experts say no single thread tells the whole story. For instance, at $100 a month, price alone keeps many off the drug, and that's just the start. Some doctors are too out of touch or overworked to write the prescriptions. Some patients are too pill-phobic to take them. And then there's the fact that the medical system often emphasizes treating disease rather than preventing it."

66. Freud 1989, 137–38.

67. Ibid., 138.

68. Laino 2002.

69. They must behave like marketers and public relations professionals, mimicking the director of the large marketing firm, Burson-Marsteller, talking to the chemical industry at a trade event about how to handle risk information: the key lies in "some very interesting psychological and sociological research on risk perception [which] suggests that the obvious, rational approach is not likely to succeed. . . . We must respond with the tools that we have for managing the emotional aspects of the human psyche. . . . The industry must be like the psychiatrist: rationally figuring out how it can help the public put things in perspective" (Rampton and Stauber 2001, 3).

70. Laino 2002.

71. Ibid.

72. Culver et al. 2012.

73. Roussouw et al. 2002.

74. Szabo 2012.

75. Lyotard defined this type of aporia as a *differend*.

76. Foucault 1988, 169.

77. On these issues, see Snyderman and Williams 2003; Brandt 2006; Rosenberg 1997.

78. Clinical trials increasingly and publicly become what Deleuze describes as the power of the false, "which replaces and supersedes the form of the true, because it poses the simultaneity of incompossible presents (good for you/bad for you), or the coexistence of not-necessarily true pasts. . . . It poses inexplicable differences to the present and alternatives which are undecidable between true and false to the past" (1989).

79. Parker-Pope 2004.

80. Agnvall 2004.

81. Mason 2003; World Health Organization 2011. See also "Pharmaceuticals and Personal Care Products as Pollutants," website at the EPA, http://www.epa.gov/ppcp/.

82. L. Thomas 1979, 49.

83. Castel 1991, 284.

Five. Moving the Lines

1. The curve is adapted from Kupfer 1991.
2. Canguilhem 1989, 198–99.
3. Morgan, Barer, and Evans 2000, 61.
4. Bloor 1983.
5. For a book-length review of these problems, see Cohen 2001.
6. Daemmrich 2004.
7. Fosket 2002, 7. Fosket goes on to note that the actual Breast Cancer Prevention Trial participants were at 3.2 percent risk, but it is the lower number that became standardized as the high-risk threshold.
8. Fosket 2002, drawing upon Press and Burke 2000: "The number is now constructed as internal to each individual woman . . . rather than a cut-off point created by the statistical needs of power calculations in a randomized clinical trial" (101).
9. Hogle 2001, 325; Lupton 1999.
10. The specific language of prevention was subsequently censored by the FDA, which decided that it misled readers and that *risk reduction* was more accurate (Hogle 2002).
11. Healy 1997.
12. Robins found that men had a prevalence of 3 percent and women 8 percent, but the figures varied greatly depending on the instrument used. Frame 1990; Public Health Service 1979; Robins et al. 1984.
13. Matthew 1990; Widmer and Cadoret 1978; Zung, Magruder-Habib, and Feussner 1990.
14. The different screens are reviewed in Attkisson and Zich 1990; Murphy 1990.
15. Screening is a tricky statistical business. The idea of a biomedical screen is to detect an existing disease or a future disease in a person who otherwise is showing no symptoms. Screens almost always have two parameters that are adjustable: sensitivity and specificity. These define how imprecise the test is and how many mistakes and what kind of mistakes will be made in using the test properly. The more sensitive a test is, the more it will flag those who have the marker. A screen that is 99 percent sensitive will miss only one in every hundred people who should be caught. Those who are missed are called false negatives (or type I errors), that is, they have been told they are acceptable when they are not. The specificity of the screen refers to how good it is at catching only those who actually have the marker. A test that is 90 percent specific will falsely indicate that ten people out of every one hundred have an unacceptable score when they are fine on that measure. These people are false positives (or type II errors). For a technical consideration of these concerns, see Shrout 1990.
16. Ibid., 95.
17. Roberts 1990.
18. Kamerow 1990.
19. Hughs 1983.

20. In 2004 nonpsychiatrists wrote 75 percent of all prescriptions for antidepressants and 30 percent of antipsychotic drugs (up from 16 percent in 2001) (Abboud 2004, D1).

21. Schacter 2006, 117.

22. Greene 2007, 197.

23. G. A. Rose, Khaw, and Marmot, 2008, 73.

24. Greener 2001, 41.

25. G. A. Rose, Khaw, and Marmot, 2008, 72.

26. Ibid., 73.

27. Ironically, cholesterol-lowering drug trials are actually quite numerous because the market is so large that almost every company competes for it (Greene 2007).

28. Armstrong 1977.

29. Schacter 2006, 115.

30. Metzl and Kirkland 2010.

31. Kolata 2001.

32. Formulation from Sunder Rajan 2006.

33. The old guidelines held that blood levels of LDL cholesterol, the bad kind that clogs arteries, should stay below 100 milligrams per deciliter (mg/dL) and, ideally, below 70 mg/dL for very high-risk patients. According to the new advisory, those guidelines are now recommended for all people with established heart disease (Edelson 2006).

34. Charan and Tichy 1998.

35. "In one simple stroke, he redefined the market and opened vast new areas of opportunity for his company" (Dan Ring, customer review of *Every Business Is a Growth Business* on http://www.amazon.com).

36. Shalo 2004.

37. Ibid.

38. Ibid. See also Landers 2002.

39. Ibid.

40. Greener 2001, 61.

41. Cook 2006, 41–42.

42. Bartfai and Lees 2006, 121.

43. Ibid., 156–57.

44. Phase IV trials are conducted after a drug has been approved. They are often small and used to study additional dosage formulations, new indications for the drug (helping doctors to prescribe the drug "off-label"), and emergent adverse reactions. Some analysts and companies distinguish phase V trials, which are conducted for postmarketing surveillance or specifically to determine new uses for existing products. In both cases these trials often "help to promote experiences with the drug to prominent physicians and the public through marketing" (Aldes 2008, 472).

45. Marini 2003.

46. Vasella, Bloomgarden, and Bloomgarden 2003; Grady 2002; Brown 2002.

47. Vedantam 2001.

48. Shalo 2004.
49. Ibid.
50. Ibid.
51. Rosenberg 1997, 44.
52. Agnvall 2004. See also Black and Yi 1996. "JNC-V [Joint National Committee 5] also adopted the word 'stage' to categorize hypertension severity, abandoning the designations of borderline, mild, moderate, and severe. The committee felt that the term 'mild' hypertension implied to both providers and patients that hypertensive individuals with BPS in that range had a benign condition that did not require excessive concern." Then "prehypertension" was introduced in JNC 7: "Prehypertension is not a disease category. Rather it is a designation chosen to identify individuals at high risk of developing hypertension, so that both patients and clinicians are alerted to this risk and encouraged to intervene and prevent or delay the disease from developing" (Chobanian et al. 2003, 1211). In 2007 the term was dropped: "Given the ominous significance of the word 'hypertension' for the layman, the term 'prehypertension' may create anxiety and request for unnecessary medical visits and examinations in many subjects" (Segura and Ruilope 2009, S284).
53. For an analysis of the role of moral valence in the rhetorical authority of medicine in singularizing conditions, see S. Kroll-Smith 2003.
54. Squires 2001.
55. Egan 2001.
56. Breitstein 2004b, 54.
57. In the 1990s a set of critiques was launched against so-called social constructivism by physicists, accusing it of denying reality and claiming that anything goes. In other fields, social constructivism has often been thought of as critiquing simple models of scientific progress by pointing out the ways in which that progress depended on and was shaped by social processes. But in the case of metabolic syndrome, social construction is seen as a positive force working alongside science in the creation of a new disease.
58. Breitstein 2004b, 49.
59. Ibid.
60. Ibid.
61. Ibid.
62. Ibid.
63. Ibid.
64. Johnson 1996, 99.
65. Dumit 2005; Dumit 2006.
66. Aronowitz 1998; Bowker and Star 1999.
67. See Greenslit 2006.
68. Breitstein 2004b, 49.
69. See, e.g., National Alliance on Mental Illness (NAMI) and Children and Adults with Attention Deficit (CHAAD).
70. Breitstein 2004b, 49.

71. Ibid., 48.

72. Ibid., 50.

73. Ibid., 54.

74. Vermilyea, Vanelli, and Adler 2002b, 71.

75. The quotation from this patient can be found at http://crystal.palace.net~llama/ angst/prozac.html.

76. Haney 1999a. One of the reasons given by patients for not continuing to take statins for the rest of their life is that they don't feel different. Only the biomarker provided by the test can tell if their cholesterol has lowered, and they can't stop just because their cholesterol falls.

77. Glenmullen 2000, 62.

78. Cartwright 1998.

79. Diller 2002, 376.

80. Glenmullen 2000, 44–45. When Prozac was introduced, one of the most striking differences between it and its predecessors was that its prescribing guidelines indicated there was no need to slowly increase the dose and balance this with the drug's side effects. Ibid., 148.

81. Healy 2002.

82. Singh 2003.

83. Vermilyea, Vanelli, and Adler 2002a, 64.

84. Kremer and Snyder 2003, 2.

85. Express Scripts 2007.

86. See Cohen 2005 on bioavailability and also the federal definition: "The rate and extent to which the active ingredient or therapeutic ingredient becomes available at the site of drug action." http://aspe.hhs.gov/mits/text/titleXI/1103.html.

87. Vermilyea, Vanelli, and Adler 2002a, 69.

88. Provocatively, "Biomarx," a word-substitution experiment with Marx's *Capital*, generates the following: "If the Patient Heals his disposable time for himself, he robs Pharma" (Dumit 2012, 82).

89. Bartfai and Lees 2006, 221.

90. See Dumit 2012.

91. With "bodily intolerance" we can recognize the same final physiological barrier that Marx's capitalists found with labor and that Goizueta found with Coke, the surprisingly expandable but not unlimited elasticity of the human body. Whereas Goizueta suggested that the target for Coke's growth was the capacity of human liquid consumption, Marx locates it in the labor humans can be pushed to do before exhaustion, and biomedicine in the intolerance to pills that the body can withstand.

92. Wald and Law 2003, 1423.

Six. Knowing Your Numbers

1. Beck 1992; Henwood et al. 2003; N. Rose 2003.

2. Linton 2001.

3. Greene 2007, 175.

4. Hogle 2002, 325, 329, 331.
5. Talaga 2000.
6. Biehl, Coutinho, and Outeiro 2001; Healy 2002.
7. Linton 2001.
8. Sorrentino 2001.
9. Snyderman and Williams 2003.
10. See Duden and Samerski 2008; Samerski 2009.
11. Stingl 2003.
12. Beck 1992.
13. Srikameswaran 2001.
14. Editorial Desk, "Predicting Heart Attacks," *New York Times*, November 17, 2002, 4–10.
15. Lund et al. 2004.
16. S. Smith 2004.
17. On tensions in things and lifestyles, see Mol and Law 2004.
18. Squires 1999.
19. Ibid.
20. On communicative and consumptive doing, see Dumit 2001; Greimas and Courtes 1982; D. Thomas 1999, 49.
21. Squires 1999.
22. Herzlich and Pierret 1987; Rosenberg 1997.
23. Crawford 2000, 231.
24. Ibid.
25. Rubin 2001.
26. Urquhart 2005, 145.
27. Ibid., 145–46.
28. Noonan et al. 2003, 52.
29. Dr. Cynthia 2003b.
30. Noonan et al. 2003, 52.
31. Iliff 2001, 2400.
32. "Science, for Canguilhem, is a 'discourse verified in a delimited sector of experience'" (Rabinow 1996, 82). "Life, whatever form it may take, involves self-perspiration by means of self-regulation" (84). "Normality is the ability to adapt to changing circumstances, to variable and varying environment" (84). "Health is not being normal; health is being normative" (85).
33. Rubin 2001.

Conclusion. Living in a World of Surplus Health

1. A recent review of the use of mass treatments to reduce risk has shown that in only one case (that of treating hypertension to reduce stroke) has there been overall effectiveness. Other cases do result in reducing biomarkers but not in helping overall health outcomes. See Greene and Jones 2011.
2. Frist 2005.
3. Harding 2000.

4. Fischer 2003.

5. Wilson 2010.

6. Bankhead 2010. The JUPITER trial is also not the first to try to justify statins for healthy people. Greene 2007 (chap. 6) describes the origins of this health logic in which reducing people's risk to a supposed normal is replaced by recommending for so-called optimal health.

7. There are exceptions to this. The question of the FDA's power and how it might be changed is a current topic of lively debate, but it is beyond the scope of this book. While I have been concentrating on the specifics of treatment growth, other analysts, such as Dan Carpenter and Marcia Angell, have been fighting over the power and limits of the FDA to shape research in the United States and worldwide.

8. My response to this query has been anticipated by Michel Foucault (2004) in a little-read talk that took place in 1974 in Brazil entitled "The Crisis of Medicine or the Crisis of Antimedicine?" Foucault said, "[Ivan] Illich and his followers point out that therapeutic medicine, which responds to a symptomatology and blocks the apparent symptoms of diseases, is bad medicine. They propose in its stead a demedicalized art of health made up of hygiene, diet, lifestyle, work and housing conditions, etc. But what is hygiene at present except a series of rules set in place and codified by biological and medical knowledge, when it is not medical authority itself that has elaborated it? Antimedicine can only oppose medicine with facts or projects that have been already set up by a certain type of medicine" (14).

9. See http://www.hhs.gov/recovery/programs/cer/index.html.

10. On the Sentinel Network, see http://healthpolicyandreform.nejm.org/?p=1232.

11. Appleby 2001.

12. Zakaria 2010.

REFERENCES

Abbasi, K. 2004. "Compulsory Registration of Clinical Trials." Vol. 329:637–38. London: BMJ Publishing Group.

Abboud, L. 2004. "Should Family Doctors Treat Serious Mental Illness? Psychiatrists Voice Concerns as More General Physicians Prescribe Antipsychotic Drugs." *Wall Street Journal*, March 24.

Abramson, J. 2004. *Overdosed America: The Broken Promise of American Medicine.* New York: HarperCollins.

Agnvall, E. 2004. "Making Us (Nearly) Sick: A Majority of Americans Are Now Considered to Have at Least One 'Pre-Disease' or 'Borderline' Condition." *Washington Post*, February 10.

Aikin, K. J. 2002. *Direct-to-Consumer Advertising of Prescription Drugs: Physician Survey Preliminary Results.* Retrieved January 25, 2003, from http://www.fda.gov/cder/ddmac/globalsummit2003/.

Akinbami L. J., X. Liu, P. N. Pastor, and C. A. Reuben. 2011. "Attention Deficit Hyperactivity Disorder among Children Aged 5–17 Years in the United States, 1998–2009." NCHS Data Brief, no 70. Hyattsville, Md.: National Center for Health Statistics. Retrieved March 15, 2012, from http://www.cdc.gov/nchs/data/databriefs/db70.htm.

Aldes, J. L. 2008. "The FDA Clinical Trial Process: Effectuating Change in the Regulatory Framework Governing Clinical Trials to Account for the Historical Shift from 'Traditional' to 'New' Phase I Trials." *Health Matrix* 18 (2), 463–500.

Alexander, T. 1996. "Still Waiting, Watchfully: A Former Fortune Writer Whose Unorthodox Choice in Facing Prostate Cancer Captivated Readers Reports on His Progress." CNN Money 133 (9), 73, May 13. Retrieved March 15, 2012, from http://money.cnn.com/magazines/fortune/fortune_archive/1996/05/13/212400/index.htm.

Allen, S., and S. Smith. 2004. "Statin Nation: Do We All Need to Lower Our 'Bad' Cholesterol?" *Boston Globe*, March 16, C1.

Althusser, L. 1984 (1970). "Ideology and Ideological State Apparatuses (Notes toward an Investigation)." *Essays on Ideology*. London: Verso.

Angell, M. 1996. *Science on Trial: The Clash of Medical Evidence and the Law in the Breast Implant Case*. New York: W. W. Norton.

————. 2004. *The Truth about the Drug Companies: How They Deceive Us and What to Do about It*. New York: Random House.

Anti-Infective Drugs Advisory Committee (AIDAC), U.S.O.A., Department of Health and Human Services, Food and Drug Administration, Center for Drug Evaluation and Research. 2002. Anti-Infective Drugs Advisory Committee (AIDAC) Meeting. Retrieved March 12, 2012, from http://www.fda.gov/ohrms/dockets/ac/02/tran scripts/3837t1.htm.

Aoki, N. 2001. "Drug Makers' Influence Pondered: Eye on US Advice to Cut Cholesterol," *Boston Globe*, May 31, A1.

Appadurai, A. 1986. "Introduction: Commodities and the Politics of Value." *The Social Life of Things: Commodities in Cultural Perspective*, ed. A. Appadurai, 3–63. Cambridge: Cambridge University Press.

Appleby, J. 2001. "Health Guides Could Raise Premiums: Report May Push More to Take Cholesterol Drug." *USA Today*, May 17.

Armstrong, J. S. 1977. "Social Irresponsibility in Management." *Journal of Business Research* 5, 185–213.

Aronowitz, R. A. 1998. *Making Sense of Illness: Science, Society, and Disease*. Cambridge: Cambridge University Press.

Attkisson, C. C., and J. M. Zich. 1990. "Depression Screening in Primary Care: Clinical Needs and Research Challenges." *Depression in Primary Care: Screening and Detection*, ed. C. C. Attkisson and J. M. Zich, 3–11. New York: Routledge.

Austin, J. L. 1962. *How to Do Things with Words*. Cambridge: Harvard University Press.

Avorn, J. 2004. *Powerful Medicines: The Benefits, Risks, and Costs of Prescription Drugs*. New York: Knopf.

Bankhead, C. 2010. "Was JUPITER Trial Data Influenced by AstraZeneca to Favor Crestor?" (originally published as "Should Healthy People Take Statins? New Studies Say No"), 2010, www.kevinmd.com.

Bartfai, T., and G. V. Lees. 2006. *Drug Discovery: From Bedside to Wall Street*. Amsterdam: Elsevier/AP.

Beck, U. 1992. *Risk Society: Towards a New Modernity*. Translated by T. B. M. Ritter. London: Sage.

Beck-Gernsheim, E. 1995. *The Social Implications of Bioengineering*. Atlantic Highlands, N.J.: Humanities Press.

Bell, A. 2002. "The Success of Science: How to Maximize the Value of Your Discovery." PowerPoint presentation for Quintiles Transnational. Retrieved February 16, 2005, from www.quintiles.com.

Bell, R. A., M. S. Wilkes, and R. L. Kravitz. 1999. "Advertisement-Induced Prescription Drug Requests: Patients' Anticipated Reactions to a Physician Who Refuses." *Journal of Family Practice* 48 (6), 446–52.

Bell, S. E. 2009. DES Daughters: Embodied Knowledge and the Transformation of Women's Health Politics. Philadelphia: Temple University Press, 2009.

Berridge, V. 2007. Marketing Health: Smoking and the Discourse of Public Health in Britain, 1945–2000. Oxford: Oxford University Press.

Best, H. W. 2001. "Simple Steps Can Bring Down Cholesterol Count." Chicago Sun-Times, May 16, 8.

Biehl, J., D. Coutinho, and A. L.Outeiro. 2001. "Technology and Effect: HIV/AIDS Testing in Brazil." Culture, Medicine, and Psychiatry 25 (1), 87–129.

Biehl, J., B. J. Good, and A. Kleinman. 2007. Subjectivity: Ethnographic Investigations. Berkeley: University of California Press.

Black, H. R., and J.-Y. Yi. 1996. "A New Classification Scheme for Hypertension Based on Relative and Absolute Risk with Implications for Treatment and Reimbursement." Hypertension 28 (5), 719–24.

Bloor, D. 1983. Wittgenstein: A Social Theory of Knowledge. New York: Columbia University Press.

Bolling, J. 2003. "DTC: A Strategy for Every Stage." Pharmaceutical Executive 23 (11), 110–17.

Bowker, G. C., and S. L. Star. 1999. Sorting Things Out: Classification and Its Consequences. Cambridge: MIT Press.

Brandt, A. M. 2006. The Cigarette Century: The Rise, Fall and Deadly Persistence of the Product that Defined America. New York: Basic Books.

Brayne, C., and P. Calloway. 1988. "Normal Ageing, Impaired Cognitive Function, and Senile Dementia of the Alzheimer's Type: A Continuum?" Lancet 1, 1265–67.

Breitstein, J. 2004a. "A Billion Brochures." Pharmaceutical Executive 24 (2), 95–96.

———. 2004b. "Metabolic Syndrome: The Making of a New Disease." Pharmaceutical Executive 24 (1), 48–54.

Broadbent, A. 2011. "Defining Neglected Disease." BioSocieties 6, 51–70.

Brown, D. 2002. "New Test for Risk of Heart Disease: Study Shifts Focus from Cholesterol." Washington Post, November 14.

Burke, K. 1984. Permanence and Change: An Anatomy of Purpose. 3rd ed. Berkeley: University of California Press.

Burns, L. R. 2005. The Business of Healthcare Innovation. Cambridge, U.K.: Cambridge University Press.

Califf, R. M. 2004. "Benefit the Patient, Manage the Risk: A System Goal." Pharmacoepidemiology and Drug Safety 13, 269–76.

Canguilhem, G. 1989. The Normal and the Pathological. Translated by C. R. Fawcett and R. S. Cohen. New York: Zone Books.

Cartwright, E. 1998. "The Logic of Heartbeats: Electronic Fetal Monitoring and Biomedically Constructed Birth." Cyborg Babies, ed. R. Davis-Floyd and J. Dumit, 240–54. New York: Routledge.

Castel, R. 1991. "From Dangerousness to Risk." The Foucault Effect: Studies in Governmentality, ed. G. Burchell, C. Gordon, and P. Miller, 281–98. Chicago: University of Chicago Press.

Centers for Medicare and Medicaid Services. 2008. *NHE Fact Sheet*. Centers for
Medicare and Medicaid Services.

———. 2011. *National Health Expenditure Projections 2010–2020*. Office of the Actu-
ary in the Centers for Medicare and Medicaid Services. Retrieved March 15, 2012,
from https://www.cms.gov/NationalHealthExpendData.

Chandler, J. K., A. I. Davidson, and H. D. Harootunian. 1994. *Questions of Evidence:
Proof, Practice, and Persuasion across the Disciplines*. Chicago: University of Chicago
Press.

Charan, R., and N. M. Tichy. 1998. *Every Business Is a Growth Business: How Your
Company Can Prosper Year after Year*. New York: Three Rivers Press.

Chobanian, A. V., et al. 2003. "Seventh Report of the Joint National Committee
on Prevention, Detection, Evaluation, and Treatment of High Blood Pressure."
Hypertension 42 (6), 1206–52.

Chomsky, N., and D. Barsamian. 2001. *Propaganda and the Public Mind: Conversations with Noam Chomsky*. Cambridge, Mass.: South End Press.

Clarke, A. 2005. *Situational Analysis: Grounded Theory after the Postmodern Turn*.
Thousand Oaks, Calif.: Sage.

Clarke, A., et al. 2003. "Biomedicalization: Theorizing Technoscientific Transformations of Health, Illness, and U.S. Biomedicine." *American Sociological Review* 68
(2), 161–94.

Clements, R. 2003. "Why It's Best for Your Body If You Assume the Worst," *Sunday
Times*, March 23, 10.

Cohen, J. S. 2001. *Over Dose: The Case against the Drug Companies: Prescription Drugs,
Side Effects, and Your Health*. New York: Jeremy P. Tarcher/Putnam.

Cohen, L. 2005. "Operability, Bioavailability, and Exception." *Global Assemblages:
Technology, Politics, and Ethics*, ed. Aihwa Ong and Stephen J. Collier, 79–90.
Malden, Mass.: Blackwell.

Conrad, P. 1992. "Medicalization and Social Control." *Annual Review of Sociology* 18,
209–32.

———. 2007. *The Medicalization of Society: On the Transformation of Human Conditions into Medical Disorders*. Baltimore: Johns Hopkins University Press.

Cook, A. G. 2006. *Forecasting for the Pharmaceutical Industry: Models for New Product
and In-Market Forecasting and How to Use Them*. Aldershot, U.K.: Gower.

Cox, T. P. 2002. "Forging Alliances." *Pharmaceutical Executive* 22 (9), 8–13. Retrieved March 15, 2012, from http://www.pharmexec.com/pharmexec/article/
articleDetail.jsp?id=29974.

Crawford, R. 2000. "Ritual of Health Promotion." In *Health, Medicine and Society:
Key Theories, Future Agendas*, ed. S. J. Williams, J. Gabe, and M. Calnan, 219–35.
New York: Routledge.

Culver, A. L., et. al. 2012. "Statin Use and Risk of Diabetes Mellitus in Postmenopausal Women in the Women's Health Initiative." *Archives of Internal Medicine* online January 9, E1–E9. doi: 10.1011/archinternmed.2011.625.

Cutting Edge Information. 2004. *Cardiovascular Marketing: Budgets, Staffing and*

Strategy (PH59) (Report Summary). Research Triangle Park, N.C.: Cutting Edge Information.

Daemmrich, A. A. 2004. *Pharmacopolitics: Drug Regulation in the United States and Germany.* Chapel Hill: University of North Carolina Press.

Daly, R., and M. Kolassa. 2003. "Start Earlier, Sell More, Sell Longer." *Pharmaceutical Executive*, March Supplement Handbook, 8–20.

De Angelis, C., et al. 2004. "Clinical Trial Registration: A Statement from the International Committee of Medical Journal Editors." *New England Journal of Medicine* 351, 1250–51.

Deleuze, G. 1989. *Cinema 2: The Time-Image.* Minneapolis: University of Minnesota Press.

Deleuze, G., and F. Guattari. 1987. *A Thousand Plateaus: Capitalism and Schizophrenia.* Translated by B. Massumi. Minneapolis: University of Minnesota Press.

Dickersin, K., and D. Rennie. 2003. "Registering Clinical Trials." *Journal of the American Medical Association* 290 (4), 516–23.

Diller, L. H. 1998. *Running on Ritalin: A Physician Reflects on Children, Society, and Performance in a Pill.* New York: Bantam.

———. 2002. *Should I Medicate My Child? Sane Solutions for Troubled Kids with, and without, Psychiatric Drugs.* New York: Basic Books.

Dixon-Woods, M. 2001. "Writing Wrongs? An Analysis of Published Discourses about the Use of Patient Information Leaflets." *Social Science and Medicine* 324, 573–77.

Doyle, C. 2002. "High Cholesterol," *Daily Telegraph* (London), July 9.

Dr. Cynthia. 2003a. "Healthy 62-Year-Old with High Ldl Considers Zocor Therapy." *Pittsburgh Post-Gazette*, April 15.

———. 2003b. "Learning about Cholesterol Is a Step toward Better Heart Health." *Pittsburgh Post-Gazette*, February 18.

Duden, B., and Samerski, S. 2008. "'Pop-Genes': The Symbolic Effects of the Release of 'Genes' into Ordinary Speech." *Women in Biotechnology*, ed. F. Mofino and F. Zucco. Netherlands: Springer, 161–70.

Dumit, J. 2001. "Playing Truths: Logics of Seeking and the Persistence of the New Age." *Focaal* 37, 63–76.

———. 2004. *Picturing Personhood: Brain Scans and Biomedical Identity.* Princeton: Princeton University Press.

———. 2005. "'Come on, people . . . we *are* the aliens. We seem to be suffering from Host-Planet Rejection Syndrome': Liminal Illnesses, Structural Damnation, and Social Creativity." *E.T. Culture: Anthropology in Outerspaces*, ed. D. Battaglia, 201–18. Durham: Duke University Press.

———. 2006. "Illnesses You Have to Fight to Get: Facts as Forces in Uncertain, Emergent Illnesses." *Social Science and Medicine* 62 (3), 577–90.

———. 2012. "Prescription Maximization and the Accumulation of Surplus Health in the Pharmaceutical Industry: The 'Biomarx' Experiment." *Lively Capital*, ed. K. Sunder Rajan, 45–92. Durham: Duke University Press.

Dumit, J., and S. Sensiper. 1998. "Living with the 'Truths' of DES: Toward an Anthropology of Facts." *Cyborg Babies: From Techno-Sex to Techno-Tots*, ed. R. Davis-Floyd and J. Dumit, 212–39. New York: Routledge.

Ecks, S. 2005. "Pharmaceutical Citizenship: Antidepressant Marketing and the Promise of Demarginalization in India." *Anthropology and Medicine* 12 (3), 239–54.

———. 2008. "Global Pharmaceutical Markets and Corporate Citizenship: The Case of Novartis' Anti-Cancer Drug Glivec." *BioSocieties* 3 (02), 165–81.

Edelson, E. 2006. "HealthDay Reporter." *Express Scripts Drug Digest*, http://www.drugdigest.org/DD/Articles/News/0,10141,532703,00.html.

Edlen-Nezin, L. 2003. "Breaking through Denial." *Pharmaceutical Executive* 23 (9), S18. Retrieved March 15, 2012, from http://www.pharmexec.com/pharmexec/Supplements/Breaking-Through-Denial/ArticleColumn/Article/detail/73310.

Egan, M. E. 2001. "The Unknown Epidemic (Research into Syndrome X)." *Forbes*. 168 (3) August, 110–11.

Epstein, S. 1996. *Impure Science: AIDS, Activism, and the Politics of Knowledge*. Berkeley: University of California Press.

———. 2007. *Inclusion: The Politics of Difference in Medical Research*. Chicago: University of Chicago Press.

Ernst & Young LLP. 2006. "Contract Research: Contracted for Trouble?" *R&D Directions* 12 (5).

Express Scripts. 2007. *2006 Drug Trend Report*.

———. 2012. *2011 Drug Trend Report*. April. Retrieved April 21, 2012 from http://express-scripts.com/research/research/dtr/.

Fackelmann, K. 2001."America Gets a Red Alert on Cholesterol Level: Heart Disease Lurks for the Complacent." *USA Today*, May 17, 8D.

Fauber, J. 2001. "U.S. Report Raises Cholesterol Fears: Guides Could Put 23 Million More on Medicines." *Milwaukee Journal Sentinel*, May 16.

Ferraro, B. Y. S. 2001. "Check Cholesterol Early and Often, Docs Urge." *New York Daily News*, May 16.

Fiely, D. 2001. "The Cholesterol Cure: New Guidelines Call for Wider Use of 'Miraculous' Drugs Known as Statins." *Columbus* (Ohio) *Dispatch*, December 13.

Fischer, M. M. J. 2003. *Emergent Forms of Life and the Anthropological Voice*. Durham: Duke University Press.

Fisher, J. A. 2009. *Medical Research for Hire: The Political Economy of Pharmaceutical Clinical Trials*. New Brunswick, N.J.: Rutgers University Press.

Fosket, J. R. 2002. "Breast Cancer Risk and the Politics of Prevention: Analysis of a Clinical Trial." PhD dissertation, University of California, San Francisco.

Foucault, M. 1986. *The Care of the Self*. Volume 3. Translated by R. Hurley. New York: Pantheon.

———. 1988. *Politics, Philosophy, Culture: Interviews and Other Writings, 1977–1984*. New York: Routledge.

———. 2004. "The Crisis of Medicine or the Crisis of Antimedicine?" *Foucault Studies*, 1, 5–19. Retrieved April 15, 2012, from http://cjas.dk/index.php/foucault-studies/article/view/562.

Fox, S., and S. Jones. 2009. *The Social Life of Health Information*. Washington, D.C.: Pew Foundation.

Frame, P. S. 1990. "Screening Procedures in Primary Care: History and Uses." *Depression in Primary Care: Screening and Detection*, ed. C. C. Attkisson and J. M. Zich, 12–30. New York: Routledge.

Frankenberg, R. 1993. "Risk: Anthropological and Epidemiological Narratives of Prevention." *Knowledge, Power, and Practice: The Anthropology of Medicine and Everyday Life*, ed. S. Lindenbaum and M. M. Lock, 219–42. Berkeley: University of California Press.

Franklin, S. 1997. *Embodied Progress: A Cultural Account of Assisted Conception*. New York: Routledge.

Freud, S. 1989. *Jokes and Their Relation to the Unconscious*. Translated by J. Strachey. New York: W. W. Norton.

Frist, W. H. 2005. "Shattuck Lecture: Health Care in the 21st Century." *New England Journal of Medicine* 352 (3), 267–72.

Garfinkel, H. 1967. *Studies in Ethnomethodology*. Englewood Cliffs, N.J.: Prentice-Hall.

Geertz, C. 1973. "Thick Description: Toward an Interpretive Theory of Culture." *The Interpretation of Cultures: Selected Essays*, 3–30. New York: Basic Books.

Gilbert, V. B. 2001. "Government Wants More People to Be Tested, Treated for High Cholesterol: Commonly Accepted Levels Are Not Safe, Report Says." *St. Louis Post-Dispatch*, May 16, A1.

Glaser, B. G., and A. L. Strauss. 1967. *The Discovery of Grounded Theory: Strategies for Qualitative Research*. Chicago: Aldine.

Glenmullen, J. 2000. *Prozac Backlash: Overcoming the Dangers of Prozac, Zoloft, Paxil, and Other Antidepressants with Safe, Effective Alternatives*. New York: Simon and Schuster.

Good, M.-J. D. 1994. *American Medicine: The Quest for Competence*. Berkeley: University of California Press.

———. 2001. "The Biotechnical Embrace." *Culture, Medicine and Psychiatry* 25 (4), 395–410.

Good, M.-J. D., et al. 1994. "Oncology and Narrative Time." *Social Science and Medicine* 38 (6), 855–62.

Gordon, D., and E. Paci. 1997. "Disclosure Practices and Cultural Narratives: Understanding Concealment and Silence around Cancer in Tuscany, Italy." *Social Science and Medicine* 44 (10), 1433–52.

Grady, D. 2002. "Study Says a Protein May Be Better Than Cholesterol in Predicting Heart Disease Risk." *New York Times*, November 14.

Greene, J. A. 2007. *Prescribing by Numbers: Drugs and the Definition of Disease*. Baltimore: Johns Hopkins University Press.

Greene, J., and D. Jones. 2011. "Is an Ounce of Prevention Worth an Ounce of Care?" Talk presented at the American Association for the History of Medicine Meetings (Philadelphia).

Greener, M. 2001. *A Healthy Business: A Guide to the Global Pharmaceutical Industry.* London: Informa Pharmaceuticals.

Greenslit, N. 2006. "DEP®ESSION and CONSUMꝘTION: Psychopharmaceuticals, Branding, and New Identity Practices." *Culture, Medicine, and Psychiatry* 29 (4), 477–502.

Grefe, E. A., and M. Linsky. 1995. *The New Corporate Activism: Harnessing the Power of Grassroots Tactics for Your Organization.* New York: McGraw-Hill.

Greider, K. 2003. *The Big Fix: How the Pharmaceutical Industry Rips Off American Consumers.* New York: Public Affairs.

Greimas, A.-J., and J. Courtes. 1982. *Semiotics and Language: An Analytical Dictionary.* Bloomington: Indiana University Press.

Grove, A. S. 1996a. *Only the Paranoid Survive: How to Exploit the Crisis Points That Challenge Every Company and Career.* New York: Currency Doubleday.

———. 1996b. "Taking on Prostate Cancer." *Fortune*, May 13. Retrieved March 15, 2012, from http://money.cnn.com/magazines/fortune/fortune_archive/1996/05/13/212394/index.htm.

Gu, Q., C. F. Dillon, and V. L. Burt. 2010. "Prescription Drug Use Continues to Increase: U.S. Prescription Drug Data for 2007–2008," NCHS Data Brief, no. 42. Retrieved March 15, 2012, from http://www.cdc.gov/nchs/products/databriefs.htm.

Hadler, N. M. 2004. *Last Well Person: How to Stay Well Despite the Health-Care System.* Montreal: McGill-Queen's University Press.

Hahn, R. A. 1995. *Sickness and Healing: An Anthropological Perspective.* New Haven: Yale University Press.

Hall, C. T. 2001. "New Rules to Fight Heart Disease: Aggressive Treatment of 'Bad' Cholesterol." *San Francisco Chronicle*, May 16, A1.

Halliday, M. A. K. 1985. *An Introduction to Functional Grammar.* London: E. Arnold.

Haney, D. 1999a. "Cardiologists Puzzled at Neglect of Cholesterol-Busting Medicine," *Spartanburg Herald Journal*, August 1.

———. 1999b. "Spreading the Word on a Lifesaver: Statin Drugs." *Los Angeles Times*, August 22.

Harding, S. 1987. "Convicted by the Holy Spirit: The Rhetoric of Fundamental Baptist Conversion." *American Ethnologist* 14 (1), 167–81.

———. 2000. *The Book of Jerry Falwell: Fundamentalist Language and Politics.* Princeton: Princeton University Press.

Hartgraves, T. 2002. "DTC Prescription Drug Advertising: The History and Impact of FDA Regulation." Manuscript. Cambridge, Mass.

Hawthorne, F. 2003. *The Merck Druggernaut: The Inside Story of a Pharmaceutical Giant.* Hoboken, N.J.: John Wiley and Sons.

Hayden, C. 2003. *When Nature Goes Public: The Making and Unmaking of Bioprospecting in Mexico.* Princeton: Princeton University Press.

Hayden, C., et al. 2007. "A Generic Solution?" *Current Anthropology* 48 (4), 475–95.

Healy, D. 1997. *The Antidepressant Era.* Cambridge: Harvard University Press.

———. 2002. *The Creation of Psychopharmacology.* Cambridge: Harvard University Press.

————. 2004. *Let Them Eat Prozac: The Unhealthy Relationship between the Pharmaceutical Industry and Depression*. New York: New York University Press.

————. 2012. *Pharmageddon*. Berkeley: University of California Press.

Heilemann, J. 2001. "Andy Grove's Rational Exuberance," interview. *Wired* 9 (6).

Henig, R. M. 1997. *The People's Health: A Memoir of Public Health and Its Evolution at Harvard*. Washington, D.C.: Joseph Henry Press.

Henwood, F., et al. 2003. "'Ignorance Is Bliss Sometimes': Constraints on the Emergence of the 'Informed Patient' in the Changing Landscapes of Health Information." *Sociology of Health and Illness* 25 (6), 589–607.

Herman, E. S., and N. Chomsky. 2002. *Manufacturing Consent: The Political Economy of the Mass Media*. New York: Pantheon.

Herzlich, C., and J. Pierret. 1987. *Illness and Self in Society*. Baltimore: Johns Hopkins University Press.

Hilts, P. J. 2003. *Protecting America's Health: The FDA, Business, and One Hundred Years of Regulation*. New York: Alfred A. Knopf.

Hogle, L. 2001. "Chemoprevention for Healthy Women: Harbinger of Things to Come?" *Health* 5 (3), 311–33.

————. 2002. "Claims and Disclaimers: Whose Expertise Counts?" *Medical Anthropology* 21, 275–306.

Holliday, L., and B. Grant. 2003. "ON THE WEB: If You're Not Everywhere, You're Nowhere." *Pharmaceutical Executive* 23 (12), 102. Retrieved March 15, 2012, from http://www.pharmexec.com/pharmexec/article/articleDetail.jsp?id=78967.

Hone, F., and R. Benson. 2004. "DTC: European Style." *Pharmaceutical Executive* 24 (3), 96–106. Retrieved March 12, 2012, from http://www.pharmexec.com/pharmexec/Current+Issue/DTC-European-Style/ArticleStandard/Article/detail/87982.

Hughs, T. P. 1983. *Networks of Power: Electrification in Western Society, 1880–1930*. Baltimore: Johns Hopkins University Press.

Iliff, D. 2001. "Guidelines for Diagnosis and Treatment of High Cholesterol [Letters]." *Journal of the American Medical Association* 286 (19), 2400–2401.

Illich, I. 1975. "The Medicalization of Life." *Journal of Medical Ethics* 1 (2), 73–77.

IMS (Institute for Healthcare Informatics). 2011. *The Use of Medicines in the United States: Review of 2010*. Report. Parsippany, NJ. Retrieved March 20, 2012, from http://www.imshealth.com/deployedfiles/ims/Global/Content/Insights/IMS%20Institute%20for%20Healthcare%20Informatics/IHII_UseOfMed_report1_.pdf.

Industrial Info Resources (IIR). 2008. *2007 Pharmaceutical Forecast, Economic Trends*. Industrial Info Resources.

Jasanoff, S. 2004. *States of Knowledge: The Co-Production of Science and Social Order*. New York: Routledge.

Johnson, H. 1996. *Osler's Web: Inside the Labyrinth of the Chronic Fatigue Syndrome Epidemic*. New York: Crown.

Kadetz, P. 2011. "Assumptions of Global Beneficence: Health-Care Disparity, the WHO and the Outcomes of Integrative Health-Care Policy at Local Levels in the Philippines." *BioSocieties* 6, 88–105.

Kaericher, C. 2007. *Pharmaceuticals and Direct to Consumer Advertising*. Bloomington: Indiana University Press.

Kahn, J. Y. 1978. "A Diagnostic Semiotic." *Semiotica* 22, 75–106.

Kamerow, D. B. 1990. "Is Screening for Depression Worthwhile in Primary Care? Screening Criteria and the Current State of Depression Research." *Depression in Primary Care: Screening and Detection*, ed. C. C. Attkisson and J. M. Zich, 21–26. New York: Routledge.

Kassirer, J. P. 2005. *On the Take: How America's Complicity with Big Business Can Endanger Your Health*. New York: Oxford University Press.

Kelleher, S., and D. Wilson. 2005. "Suddenly Sick," *Seattle Times*, June 26–June 30. Retrieved December 2, 2011, from http://seattletimes.nwsource.com/news/health/suddenlysick/.

Kelly, A. H. and Beisel, U. 2011. "Neglected Malarias: The Frontlines and Back Alleys of Global Health." *BioSocieties* 6, 71–87.

Kelly, P. 2003. "Health Literacy: A Silent Crisis." *Pharmaceutical Executive* 23 (9), S6–8.

Khan, D. F. D. B. 2000. "Two Ways to Read Cholesterol Level." *New Straits Times* (Malaysia), May 9, 5.

Klawiter, M. 2002. "Risk, Prevention and the Breast Cancer Continuum: The NCI, the FDA, Health Activism and the Pharmaceutical Industry." *History and Technology* 18 (4), 309–53.

Klein, D. F., et al. 2002. "Improving Clinical Trials: American Society of Clinical Psychopharmacology Recommendations." *Archives of General Psychiatry* 59 (3), 272–78.

Kleinman, A. 1988a. *The Illness Narratives: Suffering, Healing, and the Human Condition*. New York: Basic Books.

———. 1988b. *Rethinking Psychiatry: From Cultural Category to Personal Experience*. New York: Free Press.

Koberstein, W. 2002. "When Worlds Collide: The Unleashed Power of Marketing/R&D Collaboration." *Pharmaceutical Executive* 22 (9), 40–62. Retrieved March 15, 2012, from http://www.pharmexec.com/pharmexec/article/articleDetail.jsp?id=29963&sk=&date=&pageID=6.

Kolata, G. 2001."U.S. Panel Backs Broader Steps to Reduce Risk of Heart Attacks." *New York Times*, May 16.

Kommers, N., and L. Rainie. 2003. *Use of the Internet at Major Life Moments*. (Research Briefing). Washington. D.C.: Pew Foundation.

Kopytoff, I. 1986. "The Cultural Biography of Things: Commoditization as Process." *The Social Life of Things: Commodities in Cultural Perspective*, ed. A. Appadurai, 64–93. Cambridge: Cambridge University Press.

Kravitz, R. L., et al. 2005. "Influence of Patients' Requests for Direct-to-Consumer Advertised Antidepressants: A Randomized Controlled Trial." *Journal of the American Medical Association* 293 (16), 1995–2002.

Kremer, M., and C. M. Snyder. 2003. *Why Are Drugs More Profitable Than Vaccines?* NBER Working Paper no. 9833.

Kroll-Smith, S. 2003. "Popular Media and 'Excessive Daytime Sleepiness': A Study of Rhetorical Authority in Medical Sociology." *Sociology of Health and Illness* 25 (6), 625–43.

Kroll-Smith, S., P. Brown, and V. J. Gunter. 2000. *Illness and the Environment: A Reader in Contested Medicine.* New York: New York University Press.

Kupfer, D. J. 1991. "Long-Term Treatment of Depression." *Journal of Clinical Psychiatry* 52 Suppl, 28–34.

Laine, C., et al. 2007. "Clinical Trial Registration: Looking Back and Moving Ahead." *The Lancet* 369 (9577), 1909–11.

Laino, C. 2002. "Weighing Heart Drugs' Risks, Benefits." MSNBC, Aug 26. Retrieved November 17, 2003, from http://www.msnbc.com/news/618947.asp.

Lakoff, A. 2004. "The Anxieties of Globalization: Antidepressant Sales and Economic Crisis in Argentina." *Social Studies of Science* 34 (2), 247–69.

———. 2006. *Pharmaceutical Reason: Knowledge and Value in Global Psychiatry.* Cambridge: Cambridge University Press.

Landers, P. 2002. "Waiting for Prozac: Drug Firms Push Japan to Change View of Depression." *Wall Street Journal*, October 9.

Latour, B., and S. Woolgar. 1979. *Laboratory Life: The Construction of Scientific Facts.* Princeton: Princeton University Press.

Lee, S. 2004. "New Directions in Medical Education." *Pharmaceutical Executive* 23 (March), Supp. Handbook, 50–58.

———. 2006. "Invisible Prescribers: What You Don't Know about NPS and PAS." *Pharmaceutical Executive* 26 (3), 88–96.

Light, D. 2009. *The Risks of Prescription Drugs.* New York: Columbia University Press.

Linton, M. 2001. "Healthy Living a Numbers Game: Knowing Your Cholesterol Levels Crucial." *Toronto Sun*, November 11.

Lock, M. M. 2002. *Twice Dead: Organ Transplants and the Reinvention of Death.* Berkeley: University of California Press.

Luce, B. R., et al. 2009. "Rethinking Randomized Clinical Trials for Comparative Effectiveness Research: The Need for Transformational Change." *Annals of Internal Medicine* 151, 206–9.

Lund, E., et al. 2004. "Cancer Risk and Salmon Intake." *Science* 305 (5683), 477–78; author reply, 477–78.

Lupton, D. 1999. *Risk.* New York: Routledge.

Manuel, D. G., et al. 2006. "Effectiveness and Efficiency of Different Guidelines on Statin Treatment for Preventing Deaths from Coronary Heart Disease: Modelling Study." *British Medical Journal* 332 (7555), 1419.

Marini, R. A. 2003. "High Level of CRP Linked to Heart Disease, Stroke." *Houston Chronicle*, May 23.

Mark, T. L., K. R. Levit, and J. A. Buck. 2009. "Datapoints: Psychotropic Drug Prescriptions by Medical Specialty." *Psychiatric Services* 60 (9), 1167.

Marks, H. M. 1997. *The Progress of Experiment: Science and Therapeutic Reform in the United States, 1900–1990.* Cambridge: Cambridge University Press.

Martin, B., and E. Richards. 1995. "Scientific Knowledge, Controversy, and Public Decision-Making." *Handbook of Science and Technology Studies*, ed. S. Jasanoff, G. E. Markle, J. C. Petersen, and T. Pinch, 506–26. Thousand Oaks, Calif.: Sage.

Martin, E. 2007. *Bipolar Expeditions: Mania and Depression in American Culture.* Princeton: Princeton University Press.

Martinez-Hernáez, A. 2000. *What's behind the Symptom? On Psychiatric Observation and Anthropological Understanding.* Amsterdam: Harwood Academic.

Marx, K. 1973. *Grundrisse.* Translated by B. Fowkes. London: Penguin.

———. 1976. *Capital: A Critique of Political Economy.* Vol. 1. Translated by B. Fowkes. London: Penguin.

Mason, B. 2003. "River Fish Accumulate Human Drugs: Anti-Depressant Ingredients Found in Animals Downstream of Sewage Plant." *Nature News*, Nov 5. Retrieved March 15, 2012, from http://www.nature.com/news/2003/031105/full/news031103-8.html.

Matthew, J. 1990. "Screening for Depression in Primary Care: A Clinician's Perspective." *Depression in Primary Care: Screening and Detection*, ed. C. C. Attkisson and J. M. Zich, 251–63. New York: Routledge.

Matthews, J. R. 1995. *Quantification and the Quest for Medical Certainty.* Princeton: Princeton University Press.

Mattingly, C. 1994. "The Concept of Therapeutic 'Emplotment.'" *Social Science and Medicine* 38 (6), 811–22.

———. 1998. *Healing Dramas and Clinical Plots: The Narrative Structure of Experience.* Cambridge: Cambridge University Press.

Melucci, A. 1996. *Challenging Codes: Collective Action in the Information Age.* Cambridge: Cambridge University Press.

Metzl, J., and A. R. Kirkland. 2010. *Against Health: How Health Became the New Morality.* New York: New York University Press.

Mol, A., and J. Law. 2004. "Embodied Action, Enacted Bodies: The Example of Hypoglycaemia." *Body and Society* 10 (2), 43–62.

Morgan, S., M. Barer, and R. Evans. 2000. "Health Economists Meet the Fourth Tempter: Drug Dependency and Scientific Discourse." *Health Economics* 9 (8), 659–67.

Moynihan, R., and A. Cassels. 2005. *Selling Sickness: How the World's Biggest Pharmaceutical Companies Are Turning Us All into Patients.* New York: Nation Books.

Murphy, J. M. 1990. "Depression Screening Instruments: History and Issues." *Depression in Primary Care: Screening and Detection*, ed. C. C. Attkisson and J. M. Zich, 84–97. New York: Routledge.

Nagourney, E. 2001. "Vital Signs: Prevention in Youth, It's Not Just about Cholesterol." *New York Times*, March 27.

National Center for Health Statistics (NCHS). 2007. *Child and Adolescent Health.* Hyattsville, Md.: National Center for Health Statistics, CDC.

———. 2011. *Health, United States, 2010: With Special Feature on Death and Dying.* Hyattsville, Md., 2011. Retrieved March 15, 2012, from http://www.cdc.gov/nchs/fastats/drugs.htm.

Nelkin, D. 1979. *Controversy, Politics of Technical Decisions.* Beverly Hills, Calif.: Sage.

Nelkin, D., and M. S. Lindee. 1995. *The DNA Mystique: The Gene as a Cultural Icon.* New York: Freeman.

Nelkin, D., and L. Tancredi. 1989. *Dangerous Diagnostics: The Social Power of Biological Information.* New York: Basic Books.

Noonan, D., et al. 2003. "You Want Statins with That?" *Newsweek,* July 14, 48.

Oreskes, N. and E. M. Conway. 2010. *Merchants of Doubt: How a Handful of Scientists Obscured the Truth on Issues from Tobacco Smoke to Global Warming.* New York: Bloomsbury.

Paley, J. 2007. "New HRT Therapy and Other Topics." WomanOf.com. Retrieved October 21, 2007, from http://www.womenof.com/Articles/hc100200.asp.

Parker-Pope, T. 2004. "Personal Health (A Special Report) — Breakthrough! Ten Major Medical Advances You're Likely to See in the Coming Year." *Wall Street Journal,* January 26.

Pêcheux, M. 1982. *Language, Semantics, and Ideology: Stating the Obvious.* London: Macmillan.

Perkins, G. 2002. "Principles of Product Research and Development." *Pharmaceutical Marketing: Principles, Environment, and Practice,* ed. M. C. Smith, E. M. M. Kolassa, G. Perkins, and B. Siecker, 103–42. New York: Pharmaceutical Products Press.

Peterson, K. 2001. "Benefit Sharing for All? Bioprospecting NGOs, Intellectual Property Rights, New Governmentalities." *PoLAR: Political and Legal Anthropology Review* 24 (1), 78–91.

———. 2004. *HIV/AIDS and Democracy in Nigeria: Policies, Rights, and Therapeutic Economies.* Houston: Rice University Press.

Petryna, A. 2009. *When Experiments Travel: Clinical Trials and the Global Search for Human Subjects.* Princeton: Princeton University Press.

Petryna, A., and A. Kleinman. 2006. "Pharmaceutical Nexus." *Global Pharmaceuticals: Ethics, Markets, Practices,* ed. A. Petryna, A. Lakoff, and A. Kleinman, 1–32. Durham: Duke University Press.

Pickering, G. W. 1968. *High Blood Pressure.* 2nd ed. London: Churchill.

Pollock, A. 2012. *Medicating Race: Heart Disease and Durable Preoccupations with Difference.* Durham: Duke University Press.

Poovey, M. 1998. *A History of the Modern Fact: Problems of Knowledge in the Sciences of Wealth and Society.* Chicago: University of Chicago Press.

Pratt, L. A., D. J. Brody, and Q. Gu. 2011. "Antidepressant Use in Persons Aged 12 and Over: United States, 2005–2008." NCHS Data Brief, no 76. Hyattsville, Md.: National Center for Health Statistics.

Press, N., and W. Burke. 2000. "If You Care about Women's Health, Perhaps You Should Care about the Risks of Direct Marketing of Tamoxifen to Consumers." *Effective Clinical Practice* 7, 98–103.

Prounis, C. 2004. "The Art of Advertorial." *Pharmaceutical Executive* 24 (5), 152–64. Retrieved March 15, 2012, from http://www.pharmexec.com/pharmexec/article/articleDetail.jsp?id=99422.

Public Health Service. 1979. *Healthy People: The Surgeon General's Report on Health Promotion and Disease Prevention.* DHEW Publication, no. 79–55071. Washington, D.C.: U.S. Government Printing Office.

Rabinow, P. 1996. *Essays on the Anthropology of Reason.* Princeton: Princeton University Press.

Rampton, S., and J. Stauber. 2001. *Trust Us, We're Experts! How Industry Manipulates Science and Gambles with Your Future.* New York: Jeremy P. Tarcher/Putnam.

Ramspacher, S. 2005. "Engaging the Untreated: Identifying and Motivating Your Best Prospects." *DTC* Perspectives. Retrieved February 14, 2006, from www.dtc perspectives.com/content.asp?id=220.

Rapp, R. 1998. "Real Time Fetus: The Role of the Sonogram in the Age of Monitored Reproduction." *Cyborgs and Citadels: Anthropological Interventions in Emerging Sciences and Technologies,* ed. G. L. Downey and J. Dumit, 31–48. Santa Fe: SAR Press.

———. 1999. *Testing Women, Testing the Fetus: The Social Impact of Amniocentesis in America.* New York: Routledge.

Realto, V. 1998. "Prilosec Spot Hits All the Hot Buttons." *Pharmaceutical Executive* 18 (5), 14–19.

Rebonato, R. 2007. *Plight of the Fortune Tellers: Why We Need to Manage Financial Risk Differently.* Princeton: Princeton University Press.

Roberts, R. E. 1990. "Special Population Issues in Screening for Depression." *Depression in Primary Care: Screening and Detection,* ed. C. C. Attkisson and J. M. Zich, 84–97. New York: Routledge.

Robins, L. N., et al. 1984. "Lifetime Prevalence of Specific Psychiatric Disorders in Three Sites." *Archives of General Psychiatry* 41 (10), 949–58.

Rochon, P. A., and J. H. Gurwitz. 1997. "Optimising Drug Treatment for Elderly People: The Prescribing Cascade." *British Medical Journal* 315, 1096–99.

Rose, G. A., K.-T. Khaw, and M. G. Marmot. 2008. *Rose's Strategy of Preventive Medicine: The Complete Original Text.* Oxford: Oxford University Press.

Rose, N. 1999. *Powers of Freedom: Reframing Political Thought.* Cambridge: Cambridge University Press.

———. 2003. "Neurochemical Selves." *Society* 41 (1), 46–59.

Rosenberg, C. 1997. "Banishing Risk: Continuity and Change in the Moral Management of Disease." *Morality and Health,* ed. A. M. Brandt and P. Rozin, 35–52. New York: Routledge.

Rossouw J. E., et al. 2002. "Risks and Benefits of Estrogen Plus Progestin in Healthy Postmenopausal Women: Principal Results from the Women's Health Initiative Randomized Controlled Trial." *Journal of the American Medical Association* 288 (3): 321–33.

Rubin, R. 2001. "Lower Your Cholesterol by Any Means Necessary: There's Diet, Exercise or Medication." *USA Today,* May 16.

Sacks, H., and G. Jefferson. 1992. *Lectures on Conversation.* Oxford: Blackwell.

Samerski, S. 2009. "Genetic Counseling and the Fiction of Choice: Taught Self-Determination as a New Technique of Social Engineering." *Signs* 34 (4), 735–61.

Schacter, B. Z. 2006. *The New Medicines: How Drugs Are Created, Approved, Marketed, and Sold.* Westport, Conn.: Praeger.

Segura, J., and L. M. Ruilope. 2009. "Treatment of Prehypertension in Diabetes and Metabolic Syndrome: What Are the Pros?" *Diabetes Care* 32 (Supp. 2), S284–89.

Shah, S. 2006. *The Body Hunters: Testing New Drugs on the World's Poorest Patients.* New York: New Press.

Shalo, S. 2004. "Built for Speed." *Pharmaceutical Executive* 24 (2), 40. Retrieved March 15, 2012, from http://www.pharmexec.com/pharmexec/article/article Detail.jsp?id=84201&sk=&date=&pageID=2.

Shalo, S., and J. Breitstein. 2002. "Science + Marketing = Branding." *Pharmaceutical Executive* 22 (7), 84.

Shapin, S. 1994. *A Social History of Truth: Civility and Science in Seventeenth-Century England.* Chicago: University of Chicago Press.

Shapin, S., and S. Schaffer. 1985. *Leviathan and the Air-Pump.* Princeton: Princeton University Press.

Shrout, P. E. 1990. "Statistical Design of Screening Procedures." *Depression in Primary Care: Screening and Detection,* ed. C. C. Attkisson and J. M. Zich, 84–97. New York: Routledge.

Silverstein, K. 1999. "Millions for Viagra, Pennies for Diseases of the Poor." *The Nation,* 269 (3), 13–19. Retrieved March 15, 2012, from http://www.thenation.com/ article/millions-viagra-pennies-diseases-poor?page=full.

Singh, I. 2003. "Boys Will Be Boys: Fathers' Perspectives on ADHD Symptoms, Diagnosis, and Drug Treatment." *Harvard Review of Psychiatry* 11 (6), 308–16.

Smith, D. 1998. "It's Our Health . . . and We Want More Than Advertising." *Pharmaceutical Executive* 18 (7): 2–24. Retrieved March 12, 2012, from http://www .consumer-health.com/savvy/jul98_dtc.php.

Smith, M. C. 1968. *Principles of Pharmaceutical Marketing.* Philadelphia: Lea & Febiger.

———. 2002. "General Environment." *Pharmaceutical Marketing: Principles, Environment, and Practice,* ed. M. C. Smith, E. M. M. Kolassa, G. Perkins, and B. Siecker, 17–70. New York: Pharmaceutical Products Press.

Smith, S. 2003. "New Guidelines See Many More at Risk on Blood Pressure." *Boston Globe,* May 15.

———. 2004. "Salmon: Health Food or Pink Poison?" *Boston Globe,* January 20.

Snyderman, R., and R. S. Williams. 2003. "Prospective Medicine: The Next Health Care Transformation." *Academic Medicine* 78 (11), 1079–84.

Sorrentino, D. M. 2001."What to Ask Your Doctor." *Chicago Sun-Times,* May 16.

Spilker, B. 1989. *Multinational Drug Companies: Issues in Drug Discovery and Development.* New York: Raven Press.

Squires, S. 1999. "Designer Foods Take Off: More Products Are Being Manipulated to Pack a Medical Punch." *Washington Post View Related Topics,* May 18.

———. 2001. "NIH Revises Guidelines on Cholesterol: Drug Treatment Is Urged for Many More Americans." *Washington Post,* May 16.

Srikameswaran, A. 2001. "Blood Pressure, Cholesterol Guides Created for Type 1 Diabetes." *Pittsburgh Post-Gazette*, May 24.

Srinivasan, B. 2004. *Strategies in Drug Submissions—CRO-Sponsor Interaction, Strategic.* PowerPoint presentation to Drug Information Agency on behalf of Quintiles Transnational. Retrieved February 16, 2005, from www.quintiles.com.

Stingl, J. I. M. 2003. "Small Dose of Doubt Can Be Healthy." *Milwaukee Journal Sentinel*, May 18.

Strathern, M. 1992a. *After Nature: English Kinship in the Late Twentieth Century*. Cambridge: Cambridge University Press.

———. 1992b. *Reproducing the Future: Essays on Anthropology, Kinship, and the New Reproductive Technologies*. New York: Routledge.

Strauss, A. L. 1984. *Chronic Illness and the Quality of Life*. 2nd ed. St. Louis: Mosby.

Sturdy, S. 1998. "Reflections: Molecularization, Standardization and the History of Science." *Molecularizing Biology and Medicine: New Practices and Alliances, 1910s–1970s*, ed. S. D. Chadarevian and H. Kamminga, 273–89. Amsterdam: Harwood Academic.

Stuttaford, D. T. 2006. "Long-Life Statins." *The Times*, December 5, 2.

Sunder Rajan, K. 2006. *Biocapital: The Constitution of Postgenomic Life*. Durham: Duke University Press.

———. 2007. "Experimental Values: Indian Clinical Trials and Surplus Health." *New Left Review* 45 (May–June), 67–88.

———. 2008. "Biocapital as an Emergent Form of Life: Speculations on the Future of the Experimental Subject." *Biosocialities, Genetics and the Social Sciences: Making Biologies and Identities*, ed. S. Gibbon and C. Novas, 98–116. New York: Routledge.

Szabo, L. 2012. "Study Links Statins to Higher Diabetes in Older Women." *USA Today*, January 9. Retrieved March 15, 2012, from http://yourlife.usatoday.com/health/medical/diabetes/story/2012-01-09/Study-links-statins-to-higher-diabetes-in-older-women/52470838/1.

Talaga, T. 2000. "Skin Test Makes Cholesterol Check Quick and Painless." *Toronto Star*, November 15.

Thomas, D. 1999. "Cholesterol-Fighting Margarines Get Good Reviews." *Omaha World Herald*, May 26.

Thomas, L. 1979. *The Medusa and the Snail: More Notes of a Biology Watcher*. New York: Viking.

Tone, A., and E. S. Watkins. 2007. *Medicating Modern America: Prescription Drugs in History*. New York: New York University Press.

Turett, N. 2002. "Thriving Amid Uncertainty: Relationships Reign." *Pharmaceutical Executive* 22 (9). Retrieved March 15, 2012, from http://www.pharmexec.com/pharmexec/PE+Features/Thriving-Amid-Uncertainty/ArticleStandard/Article/detail/29984.

Turner, V. 1982. *From Ritual to Theatre: The Human Seriousness of Play*. New York: Performing Arts Journal Publications.

Turner, V. W., and E. L. B. Turner. 1992. *Blazing the Trail: Way Marks in the Exploration of Symbols*. Tucson: University of Arizona Press.

Tye, L. 1998. *The Father of Spin: Edward L. Bernays and the Birth of Public Relations.* New York: Crown.

Urquhart, J. 2005. "Some Key Points Emerging from the COX-2 Controversy: No Conflict of Interest Was Declared." *Pharmacoepidemiology and Drug Safety* 14 (3), 145–47.

Vasella, D., N. Bloomgarden, and K. Bloomgarden. 2003. "Courage under Fire." *Pharmaceutical Executive* 23 (4), S14–17.

Vedantam, S. 2001. "Blood Test May Help Spot Hearts at Risk, Scientists Say." *Washington Post*, June 28.

Vermilyea, J., M. Vanelli, and S. Adler. 2002a. "Moving beyond Market Share." *In Vivo: The Business and Medicine Report* 20 (3), 69.

———. 2002b. "Reconfiguring DTC with Patient Behavior in Mind." *In Vivo: The Business and Medicine Report* 20 (9), 71.

Wald, N., and M. Law. 2003. "A Strategy to Reduce Cardiovascular Disease by More Than 80%." *British Medical Journal* 326 (7404), 1419–24.

Walker, K. 2000. "Stress Can Send Your Blood Cholesterol Soaring, Raising Chance of Heart Attack." *Chicago Sun-Times*, July 16, 4.

Weber, L. J. 2006. *Profits before People? Ethical Standards and the Marketing of Prescription Drugs.* Bloomington: Indiana University Press.

Welch, H. G. 2004. *Should I Be Tested for Cancer? Maybe Not and Here's Why.* Berkeley: University of California Press.

White, H. 1973. *Metahistory: The Historical Imagination in Nineteenth-Century Europe.* Baltimore: Johns Hopkins University Press.

Whyte, S., S. Van der Geest, and A. Hardon. 2003. *Social Lives of Medicines*: Cambridge: Cambridge University Press.

Widmer, R. B., and R. J. Cadoret. 1978. "Depression in Primary Care: Changes in Pattern of Patient Visits and Complaints during a Developing Depression." *Journal of Family Practice* 7 (2), 293–302.

Wilkes, M. S., R. A. Bell, and R. L. Kravitz. 2000. "Direct-to-Consumer Prescription Drug Advertising: Trends, Impact, and Implications." *Health Affairs (Millwood)* 19 (2), 110–28.

Wilkes, M. S., and M. Shuchman. 1989. "Pitching Doctors." *New York Times Magazine*, November 5.

Wilson, D. 2010. "Risks Seen in Cholesterol Drug Use in Healthy People." *New York Times*, March 30.

Winslow, R. 2004. "Blood Feud: For Bristol-Myers, Challenging Pfizer Was a Big Mistake—In Rare Head-to-Head Study, Lipitor Beats Pravachol at Reducing Heart Risk—A New Push on Cholesterol." *Wall Street Journal*, March 9, A1.

Wittgenstein, L. 1991. *On Certainty.* San Francisco: Arion Press.

World Health Organization. 2011. *Pharmaceuticals in Drinking-water: Public Health and Environment Water, Sanitation, Hygiene and Health.* Geneva: WHO Press.

Zakaria, T. 2010. "Obama Says U.S. Economy Has to Grow Faster." *Reuters*, August 2. Retrieved March 15, 2012, from http://www.reuters.com/article/2010/08/02/obama-economy-idUSN0225722520100802.

Zola, I. K. 1972. "Medicine as an Institution of Social Control." *Sociological Review* 20 (4), 487–504.

Zung, W. W. K., K. Magruder-Habib, and J. R. Feussner. 1990. "Screening for Depression in General Medical Care." *Depression in Primary Care: Screening and Detection*, ed. C. C. Attkisson and J. M. Zich, 155–68. New York: Routledge.

INDEX

Joseph Dumit is Director of Science and Technology Studies
and Professor of Anthropology at the University of California,
Davis. He is the author of *Picturing Personhood: Brain Scans and
Biomedical Identity*, and the editor, with Regula Valérie Burri,
of *Biomedicine as Culture: Instrumental Practices, Technoscientific
Knowledge, and New Modes of Life*.

Library of Congress Cataloging-in-Publication Data
Dumit, Joseph.
Drugs for life : how pharmaceutical companies define our health /
Joseph Dumit.
p. cm. — (Experimental futures)
Includes bibliographical references and index.
ISBN 978-0-8223-4860-3 (cloth : alk. paper)
ISBN 978-0-8223-4871-9 (pbk. : alk. paper)
1. Pharmaceutical industry — Social aspects — United States.
2. Drugs — Social aspects — United States. 3. Drug utilization —
United States. I. Title. II. Series: Experimental futures.
HD9666.5.D86 2012
338.4'761510973 — dc23   2012011596